BIBLE STUDY LESSONS

Beliefs Important to Baptists

SECOND EDITION

Study Guide

William M. Pinson, Jr.
Rosalie Beck
James Semple
Ebbie Smith

Dallas, Texas

Beliefs Important to Baptists—Study Guide

Printed in the United States of America.

BAPTISTWAY PRESS® Leadership Team
Executive Director, Baptist General Convention of Texas: David Hardage
Director, Great Commission Team: Delvin Atchison
Interim Publisher, BaptistWay Press®: Scott Stevens

Cover and Interior Design and Production: Desktop Miracles, Inc.
Printing: Data Reproductions Corporation

Second printing: November 2017
ISBN: 978-1-934731-69-7

Beliefs Important to Baptists

HOW TO USE THIS EDITION OF

Beliefs Important to Baptists

This *Study Guide* is intended to provide guidance and content as you study the biblical bases of some beliefs that are important to Baptists. The twelve beliefs to be studied are listed alphabetically on the preceding page after an introductory lesson, "Who in the World Are Baptists, Anyway?" The lessons provide studies of twelve beliefs important to Baptists. This list of basic Baptist beliefs is not an "official" list, but the beliefs listed are representative of what many Baptists believe.

The twelve Baptist beliefs to be studied are listed and published in alphabetical order so as not to suggest an "official" listing of beliefs from more important to less important. In studying these Baptist beliefs, you are encouraged to study first, "Who in the World Are Baptists, Anyway?" After that, the twelve beliefs important to Baptists can be studied in any order.

You will note that this study is a Bible study. The intention of these study materials is that you study the Bible carefully with the aid of these comments as you seek to understand these beliefs important to Baptists.

Leading the Study Sessions

A FREE *Teaching Guide* for leading study sessions on *Beliefs Important to Baptists* is available at www.baptistwaypress.org.

Spanish Edition

A Spanish edition of *Beliefs Important to Baptists—Doctrinas Importantes de los Bautistas*—is available free at www.baptistwaypress.org, along with a *Teaching Guide* in Spanish.

The Writers

William M. Pinson, Jr., executive director emeritus of the Executive Board of the Baptist General Convention of Texas, wrote the introductory lesson, "Who in the World Are Baptists, Anyway?"

Rosalie Beck, associate professor in the religion department, Baylor University, Waco, Texas, wrote these lessons: "The Autonomy of the Local Congregation of Believers"; "Salvation Only by Grace Through Faith"; "Soul Competency and the Priesthood of the Believer"; "Symbolic Understanding of Baptism and the Lord's Supper."

James Semple, retired as director of the State Missions Commission of the Baptist General Convention of Texas, wrote these lessons: "The Deity and Lordship of Jesus Christ"; "Religious Freedom and Separation of Church and State"; "The Security of the Believer"; "Voluntary Cooperation Among Churches."

Ebbie Smith, who formerly served as a missionary in Indonesia and is retired as a professor at Southwestern Baptist Theological Seminary, Fort Worth, Texas, wrote these lessons: "The Authority of the Bible"; "Believer's Baptism and Church Membership"; "Congregational Church Government"; "Evangelism and Missions."

LESSON ONE

Who in the World Are Baptists, Anyway?

BACKGROUND SCRIPTURES

Genesis 1:26–27; Matthew 16:13–17; John 3:1–16; Ephesians 2:1–19

FOCAL TEXT

Ephesians 2:1–19

MAIN IDEA

"The doctrine of the soul's competency in religion under God is the historical significance of the Baptists"[1] and means that God provides each person with the ability and freedom to make decisions in matters relating to God.

STUDY AIM

To summarize some basic biblical understandings that are the source of who Baptists are, what they believe, and how they live

QUICK READ

This lesson provides an introduction to the biblical basis for principles that describe what it means to be a Baptist Christian with a primary emphasis on soul competency before God.

Baptists frequently make the headlines and the newscasts. Some of the stories are positive, such as those about Baptist relief efforts in the midst of disasters. Unfortunately, other stories paint Baptists as "feuding, fussing, and fighting" most of the time. People who are not Baptists wonder, "Who in the world are Baptists, anyway?" In fact, a number of Baptists seem to wonder the same thing!

To further complicate matters, people with very diverse beliefs and actions wear the name "Baptist." Baptists can be found in various political parties in our nation. Baptists advocate a wide variety of views on social and moral issues. Baptists hold differing convictions about theology and interpretation of the Bible.

So what makes a Baptist a Baptist? And why are Baptists so diverse? Those are difficult questions without simple answers. In fact, no single doctrine or belief can describe what it means to be a Baptist. Much like a recipe, a combination of doctrines and beliefs actually goes into describing a Baptist. And people hold different ideas about what should go into the Baptist mix. Yet most Baptists agree on the core ingredients. This lesson will explore the biblical foundation for a number of these basic Baptist beliefs, recognizing that such a brief space provides only for a limited discussion.

Soul Competency (Ephesians 2:1-7)

The Holy Spirit led Paul, the great missionary of the first century, to write to the Christians at Ephesus about their life in Christ. He emphasized that apart from Christ there is no salvation from sin and death. Paul also stressed that each person possesses the capacity to decide whether to follow Jesus or not. He indicated that the Ephesian Christians through faith in Christ had determined to leave the ways of the world (Ephesians 2:2–3), to respond to God's love in Christ, and to live lives worthy of heaven (Eph. 2:4–7). Throughout this letter Paul indicated that the Ephesians had choices to make,

Ephesians 2:1–19 (NIV)

1 As for you, you were dead in your transgressions and sins, 2 in
which you used to live when you followed the ways of this world and of
the ruler of the kingdom of the air, the spirit who is now at work in
those who are disobedient. 3 All of us also lived among them at one
time, gratifying the cravings of our sinful nature and following its
desires and thoughts. Like the rest, we were by nature objects of
wrath. 4 But because of his great love for us, God, who is rich in mercy,
5 made us alive with Christ even when we were dead in transgressions—
it is by grace you have been saved. 6 And God raised us up with Christ
and seated us with him in the heavenly realms in Christ Jesus, 7 in
order that in the coming ages he might show the incomparable riches
of his grace, expressed in his kindness to us in Christ Jesus. 8 For it is
by grace you have been saved, through faith—and this not from yourselves, it is the gift of God—9 not by works, so that no one can boast.
10 For we are God's workmanship, created in Christ Jesus to do good
works, which God prepared in advance for us to do.

11 Therefore, remember that formerly you who are Gentiles by birth
and called "uncircumcised" by those who call themselves "the circumcision" (that done in the body by the hands of men)—12 remember that
at that time you were separate from Christ, excluded from citizenship
in Israel and foreigners to the covenants of the promise, without hope
and without God in the world. 13 But now in Christ Jesus you who once
were far away have been brought near through the blood of Christ.

14 For he himself is our peace, who has made the two one and has
destroyed the barrier, the dividing wall of hostility, 15 by abolishing in
his flesh the law with its commandments and regulations. His purpose
was to create in himself one new man out of the two, thus making
peace, 16 and in this one body to reconcile both of them to God through
the cross, by which he put to death their hostility. 17 He came and
preached peace to you who were far away and peace to those who
were near. 18 For through him we both have access to the Father by one
Spirit.

19 Consequently, you are no longer foreigners and aliens, but fellow
citizens with God's people and members of God's household . . . .

such as his appeal to "live a life worthy of the calling you have received" (Eph. 4:1).

Paul based his assumption that the Ephesians possessed the ability to respond to his appeals solidly on the writings of the Old Testament and the teachings of the Lord Jesus Christ. Genesis reveals that God created human beings with the freedom of choice (Genesis 1:26–27). The Old Testament prophets called on the people of Israel to turn from their wicked ways to God's ways. Jesus' initial preaching urged people to repent. Moreover, Jesus asked Peter to make a personal decision regarding who Jesus was (Matthew 16:13–17). These appeals for people to decide for God would be cruel farces if human beings did not have the capacity to choose to respond.

Therefore a basic Baptist belief is "the doctrine of the soul's competency in religion under God."[2] This belief is not an emphasis on human self-sufficiency. Rather, it stresses that the ability to decide—that is, the

George W. Truett and Religious Liberty

Many historians consider George W. Truett, pastor of the First Baptist Church in Dallas from 1898 to 1944, as one of the greatest, if not the greatest, pastor in Southern Baptist life. Never provincial in his outlook, he served as president of both the Southern Baptist Convention and of the Baptist World Alliance. He also gave strong support to the Baptist General Convention of Texas and to institutions related to the convention. When Truett died, the entire Dallas community expressed love and appreciation for him. City and county offices were closed in his honor, and a huge crowd attended his funeral.

In 1920 Truett delivered one of the most famous sermons in Baptist history from the east steps of the Capitol in Washington, D. C. His theme was religious liberty. In the sermon, he quoted Jesus' statement, "Render unto Caesar the things which are Caesar's, and unto God the things that are God's" (Matthew 22:21, KJV). He then declared: "That utterance, once and for all, marked the divorcement of church and state."[3]

competency of the soul—is a gift from God. Thus we have freedom of choice because God has so gifted us. Furthermore, the choice cannot be delegated. Each person must decide for herself or himself to follow Jesus or not. No one can make that choice for another. Baptists declare that no one should try to coerce another in a decision for Christ. Neither church nor government, Baptists believe, has any right to attempt to force a religious decision on anyone. Certainly Baptists seek to persuade people to follow Christ, but they realize that such commitment is a voluntary individual decision.

Many Baptists believe that the doctrine of soul competency is basic to other Baptist beliefs. It relates to many other doctrines that Baptists cherish, in a sense tying them together.

Salvation by Grace Through Faith (Eph. 2:8–10)

The Bible teaches that salvation is in Christ by grace through faith alone. This certainly relates to soul competency. Paul stated to the Ephesians: "For it is by grace you have been saved, through faith—and this not from yourselves, it is the gift of God—not by works, so that no one can boast" (Eph. 2:8–9). Baptists believe in the deity and lordship of Jesus Christ. Baptists insist that salvation from sin and death to forgiveness and life is only found in Jesus Christ, who declared, "I am the way and the truth and the life. No one comes to the Father except through me" (John 14:6).

God's grace—God's unmerited love for lost humanity—led God to send his Son to be our Savior. As Jesus told Nicodemus, the Jewish leader who came to him by night, "For God so loved the world that he gave his one and only Son, that whoever believes in him shall not perish but have eternal life" (John 3:16). Baptists believe that it is grace/faith plus nothing that results in salvation—not grace/faith plus good works, or church membership, or baptism, or sacrament, or anything else. People are free to believe or not to believe in Jesus as personal Lord and Savior. Those who believe in Jesus as Savior pass from death that is the result of sin to eternal and abundant life that is the result of faith in

Christ. Baptists declare also that this salvation is secure for eternity in Christ.

Each believer is to express through believer's baptism, another major belief of Baptists, that he or she has been made "alive with Christ" (Eph. 2:5). Both words are important: *believer's* and *baptism*. Baptists declare that only those who have personally made a decision to believe in Christ should be baptized because only through belief do we pass from death to life as is symbolized in baptism. That is why Baptists reject infant baptism. The word *baptize* means to immerse. Therefore, Baptists immerse believers as a beautiful picture of their death to an old way of life and being "raised . . . up with Christ" (Eph. 2:6). Baptism also enables the believer to identify with the death, burial, and resurrection of Jesus. Baptism is a symbol of what has taken place in the person through belief in Christ. Baptism does not save but is a picture of salvation. It is also a covenant with God and with fellow believers to live worthy of Christ. Similarly, Baptists believe that the Lord's Supper is not a sacrament or necessary for salvation but symbolizes the broken body and shed blood of Jesus for our salvation.

Baptism takes place within the community of believers, a church. Paul wrote to the Ephesians about people of diverse background, such as Jews and Gentiles, being brought together as one in Christ. Thus, a church is to be made up of people who have "been brought near through the blood of Christ" (Eph. 2:13). As such, a church is a divine-human organization. It is divine in the sense that it is the "body of Christ" and only those who have been saved in Christ are to be members. It is human in that it is made up of people who are saved but who are still imperfect.

Another way to state this conviction is that Baptists hold to the concept of a "believers' church," a regenerate church membership. Only people who have been saved by grace through faith and who have testified to that experience are to be members of a church. This means that each member of the local body of baptized believers has come into the fellowship in the same way. There is equality in salvation and church membership.

This leads to the Baptist emphasis on *theo-democratic* church governance. Baptist churches have no hierarchy. No individual or group of people decides for the entire body of members what they are to believe and to do. Rather each member of the body shares in the decisions. Yet, ideally, the decisions are not to be what the people want, but what Christ, the head of the church, wants. Thus the use of the term *theo-* (the Greek word for God) *democracy* (the word for rule by the people). Through Bible study, prayer, discussion, and meditation the members are to seek the will of God as they participate in congregational church governance.

Furthermore, each church is autonomous—that is, independent. Baptist churches are not subject to rule or governance by any outside body in regard to faith and religious practice. No "denominational headquarters" or government agency dictates to a church what to believe or

Beliefs Important to Baptists

The Baptist Distinctives Committee of the Baptist General Convention of Texas has developed a list of basic Baptist beliefs that are considered not "official" but representative of what many Baptists believe. In alphabetical order, not by priority, these are the beliefs:

Authority of the Bible
Autonomy of the local congregation of believers
Believer's baptism and church membership
Congregational church government
Deity and lordship of Jesus Christ
Evangelism and missions: the Great Commission
Religious freedom and separation of church and state
Salvation only by grace through faith
Security of the believer
Soul competency and the priesthood of the believer
Symbolic understanding of baptism and the Lord's Supper
Voluntary cooperation among churches.

how to worship. How could it be otherwise? The Bible indicates that each believer is competent in religion under God. Therefore each church made up of Baptists is equal before God and has no authority over another.

However, a local body of baptized believers on its own cannot adequately carry out the Great Commission of the Lord Jesus Christ (Matthew 28:18–20). Therefore, Baptist churches cooperate with one another for the sake of missions, evangelism, Christian education, ministry, and other causes. This cooperation is purely voluntary, as it was in New Testament times among churches. Voluntary cooperation among Baptist churches began with associations of churches, expanded to state conventions, and finally to national conventions and bodies of Baptists. Each church relates directly to any organization of Baptists beyond it, and that relationship is always voluntary. Baptist organizations beyond local congregations are also autonomous and relate voluntarily with one another. Through such voluntary cooperation, Baptists have been able to have an impact for good on millions of people throughout the world.

Priesthood of the Believers (Eph. 2:11-19)

Saved by grace through faith and competent in religion under God, each Baptist through Christ has "access to the Father by one Spirit" (Eph. 2:18). Paul declared to the Ephesians that each believer in Christ has access to God in the same way. There is not one way for the Gentile and another for the Jew. In Christ such distinctions disappear, and every believer has equal access to God.

The New Testament reveals that in Christ we become "priests." Peter stated that those in Christ are a "holy priesthood" (1 Peter 2:5) and a "royal priesthood" (1 Peter 2:9). In the Old Testament the people had access to God through priests. In the New Testament every disciple of Jesus has access to God directly. Thus a major emphasis of Baptists is the "priesthood of believers."

Being a priest carries both opportunity and responsibility. The opportunity is to relate directly with God through prayer, worship, meditation, trust, and obedience. No special clerical class is needed to represent us to God or to serve as a mediator between God and ourselves. However, with this opportunity goes responsibility. We are to take the knowledge of God that is ours and share it with everyone in witness and ministry. That is, we are to be priests to others, loving and caring for them in Jesus' name. Therefore, Baptists take seriously their individual responsibility for evangelism, mission, and ministry to all people.

The doctrine of the priesthood of believers coupled with the doctrine of soul competency calls for religious freedom and the separation of church and state. Under God, people ought to be free to exercise both their competency in matters of faith and religious practice as well as their opportunity and responsibility as believer priests. No ecclesiastical or governmental body ought to interfere with these practices or attempt to dictate to the followers of Christ what to believe or how to respond to what they perceive as the will of God.

When Baptists first proclaimed religious liberty, they met terrible resistance. Religious authorities viewed the concept as heretical. Governmental authorities viewed it as treasonous. They thought that allowing people religious freedom would weaken the power of the government and possibly cause people to demand political as well as religious freedom. Baptists were seen as a threat both to despotic monarchs and to dictatorial clergy. Therefore Baptists suffered persecution at the hands of both church and state. Ridicule, abuse, imprisonment, torture, and death did not silence the Baptists, however. They persisted in their struggle for religious freedom for all, not just for themselves.

Largely due to the efforts of Baptists and others of similar views, we enjoy religious freedom in the United States. The Bill of Rights in the Constitution of the United States guarantees that our nation will have no established—that is, government-supported—religion. In many places in the world, governments support a particular religion or Christian denomination in various ways, such as through taxation.

Baptists insist that the support of a church ought to be by the voluntary tithes and offerings of the members, not by government-coerced taxation.

We can be grateful that church and state are separate in our nation, with churches supported voluntarily by members and not through government coercion. People of all religious persuasions and those with none are to be free from government interference in matters of faith. Soul competency and the priesthood of believers are best practiced when there is a free church in a free state.

So Who in the World Are Baptists, Anyway?

Basic to all of these beliefs is the Baptist insistence that the Bible is the Word of God and our sole written authority for faith and practice. Baptists declare that we have no creed but the Bible. Baptists reject all creeds as spurious efforts to capture the truth of the Holy Bible in a human document. Indeed, Baptists have developed confessions of faith, but these are intended to serve only as broad guides to interpretation and never as an authoritative or official expression of biblical truth. Such confessions are merely that—confessions of what a particular group of Baptists believe. They have no authority over any individual or church.

Thus we return to a core Baptist conviction: freedom of the soul before God. This freedom includes freedom to interpret the Bible. With that freedom goes responsibility, of course, such as the responsibility to seek the guidance of the Holy Spirit in interpreting Scripture and to use sound principles of biblical interpretation.

So who in the world are Baptists, anyway? Certainly we have much in common with all followers of Jesus Christ, such as a belief in God, the Bible, Jesus, and the importance of church. However, we differ on certain matters and emphasize particular doctrines. These differences and emphases taken as a whole set Baptists apart as distinctive. We believe these beliefs that define us are based on the Bible. We also believe that each person ought to be free to determine his or her own beliefs apart from coercion of church or state. Thus Baptists share enthusiastically our view of God, salvation, and other key doctrines while granting to others the freedom to share their views. In fact, Baptists have been willing to die for the freedom of all people to express through word and deed their religious convictions. That is a heritage worth preserving for the generations to follow.

QUESTIONS

1. Consider the list in the sidebar, "Beliefs Important to Baptists," set forth by the Baptist Distinctives Committee of the Baptist General Convention of Texas. Would you add any? Take away?

2. Why is the concept of soul competency basic to many of the other Baptist doctrines?

3. Which of the Baptist beliefs and doctrines would you describe as the most basic and why?

4. Some people believe that the sovereignty of God rules out the freedom of choice in human beings. How do you respond to this?

5. What evidence, if any, do you see that some Baptist bodies today are endeavoring to dictate to other Baptist bodies what to believe? What basic Baptist beliefs would such practices violate?

6. How would you describe what it means to be a Baptist to someone who is not a Baptist?

NOTES

1. E. Y. Mullins, *Axioms of Religion,* Baptist Classics Series (Nashville: Broadman and Holman, Publishers, 1997), 66.
2. Mullins, 66.
3. The full text of George W. Truett's sermon, "Baptists and Religious Liberty," can be accessed on the internet at this address: www.bjconline.org. See "Sermons" under "Resources." Accessed 12/3/2010

LESSON TWO

The Authority of the Bible

BACKGROUND SCRIPTURES

Psalm 19:7-10; 119:11, 97-112; Isaiah 40:8; Jeremiah 36; Matthew 5:17-18; Luke 21:33; 24:13-49; Acts 17:10-12; Romans 15:4; 2 Timothy 3:14-17; Hebrews 4:12-13; 2 Peter 1:19-21

FOCAL TEXTS

Psalm 119:97-112; Luke 24:13-45; Romans 15:4; 2 Timothy 3:14-17; 2 Peter 1:19-21

MAIN IDEA

". . . The authority of the Bible is the authority of Christ. . . . Christ speaks to us through the Bible. Our ultimate authority in Christianity is the authority of Christ as the revelation of God."[1]

STUDY AIM

To describe how the Scriptures are authoritative for our lives

QUICK READ

Authority establishes truth and prescribes practice. Baptists accept the Bible as authority because it is God's revelation in Jesus Christ and can therefore guide in all Christian belief and behavior.

During a study time at church for youth, somehow I unexpectedly found myself as the youth teacher. Trying to be relevant, I asked the group what they would like to talk about. One young woman declared that she would like to talk about interracial marriage.

"Ok," I said, "What do you think about it?"

"Well," she answered, "we know it is wrong because the Bible says it is!"

"And where does the Bible say that?" I asked.

"I don't know," she rejoined, "but I know it does because I have always been told it does."

We began to try to find what the Bible actually says about interracial marriage. We looked at Deuteronomy 7:3–4; Ezra 9:1—10:44; and Nehemiah 10:28–30. We found that in every case, the prohibition of marriage with other peoples was based on religious factors, not racial. "Do not intermarry with them . . . for they will turn your sons away from following me to serve other gods" (Deuteronomy 7:3–4).

What had been the problem? This fine young woman was allowing what she had always been told to serve as the authority for what she believed. Authority for believers rests in the Word of God, not in any other source.

In a religious sense, authority is that which establishes belief and guides conduct. Baptist leader Russell H. Dilday, Jr., defines authority as "*that right or power to command action or compliance or to determine belief or custom in matters of religion*."[2] Some people and groups base their authority on inadequate sources such as tradition, the church, culture, worldview, reason, creeds, prestigious people, or even personal experience. Baptists consider Scripture, rather than such inadequate sources, to be their full authority.

Baptists consider the Bible authoritative for all they believe and everything they should do. The Bible remains and will remain "the supreme standard by which all human conduct, creeds, and religious opinions should be tried."[3] Scripture constitutes the authority for Baptists because it is God's revelation of his truth and his will.

Psalm 119:97-112 (NIV)

97 Oh, how I love your law!
I meditate on it all day long.
98 Your commands make me wiser than my enemies,
for they are ever with me.
99 I have more insight than all my teachers,
for I meditate on your statutes.
100 I have more understanding than the elders,
for I obey your precepts.
101 I have kept my feet from every evil path
so that I might obey your word.
102 I have not departed from your laws,
for you yourself have taught me.
103 How sweet are your words to my taste,
sweeter than honey to my mouth!
104 I gain understanding from your precepts;
therefore I hate every wrong path.
105 Your word is a lamp to my feet
and a light for my path.
106 I have taken an oath and confirmed it,
that I will follow your righteous laws.
107 I have suffered much;
preserve my life, O LORD, according to your
word.
108 Accept, O LORD, the willing praise of my mouth,
and teach me your laws.
109 Though I constantly take my life in my hands,
I will not forget your law.
110 The wicked have set a snare for me,
but I have not strayed from your precepts.
111 Your statutes are my heritage forever;
they are the joy of my heart.
112 My heart is set on keeping your decrees
to the very end.

It is one thing for Christians as a whole or as a group (such as Baptists) to affirm the Bible as authoritative. It is another for you as an individual, however, to make the Bible God's ultimate authority for your belief and behavior. This lesson centers on the question, "How can the Bible become the central authority in your life?"

Luke 24:13-45

13 Now that same day two of them were going to a village called
Emmaus, about seven miles from Jerusalem. 14 They were talking with
each other about everything that had happened. 15 As they talked and
discussed these things with each other, Jesus himself came up and
walked along with them; 16 but they were kept from recognizing him.

17 He asked them, "What are you discussing together as you walk
along?"

They stood still, their faces downcast. 18 One of them, named
Cleopas, asked him, "Are you only a visitor to Jerusalem and do not
know the things that have happened there in these days?"

19 "What things?" he asked.

"About Jesus of Nazareth," they replied. "He was a prophet, powerful in word and deed before God and all the people. 20 The chief priests
and our rulers handed him over to be sentenced to death, and they
crucified him; 21 but we had hoped that he was the one who was going
to redeem Israel. And what is more, it is the third day since all this took
place. 22 In addition, some of our women amazed us. They went to the
tomb early this morning 23 but didn't find his body. They came and told
us that they had seen a vision of angels, who said he was alive. 24 Then
some of our companions went to the tomb and found it just as the
women had said, but him they did not see."

25 He said to them, "How foolish you are, and how slow of heart to
believe all that the prophets have spoken! 26 Did not the Christ have to
suffer these things and then enter his glory?" 27 And beginning with
Moses and all the Prophets, he explained to them what was said in all
the Scriptures concerning himself.

28 As they approached the village to which they were going, Jesus
acted as if he were going farther. 29 But they urged him strongly, "Stay
with us, for it is nearly evening; the day is almost over." So he went in
to stay with them.
30 When he was at the table with them, he took bread, gave thanks,
broke it and began to give it to them. 31 Then their eyes were opened
and they recognized him, and he disappeared from their sight. 32 They
asked each other, "Were not our hearts burning within us while he
talked with us on the road and opened the Scriptures to us?"
33 They got up and returned at once to Jerusalem. There they found
the Eleven and those with them, assembled together 34 and saying, "It
is true! The Lord has risen and has appeared to Simon." 35 Then the
two told what had happened on the way, and how Jesus was recognized by them when he broke the bread.
36 While they were still talking about this, Jesus himself stood
among them and said to them, "Peace be with you."
37 They were startled and frightened, thinking they saw a ghost.
38 He said to them, "Why are you troubled, and why do doubts rise in
your minds? 39 Look at my hands and my feet. It is I myself! Touch me
and see; a ghost does not have flesh and bones, as you see I have."
40 When he had said this, he showed them his hands and feet. 41 And
while they still did not believe it because of joy and amazement, he
asked them, "Do you have anything here to eat?" 42 They gave him a
piece of broiled fish, 43 and he took it and ate it in their presence.
44 He said to them, "This is what I told you while I was still with you:
Everything must be fulfilled that is written about me in the Law of
Moses, the Prophets and the Psalms."
45 Then he opened their minds so they could understand the
Scriptures.

Romans 15:4

For everything that was written in the past was written to teach us, so that through endurance and the encouragement of the Scriptures we might have hope.

2 Timothy 3:14-17

14 But as for you, continue in what you have learned and have become convinced of, because you know those from whom you learned it, 15 and how from infancy you have known the holy Scriptures, which are able to make you wise for salvation through faith in Christ Jesus. 16 All Scripture is God-breathed and is useful for teaching, rebuking, correcting and training in righteousness, 17 so that the man of God may be thoroughly equipped for every good work.

2 Peter 1:19-21

19 And we have the word of the prophets made more certain, and you will do well to pay attention to it, as to a light shining in a dark place, until the day dawns and the morning star rises in your hearts. 20 Above all, you must understand that no prophecy of Scripture came about by the prophet's own interpretation. 21 For prophecy never had its origin in the will of man, but men spoke from God as they were carried along by the Holy Spirit.

Leading to Personal Faith in Christ (Luke 24:13-45)

Scripture will become the central authority in your life only as the Bible's message leads you to personal relationship with Jesus. God the Father remains the one supreme, eternal, and all-knowing Being and therefore the ultimate source of authority. He has, however, revealed himself, his nature and will, through his Spirit in the person of his Son Jesus Christ.[4] Baptist leader Russell Dilday summarizes these truths in these words: "Our authority then is the sovereign, triune God, revealed in Jesus Christ, communicated through his inspired Word, and confirmed by the Holy Spirit in Christian experience."[5]

The account of the disciples on the road to Emmaus (Luke 24:13–45) demonstrates how God's Word leads believers to personal relationship with Jesus and through that experience to apprehend and practice biblical truth. On the day of Jesus' resurrection, these disciples were traveling from Jerusalem to the village of Emmaus. They were discussing the events of Jesus' death. They spoke of reports of the missing body. Jesus joined the two, but God prevented them from recognizing him.

Jesus entered into their conversation. Cleopas revealed his and his friend's hesitation to affirm either belief or disbelief in Jesus' promise of resurrection. They reported that "some of our women" (Luke 24:22) said they did not find the body at the tomb but rather saw a vision of angels who said Jesus was alive. The two also reported that the apostles had found the grave empty. The Emmaus-bound disciples expressed their dimming hope that Jesus was Messiah (the redeemer of Israel). Three days had passed since the cross. They felt that if Jesus had been Messiah, it would have been confirmed by this time.

Saying they were "slow of heart" to believe the prophets' words (Luke 24:25), Jesus unfolded the biblical teachings. Beginning with "Moses and all the Prophets" (Luke 24:27), Jesus explained to them what the Scriptures taught about the Christ—that the death of Messiah was predicted as part of God's redemptive plan. The prophecies taught, said Jesus, that the Messiah (Christ), by divine necessity, had to suffer the agonies of betrayal, mockery, and death before entering his glory.

Jesus paused and ate with the struggling believers. As Jesus blessed the bread, their eyes were opened. They recognized the Master! Jesus then vanished from their sight. They exclaimed to each other, "'Were not our hearts burning within us while he talked with us on the road and opened the Scriptures to us?'" (Luke 24:32).

All doubt was erased after Jesus explained to them the message of the Scriptures. The disciples immediately returned to Jerusalem, unafraid of the danger of night travel. They proclaimed their experience to the apostles and other disciples who also were testifying that Jesus had indeed risen. Understanding the message of Scripture led these disciples to a new faith and relationship with Christ.

The Bible becomes authoritative for you today when you, too, allow Scripture to draw you to an experience with Jesus. For believers, Jesus becomes more than a historical person, though he is certainly that. Jesus becomes the living Lord who saves, directs, and guides. Jesus, whose will is revealed in the Scriptures, constitutes authority. The Bible becomes authoritative when the Holy Spirit through Scripture makes Christ known in experience. Do you desire the Bible to guide and help you more? The Bible will become more authoritative for you as you experience Christ through the Bible's message.

Understanding the Nature of Scripture (2 Timothy 3:14-17)

Scripture will become the central authority for your life as you comprehend and accept the true nature of Scripture. The true nature of Scripture includes Scripture's divine origin, its incredible unity, its miraculous preservation, its incredible power, its continuing relevance, and its errorless revelation of truth. Each of these principles holds immense importance, but let us give attention especially just now to the first and the last. As you comprehend the nature of Scripture, you will find adequate reason to accept biblical authority for your belief and practice.

Understanding the Bible's nature begins with comprehending the truth of its divine origin. The Scriptures are "God-breathed" (2 Timothy 3:16). The metaphor here is of the breath of God rendering a quiet, unseen influence through the compulsive power of the Holy Spirit to produce the unique revelation God intended. The meaning is that Scripture is inherently inspired rather than that Scripture has an inspiring effect.

Paul used two terms for Scripture in 2 Timothy 3:15–16. He wrote "holy Scriptures" or holy writings in verse 15. He was referring to the Old Testament, which the Jewish people considered the authoritative Word of God. In verse 16, "all scripture" (NIV) or "every scripture" translates another word, "writing." This word may simply be a further reference to the Old Testament. It might, however, also include other inspired writings such as New Testament sections. Peter spoke of Paul's epistles, which "contain some things that are hard to understand, which ignorant and unstable people distort, as they do the other Scriptures, to their own destruction" (2 Peter 3:16). So Peter placed Paul's epistles on the same level as the Old Testament.[6] "All Scripture" in verse 16 therefore likely includes both Old and New Testaments.

The Bible in Action

Until 1954, the West Danis of Irian Jaya (Indonesia) had little contact with the outside world. Evangelistic work at first saw little response. Then, 2,000 Danis came to Christian faith, burned their traditional fetishes, and began to share the gospel with other Danis. On one day, in 1960, 8,000 Danis declared their faith in Christ and burned their fetishes.

Missionary James Sunda began meeting for prayer and Bible study with Dani leaders. One morning the Dani leaders said to Sunda, "We have been reading the Bible. It seems to teach that Christians should not kill others. Is that right?"

"Yes, that is right," answered Sunda.

"But," rejoined the Dani leaders, "Our way of life demands that we raise pigs, sacrifice them for our ancestors, hold a great feast, and then make war on the people in the next valley. That is what we have always believed and what we have always done. Now that we are Christians, should we not stop this?"

"That is correct," said Sunda. "What *are* you going to do?"

"We plan to have a big feast, invite our enemies, and while they are here, tell them we have become Christians and Christians do not kill others. We will burn one-half our weapons. They will know we cannot attack them but that if they attack us, we have enough weapons to defend ourselves."

What happened? The West Danis accepted a new authority. They changed from basing their beliefs (sacrificing to ancestors) and their practices (war) on their traditions to a new authority, the Bible.[15]

The biblical teachings as to the origin of Scripture follow a pattern. God revealed himself through his mighty acts—such as creation, exodus, incarnation, transfiguration, crucifixion, and resurrection. The Spirit of God moved writers to observe and comprehend what God was saying in the events. The same Spirit then guided these writers to write exactly the message God intended. God preserved these writings, and now the Spirit guides believers in understanding them. The Bible is, therefore, a revelation of divine origin, a revelation that is, as Baptist seminary professor T. B. Maston said, "from God, of God, to man, through man."[7] The Bible thus constitutes the inspired, infallible Word of God.

The truth of its divine origin establishes the Bible as a unique authority for you—an authority that can be claimed by no other source. Baptist pastor George W. Truett said, "Not traditions, nor customs, nor councils, nor confessions, nor ecclesiastical formularies, however venerable and pretentious, guide Baptists, but simply and solely the will of Christ as they find it revealed in the New Testament."[8]

The Bible also claims authority in your life because it represents ultimate truth. Scripture is the record of God's revelation of himself through inspired writers. Baptists, therefore, affirm the Scriptures as a "perfect treasure of divine instruction."[9] The Bible's authority in believers' lives stems from the conviction that the Scriptures constitute "truth, without any mixture of error."[10]

Some Notable Statements Concerning Biblical Authority:[16]

- "The ultimate source of authority is Jesus Christ the Lord, and every area of life is to be subject to his Lordship."
- "The Bible as the inspired revelation of God's will and way, made full and complete in the life and teachings of Christ, is our authoritative rule of faith and practice."
- "The Holy Spirit is God actively revealing himself and his will to people. He therefore interprets and confirms the voice of divine authority."

Baptist statements of belief over the years have affirmed consistently that the Bible is the sole authority for faith and practice. "Sole authority" does not mean that Baptists find truth in no other source. Rather, it means that the Bible, when interpreted by the same Spirit who inspired it, is sufficient and able to guide believers to everything necessary for belief and behavior—for faith and practice. Christians accept other sources of truth only as they conform to the overall teachings of Scripture.

The assurance of the reliability, trustworthiness, and infallibility of Scripture assures believers that what the Bible teaches them to believe and practice will never be wrong. The totally inspired Bible never contradicts itself. No human statement of doctrine or the pronouncements of any Christian leader hold authority equal to the Bible.

The Bible will become authoritative in your life as you accept it as the Word of God leading without error to all matters of doctrine and behavior.

Flowing from Accurate Interpretation (2 Peter 1:19–21)

Scripture will become authoritative in your life as its teachings flow from accurate interpretation. In 2 Peter 1:19–21 the apostle was probably combating the gnostic heresy that regarded Christ as a lower manifestation of the highest deity. Peter declared that his being an eyewitness of the transfiguration gave a personal and dynamic insight to the majesty of Christ (2 Pet. 1:16–18).

In verse 19, "the word of the prophets made more certain," might mean that the prophetic witness had greater force than did Peter's eyewitness to the transfiguration. More likely, Peter's words mean that the transfiguration confirmed the messianic prophecies and made clear Christ's deity.[11]

Peter declared that the Scriptures did not come into being by the impulses or will of humans but rather by those "carried along" by the Spirit (2 Pet. 1:21) so that they wrote the true and accurate Word of God. Peter did not argue for Scripture's inspiration; he assumed it.

To the conviction that the Holy Spirit directed the writing of Scripture, Peter added that the Spirit must also guide humans to understand and interpret the Word. The New International Version of verse 20 is, "no prophecy of Scripture came about by the prophet's own interpretation." Consider these other possible translations, too: "There is no prophetic teaching found in scripture that can be interpreted by man's unaided reason" (The Twentieth Century New Testament) and " . . . No prophetic scripture allows a man to interpret it by himself" (Moffatt). The Holy Spirit moved authors to write the Scriptures; the Spirit will also move people to understand and interpret it.

The Bible will assume a place of authority in your life only as you develop adequate methods of Bible study. When your interpretations flow from the Spirit who inspired the Scriptures, the teachings will assume a more powerful place in your life.

Providing Solid Guidance for Christian Living
(Psalm 119:97-112; Romans 15:4; 2 Timothy 3:14-17)

Scripture will become authoritative in your life as it provides solid and practical guidance for Christian living. Paul declared the Word "useful," that is, having potential to result in proper living (2 Tim. 3:16).

The Bible is useful in providing guidance for life. The guidance of the Scriptures assures believers that they will find and follow the will of God if they are faithful to biblical teachings (Psalm 119:104–105). Baptist leader Charles Wade has written, "We must always go to the Scriptures to find guidance and answers. . . . We must use the Bible as our plumb line, the standard by which we evaluate our own personal opinions and attitudes about a given issue."[12]

The Bible is useful in providing hope that leads to endurance. Paul, in Romans 15:4, indicated that Scripture was written "to teach us, so that through endurance and the encouragement of the Scriptures we might have hope."

The Bible is useful in providing conviction of sin. The words of Scripture bring to light the hidden sinfulness of our hearts and drive us to repentance (Hebrews 4:12–13). Few lessons are more advantageous than this.

The Bible is useful in warning against sin. The psalmist considered the Word of God as of great benefit and power because in this Law the psalmist found wisdom, insight, and protection from sinful behavior (Ps. 119:97–102). God's Word guided the psalmist to hate sin and thereby avoid wrong paths (Ps. 19:10–13; 119:104). For this reason, the psalmist had "hidden" (stored up and protected) the Word in his heart so that he would not sin against God (Ps. 119:11).

The Bible is useful in leading to the full meaning of salvation. In 2 Timothy 3:14–17, the Apostle Paul declared that the Scriptures are able to "make you wise for salvation through faith in Christ Jesus" (2 Tim. 3:15). The Bible leads believers in the dual dimensions of salvation—that is, how to be saved and how to live as a saved person.

The Bible is useful for teaching (instruction) in religious and ethical insight and for stimulating to deeper discipleship (2 Tim. 3:16). The presence of heresy in Timothy's day made sound doctrinal teaching imperative. Is this situation not also reflected today?

The Bible Becomes Authoritative for Any Christian:

- When that Christian comes to a personal experience with Christ through the Scriptures
- When that believer understands the nature of the Bible and accepts its divine origin and authority
- When that believer's understanding of the Bible flows from accurate interpretation of the Word
- When the believer understands and avails himself or herself of the living usefulness of Scripture

Allow the Spirit to make the Bible authoritative in your life!

The Scriptures are useful for reproof ("rebuking"). Reproof exposes false teaching, reveals inadequate understanding, and unmasks false teachers. The term likely relates both to exposing false teachers and to exposing errors in our personal lives. "Scripture can show sinners their failures, clarify the point of the mistake, and lead them to a new sense of peace and wholeness."[13]

The Bible is useful for correction. This term suggests that the Bible helps Christians restore their doctrine and/or personal practice to conformity to the will of God. Correction involves a most positive factor in the use of Scripture.

Scripture also is useful in providing moral "training" that leads to righteous living. Paul employed this parental term for disciplining a child and developing his or her character. The term carries the idea of a system of discipline that leads to a divinely acceptable lifestyle.

The Bible is useful in equipping the people of God. As believers avail themselves of this profitable revelation, they will be "thoroughly equipped for every good work" (2 Tim. 3:17). "Thoroughly equipped" means *in fit shape or condition*. The result is that the worker is totally enabled to do whatever God calls on him or her to do and that this equipping is an abiding condition.[14] The Christian leader who accepts

The Uses of the Bible in the Believer's Life

- Guiding in life and thought
- Providing hope that leads to endurance
- Instructing in the fullest meaning of salvation
- Warning against the evils of sin
- Producing conviction of sin
- Instructing in religious and ethical thought
- Exposing errors in thought and life (reproof)
- Restoring doctrinal truth and ethical behavior (correction)
- Training in moral living that leads to righteousness
- Equipping for service

and lives by the authoritative Word of God will have the tools to deal with any task he or she might face.

The Scripture will assume authority in your life as you accept and act on its tremendous usefulness as a guide for Christian living.

The Bible, Our Sole and Sufficient Guide

For Baptists, the Bible is the sole and sufficient guide to all matters of belief and behavior—to faith and practice. Baptists, therefore, neither hold to a creed nor give total deference to the pronouncements of any leader. The authority for Baptists rests in Christ as Christ is revealed in the Scriptures.[17] As you allow the Spirit to work in your life, you will affirm the Bible, and it will become more and more authoritative for you.

QUESTIONS

1. Are there areas of your life that are governed more by tradition, that is, what you have always believed or always been told, than by Scripture? List any such areas and write plans by which you might reverse this trend.

2. Of the ways described by which a believer might develop a deeper commitment to biblical authority, which do you think would be most profitable in your life?

3. Often we say Baptists accept the Scriptures as the sole authority for all matters of faith and practice. What problems do you see in the term, "sole"?

4. What do you think allows sincere, Bible-loving Christians to come to differing interpretations of Scripture? What should be done in such situations?

NOTES

1. Walter Thomas Conner, *Christian Doctrine* (Nashville, Tennessee: Broadman Press, 1937), 42.
2. Russell H. Dilday, Jr., *The Doctrine of Biblical Authority* (Nashville: Convention Press, 1982), 20, italics in original.
3. Article 1, "The Baptist Faith and Message," 1963. For a copy of "The Baptist Faith and Message," 1963, see http://texasbaptists.org/files/2010/08/1963BaptistFaithandMessage1.pdf. Accessed 12/8/2010.
4. Herschel H. Hobbs, "The Authority of the Bible," Address at the Conference on Biblical Authority, Southeastern Baptist Theological Seminary, January 29–30, 1980, pages 5–7, and W. T. Conner, *Revelation and God* (Nashville: Broadman Press, 1936), 96.
5. Dilday, 29.
6. A. T. Robertson, *Word Pictures in the New Testament* (Nashville, Tennessee: Broadman Press, 1933), VI:179.
7. T. B. Maston, *Why Live the Christian Life?* (Nashville: Thomas Nelson, 1974), 47.
8. "Baptists and Religious Liberty," in *A Sourcebook for Baptist Heritage*, ed. H. Leon McBeth (Nashville: Broadman Press, 1990), 470. The full text of George W. Truett's sermon, "Baptists and Religious Liberty," can also be accessed on the internet at this address: www.bjconline.org. See "Sermons" under "Resources." Accessed 12/3/2010
9. Article 1, "The Baptist Faith and Message," 1963.
10. Article 1, "The Baptist Faith and Message," 1963.
11. A. T. Robertson, VI:157.
12. Charles R. Wade, with Lee and Carol Bowman, *The Jesus Principle: Building Churches in the Likeness of Christ* (Arlington, TX: Clear Stream Publishing Inc., 1998), 169.
13. Thomas D. Lea, *1 & 2 Timothy*, The New American Commentary (Nashville: Broadman Press, 1992), 237.
14. Lea, 237.
15. See James Sunda, *Church Growth in West New Guinea* (Lucknow, India: Lucknow Publishing House, 1963), 22–45; Donald A. McGavran, *Understanding Church Growth*, 3d ed. (Grand Rapids: Eerdmans, 1990), 128, 241, 256–57.
16. From "Baptist Ideals" a statement prepared for the 1964 celebration of the one hundred and fiftieth anniversary of the organization of the first Baptist national organization in America. Prepared by a committee chaired by Ralph A Herring. Contained in Walter B. Shurden, *The Baptist Identity: Four Fragile Freedoms* (Macon, Georgia: Smyth & Helwys Publishing,1993), 103–104.
17. For additional assistance on the topic of this lesson, see *The Bible—You Can Believe It* by James C. Denison (Dallas, TX: BaptistWay Press, 2005). Call 1-866-249-1799 or see www.baptistwaypress.org.

LESSON THREE

The Autonomy of the Local Congregation of Believers

BACKGROUND SCRIPTURES

Matthew 18:15-20; Acts 6:3-6; 13:1-3; 14:23,27; 15:1-30; 16:5; 20:28; 1 Corinthians 1:2; 5:1-5; Revelation 2–3

FOCAL TEXTS

Matthew 18:15-20; Acts 6:3-6; 13:1-3; 1 Corinthians 5:1-5

MAIN IDEA

"Each local church is self-governing and independent in the management of its affairs."[1]

STUDY AIM

To explain why Baptists believe that each local church is autonomous and identify implications of this idea

QUICK READ

Members of a local Baptist church have the responsibility and privilege of making the decisions that chart the church's course. No external authority can tell a Baptist church what to do

People unfamiliar with Baptists often do not understand the nature of Baptist churches and how they relate to one another. They especially may not comprehend a people whose national, state, or other organization beyond the local church does not dictate the actions of the local church. Decisions made in these organizations beyond the local church hold no power over the local church to make changes.

Baptists structure their churches as congregations in which the members make the decisions and choose to cooperate with other like-minded churches. This polity (structure) makes sense when you look at the Baptist doctrines we're studying. Salvation by grace, soul competency, priesthood of the believers, symbolic ordinances—it makes sense that Baptist church structure reflects the basic belief in the individual responsibility of a believer to work for the kingdom of God, share the gospel, and join a community of faith for nurture and growth. Of course the individual believer would have a voice in the governance of the church! We call this way of doing a church's work the autonomy of the local church. "Autonomy" comes from the Greek words *autos* and *nomos*, meaning "self" and "law." An autonomous church rules itself.

Many Christian denominations structure their churches and the relationships between congregations differently than Baptists do. Each type of church structure rests on a certain interpretation of biblical passages. When Baptists developed in the early 1600s and searched Scripture for their model of church polity, they understood the overall sense of Scripture to support a congregational model as we have today. Acts 6:3–6 taught them that churches choose their own leaders. Matthew 18:15–20 and 1 Corinthians 5:1–5 taught them that churches decide how to discipline members. And Acts 13:1–3 taught them that local churches choose people for ministry as led by the Holy Spirit.

Matthew 18:15–20 (NRSV)

15 "If another member of the church sins against you, go and point
out the fault when the two of you are alone. If the member listens to
you, you have regained that one. 16 But if you are not listened to, take
one or two others along with you, so that every word may be confirmed
by the evidence of two or three witnesses. 17 If the member refuses to
listen to them, tell it to the church; and if the offender refuses to listen
even to the church, let such a one be to you as a Gentile and a tax collector. 18 Truly I tell you, whatever you bind on earth will be bound in
heaven, and whatever you loose on earth will be loosed in heaven.
19 Again, truly I tell you, if two of you agree on earth about anything you
ask, it will be done for you by my Father in heaven. 20 For where two or
three are gathered in my name, I am there among them."

Acts 6:3–6

3 Therefore, friends, select from among yourselves seven men of
good standing, full of the Spirit and of wisdom, whom we may appoint
to this task, 4 while we, for our part, will devote ourselves to prayer and
to serving the word." 5 What they said pleased the whole community,
and they chose Stephen, a man full of faith and the Holy Spirit,
together with Philip, Prochorus, Nicanor, Timon, Parmenas, and
Nicolaus, a proselyte of Antioch. 6 They had these men stand before
the apostles, who prayed and laid their hands on them.

Acts 13:1–3

1 Now in the church at Antioch there were prophets and teachers:
Barnabas, Simeon who was called Niger, Lucius of Cyrene, Manaen a
member of the court of Herod the ruler, and Saul. 2 While they were
worshiping the Lord and fasting, the Holy Spirit said, "Set apart for
me Barnabas and Saul for the work to which I have called them."
3 Then after fasting and praying they laid their hands on them and
sent them off.

1 Corinthians 5:1–5

[1]It is actually reported that there is sexual immorality among you, and of a kind that is not found even among pagans; for a man is living with his father's wife. [2]And you are arrogant! Should you not rather have mourned, so that he who has done this would have been removed from among you?

[3]For though absent in body, I am present in spirit; and as if present I have already pronounced judgment [4]in the name of the Lord Jesus on the man who has done such a thing. When you are assembled, and my spirit is present with the power of our Lord Jesus, [5]you are to hand this man over to Satan for the destruction of the flesh, so that his spirit may be saved in the day of the Lord.

God Is Present . . . (Acts 6:3–6)

God is present where two or three are gathered in the Lord's name (Matthew 18:20). So, wherever believers gather, they have the leadership of the Holy Spirit as a community of faith. They thus can make all the decisions necessary as a congregation. As individuals, each person carries the responsibility to live for God, to interpret Scripture, and to be Christ in the world. But as a community of faith, God's presence sharpens those responsibilities and focuses them for the good of the church.

In Acts 6:3–6, God focused the concept of service for the Jerusalem church. The apostles spent their time in worship and teaching the new Christians. They didn't have time to take care of the needy of the congregation. Under Jewish law, God required believers to take special care of widows and orphans. The Greek-speaking widows in the Jerusalem church felt neglected by the leaders. The church solved the problem by choosing from the congregation seven people to act as servants in distributing food and other necessities to the needy. For this lesson, the important point is that the people chose the servants. Peter and the other apostles did not say, "You, you, and you." Rather, they relied on the Holy Spirit working in the average church member to choose wisely.

The folks in the congregation looked for Spirit-filled and God-directed believers who could do the job. The members worked from their knowledge of each other and what the job required. Once the congregation chose the seven servants, the apostles set the men aside for special duties in a public ceremony. The public ceremony did not give the men special power. The laying on of hands simply indicated to the assembly that the servants accepted their new responsibilities and that the church made a covenant with them to help with the work. The members of the congregation chose wisely, for the servants did the job and did it well.

In Acts 6:3–6, the autonomy of the local church shines through. People perceived a need. The congregation, under the leadership of the Holy Spirit, determined a way to meet the need. The members chose people to do the actual work. No one told the congregation what they must do. No one ordered the selection of certain people. No one said, "If you don't do it this way, you aren't a true believer."

For Baptists, the Bible affirms that the local church is responsible for its own business, both spiritual and practical. The congregation may choose to cooperate with others, as in an association or convention, but "other groups or churches cannot take away the decision-making responsibilities of the local congregation."[2] God is present where two or three are gathered, and those two or three must make their own decisions under God's leadership.

When Decisions Have to Be Made . . .
(Matthew 18:15-20; 1 Corinthians 5:1-5)

When I teach Church History or Baptist History and come to the lecture on church discipline, the topic always creates discomfort. No one wants to be seen as judgmental or fanatical. Saying to fellow church members that they need to mend their ways requires special care. Thankfully, this lesson centers on the autonomy of the local church. So I don't have to deal specifically with the issue of church discipline. But we will focus on these passages as they make the point that the local church, and not some external agency or group, chooses what shall and shall not require discipline.

The New Testament teaches that the local church has responsibility for taking care of both practical and spiritual matters in its midst. Both Matthew 18:15–20 and 1 Corinthians 5:1–5 clearly note that the local folks must make decisions for the good of the congregation as well as the good of individual members. In some denominations, discipline is ordered by a hierarchy outside the local church. For Baptists, discipline remains within the control of the local congregation. Furthermore, discipline is a congregational decision, not the decision of one or two people.

These passages assert that God's presence with a group of believers establishes the necessary power for making decisions. Matthew 18 does not say you must wait until an outside authority gives an order before your congregation can act. In 1 Corinthians 5, Paul urged the community of faith to remove an immoral member. Paul, however, also recognized that the action must result from the leadership of God. Central to Baptist thought lies the idea that the corporate consciousness of Christ comes through when a congregation meets to make a decision. Paul's concerns, aired in a meeting and commented on, might galvanize the Corinthian church to take action. Still, Paul could only suggest action. The final decision rested with the folks in Corinth and how they perceived God's leadership.

From the days of the New Testament, local churches have cooperated with one another to accomplish greater good. In Romans 16:1–2, we learn that churches accepted members from other congregations. First Corinthians 16:1–4 shows that churches pooled their resources in a good cause. And the existence of the New Testament itself proves that churches shared letters and information among themselves for the good of all (Colossians 4:16–17).[3] While acting as autonomous churches, congregations still cooperated in many endeavors.

For modern Baptists, the issue becomes complicated because autonomous local churches have chosen to relate to one another and cooperate to accomplish tasks that single congregations could not. We relate to other Baptist churches in our geographical area through the local association and the state convention. Each group we relate to has the right and responsibility to set standards for the relationship. We as a church have a voice in establishing those standards. If for some reason we deviate from the standards set, then the association or convention has the authority to "dis-fellowship" us, to withdraw cooperation, and we must go on our way. Each level of relationship makes its own decisions based on what the members believe to be right.

For example, one Baptist association chose to welcome a woman as pastor of one of the churches. Affirming the local congregation members' right to choose their own pastor, the association treated and worked with her church as it had for decades. Another association nearby chose to "dis-fellowship" a church for calling a woman minister. For the members of that association, the standard of who could be a church minister did not include women. Thus that association excluded the congregation in question. For our purposes in this lesson, I must affirm both decisions. Both decisions recognized that the local church must make its own choices, but also that those choices carry consequences. However I feel personally about the "right" or "wrong" of

Setting People Apart for Service

In the New Testament, a church would set people apart in public ceremonies for special tasks, as with the Antioch congregation laying hands on Paul and Barnabas (Acts 13:1–3). Such a ceremony was not a requirement to be met before becoming a minister. The Bible emphasizes that the lives of the people chosen for special work, whether Phoebe of Cenchreae (Romans 16:1), Philip of Samaria (Acts 6:5), or Epaphroditus of Philippi (Philippians 2:25), bore testimony to God's presence. The Holy Spirit led and reinforced the congregation's decision.

women in ministry—and as a woman minister in the teaching profession, I have strong opinions!—both associations acted within mainstream Baptist doctrine because neither dictated to the local church who must be their pastor.

Baptists historically have affirmed local church autonomy, but we also have asserted cooperation for missions, evangelism, and so forth. Many churches working together accomplish more than one church. In 1814 churches across America joined together to support Anne Hazeltine and Adoniram Judson as missionaries by forming the Baptist General Missionary Convention. When these churches joined together, they agreed to work together for missions. Note that as individual churches they differed greatly! They worshiped in different ways. They had different concepts of who should be church leaders. They felt differently about including people of other races in their memberships. They had different concepts of the atonement and the work of the Holy Spirit. However, they all agreed that God wanted them to support and do missions. So they put aside their differences, differences they saw as less important than missions. They focused on the all-important task of missions.

Mainstream Baptists have worked to accept diversity while maintaining cooperation among congregations. In 1845, the Southern Baptist Convention split from the General Missionary Convention because the difference in the Northern and Southern views of slavery caused too much trouble.

Your Spiritual Gifts

Knowing your spiritual gifts will help you decide in which areas of church service to engage. Determine your gifts by talking with Christian friends who know you well, thinking about what you like to do and do well in the church, and praying for God to show you what gifts the Spirit has placed in your life. Read 1 Corinthians 12:4–11 and Ephesians 4:11–13 to see whether one or more of those gifts fits you.

In recent years, splits have occurred among Baptists because a church's concept of Scripture or of ministry or of missions or of ministerial authority differed too much from what a group accepted as true. A tough question facing twenty-first-century Baptists is, "How much difference is too much?" In the past, Baptists have accepted a great deal of difference and still cooperated. Today, mainstream Baptists still accept differences and cooperate. How much difference is "too much"? And who answers that question for you?

Concerning the Work of the Kingdom . . . (Acts 13:1-3)

I grew up attending the mission organizations for children and youth—Sunbeams, GAs, and YWAs. I served as a Journeyman missionary. Missions was, is, and always will be important to me. So, with great pleasure, I turn our attention to the concept of local church autonomy as it worked out in missions in the first century.

The story should be familiar to you. Barnabas, the Son of Encouragement, traveled to Antioch of Syria because the Jerusalem church heard that a Christian congregation had taken root there and was growing rapidly. Barnabas found the young congregation thriving and on target with their understanding of the gospel. Calling in Paul to help teach and nurture the young believers, the two men worked with the church for more than a year (Acts 11:19–30).

As the congregation was worshiping and fasting, the Holy Spirit led the congregation to "set apart" these two leaders "for the work to which I have called them" (Acts 13:2). In Judaism and early Christianity, a person fasted to emphasize the importance of a serious request. A person also fasted to focus on prayer and the will of God. So, because the people in Antioch wanted to know God's will, and they were serious about the effort, the Holy Spirit led the congregation to set aside Barnabas and Paul for special work. The Antioch folks became the first missionary sending organization! And Paul and Barnabas, the first full-fledged missionaries!

The local church made the choice under God's leadership. The local congregation responded to the prompting of the Holy Spirit in choosing the ones to be sent. The local church thus is seen to be the basic organizational building block of Baptist missionary efforts.

Over the years, the way churches did missions changed. In 1792, British Baptists formed the Baptist Missionary Society to send William and Dorothy Carey, and others, to India to preach the gospel. In 1814, the General Missionary Convention was formed in America to support Anne Hazeltine and Adoniram Judson's work in Burma. In 1845, when Southern Baptists split from the General Convention, the messengers to the formation convention established the Foreign Mission Board and the Domestic Mission Board before anything else. Why the move away from the Antioch model of an individual church sending missionaries?

The basic answer is that Baptists are a practical people. They figured out that by pooling funds, they could send more missionaries, and equip them better, than a single church could. Because missions carried such importance, most Baptist churches modified their concern for absolute local autonomy to participate in the larger missions effort. However, some folks did not believe the Bible authorized any agency beyond the local church. Thus they refused to be part of missionary societies or conventions. These congregations, known as Anti-Mission Baptists, acted true to their Baptist heritage of local church decision-making. They chose not to join associations or conventions. If one of these churches engaged in missions or evangelism, it pursued the activity without help from others.

For the Anti-Mission Baptists, the cooperating Baptists moved too far from a certain interpretation of Scripture, and so fellowship was broken. For the cooperating Baptists, the Anti-Mission folks interpreted the Bible too narrowly. The command to preach the gospel to the world held more importance than an interpretation condemning missionary organizations beyond the local church. Both groups took seriously the autonomy of the local church, but they understood that autonomy differently when they related it to the Great Commission.

A Current Concern

A modern development threatening the Baptist doctrine of the autonomy of the local church is the adoption by some congregations of the business model with a CEO running the operation. If the pastor functions as a CEO, and the paid ministerial staff work for the pastor, what role does the congregational member have? When the CEO makes all the decisions and simply informs the congregation, what remains for the member to do besides supply money? This increasingly popular organizational model is not Baptist, and it undercuts the rights and privileges of individual members of the congregation. Ministers, in Baptist life, are not "rulers." They are "servants." Remember, ultimately we are all priests.

QUESTIONS

1. What do you think of the CEO model for a pastor? Why might folks prefer that model to the historical Baptist model?

2. How seriously do you take your responsibilities as a church member?

3. Whose responsibility is the running of the church? the mission of the church? the finances of the church?

NOTES

1. Walter Thomas Conner, *Christian Doctrine* (Nashville, Tennessee: Broadman Press, 1937), 266.
2. Rosalie Beck, "The Church is Free to Make Its Own Decisions under the Lordship of Christ," in *Defining Baptist Convictions for the Twenty-First Century*, ed. Charles W. Deweese (Franklin, Tennessee: Providence House Publishers, 1996), 131.
3. H. Leon McBeth, "Autonomy and Cooperation," in the *Foundations of Baptist Heritage Series* (Nashville, Tennessee: The Historical Commission of the Southern Baptist Convention, 1989), 1.

LESSON FOUR

Believer's Baptism and Church Membership

BACKGROUND SCRIPTURES

Matthew 28:19-20; Mark 1:9-11; Luke 3:21-22; John 3:23; Acts 2:14-47; 5:11-14; 8:26-39; 16:11-15, 25-34; Romans 1:7; 6:3-5; 1 Corinthians 1:2; 3:16; Colossians 2:12

FOCAL TEXTS

Acts 8:26-38; 16:11-15, 25-34

MAIN IDEA

" . . . The only person properly qualified for baptism is one who has heard the gospel, accepted its message, and believed in Christ as . . . Savior."[1] "Only those should be received into church membership who give credible evidence that they have received Christ as Savior and Lord."[2]

STUDY AIM

To state the meaning of believer's baptism and why it is important

QUICK READ

Baptism, the immersion of a believer in water in the name of the Holy Trinity, symbolizes the total salvation experience, testifies of the believer's commitment to Jesus, and provides access to church membership.

The baptismal service had been announced, the baptismal pool had been prepared, and the two teenage women candidates were present and ready. What was more, the unsaved father of one of the young women together with three unsaved friends of both were present. It promised to be a significant worship experience and a tremendous witnessing opportunity.

As is too often the case, a problem also arose. For reasons still undetermined, the water in the baptismal pool was near the boiling point. Deacons said we would just have to postpone the service. I told them that the unsaved father and the unsaved friends were present and that we must have the baptismal service that morning. We could wait until the end of the morning rather than early in the service, but we had to do it that morning.

"What will we do?" asked the deacons.

"I don't know," I answered. "I must begin the service. You are the deacons. You will work it out."

We heard strange noises from the baptistery during the service. At the time for the baptismal service, the minister of youth proceeded to baptize both young women—one by her baptism testifying to her own father and both of them to their friends.

What had happened to make the baptismal pool usable? During the service, the deacons had purchased fifty-two bags of ice and put them into it. The water was then cool enough for the service to proceed.

What was the big deal? Why not postpone the service? The young women were believers; their salvation did not depend on their baptism. The young women needed in obedience to their Lord to follow him in baptism, but that could wait a week. The baptism had to be Scriptural; immersion was necessary. The witness of baptism was imperative, though, especially in view of the presence of the unsaved father and their unsaved friends. The church was prepared to receive the two into membership. Baptism that day was important!

What actually is baptism and why is it important in the Christian life? This lesson seeks to guide you to understand fully, accept personally, and explain adequately the biblical meaning of baptism—its religious significance and its eternal importance.

Acts 8:26-38 (NIV)

26Now an angel of the Lord said to Philip, "Go south to the road—the
desert road—that goes down from Jerusalem to Gaza." 27So he started
out, and on his way he met an Ethiopian eunuch, an important official
in charge of all the treasury of Candace, queen of the Ethiopians. This
man had gone to Jerusalem to worship, 28and on his way home was
sitting in his chariot reading the book of Isaiah the prophet. 29The
Spirit told Philip, "Go to that chariot and stay near it."

30Then Philip ran up to the chariot and heard the man reading
Isaiah the prophet. "Do you understand what you are reading?" Philip
asked.

31"How can I," he said, "unless someone explains it to me?" So he
invited Philip to come up and sit with him.

32The eunuch was reading this passage of Scripture:

"He was led like a sheep to the slaughter,
and as a lamb before the shearer is silent,
so he did not open his mouth.
33In his humiliation he was deprived of justice.
Who can speak of his descendants?
For his life was taken from the earth."

34The eunuch asked Philip, "Tell me, please, who is the prophet talking about, himself or someone else?" 35Then Philip began with that
very passage of Scripture and told him the good news about Jesus.

36As they traveled along the road, they came to some water and
the eunuch said, "Look, here is water. Why shouldn't I be baptized?"
38And he gave orders to stop the chariot. Then both Philip and the
eunuch went down into the water and Philip baptized him.

Acts 16:11-15, 25-34

11From Troas we put out to sea and sailed straight for Samothrace,
and the next day on to Neapolis. 12From there we traveled to Philippi, a
Roman colony and the leading city of that district of Macedonia. And
we stayed there several days.

[13]On the Sabbath we went outside the city gate to the river, where we
expected to find a place of prayer. We sat down and began to speak to
the women who had gathered there. [14]One of those listening was a
woman named Lydia, a dealer in purple cloth from the city of Thyatira,
who was a worshiper of God. The Lord opened her heart to respond to
Paul's message. [15]When she and the members of her household were
baptized, she invited us to her home. "If you consider me a believer in the
Lord," she said, "come and stay at my house." And she persuaded us.

• •

[25]About midnight Paul and Silas were praying and singing hymns to
God, and the other prisoners were listening to them. [26]Suddenly there
was such a violent earthquake that the foundations of the prison were
shaken. At once all the prison doors flew open, and everybody's chains
came loose. [27]The jailer woke up, and when he saw the prison doors
open, he drew his sword and was about to kill himself because he
thought the prisoners had escaped. [28]But Paul shouted, "Don't harm
yourself! We are all here!"

[29]The jailer called for lights, rushed in and fell trembling before Paul
and Silas. [30]He then brought them out and asked, "Sirs, what must I
do to be saved?"

[31]They replied, "Believe in the Lord Jesus, and you will be saved—
you and your household." [32]Then they spoke the word of the Lord to
him and to all the others in his house. [33]At that hour of the night the
jailer took them and washed their wounds; then immediately he and all
his family were baptized. [34]The jailer brought them into his house and
set a meal before them; he was filled with joy because he had come to
believe in God—he and his whole family.

The Meaning of Baptism (Acts 8:26–38; 16:11–15, 25–34)

What is the biblical meaning of baptism? We can capsule this meaning by considering two significant words—*believer* and *symbolic*. Biblical teachings restrict baptism to people who have repented of their sins, accepted Christ as Savior, and determined to follow him as Lord. The passages for study present accounts of salvation experiences in the New Testament—each of which point to salvation coming before baptism.

On the day of Pentecost a miraculous event empowered the gathered disciples to proclaim the gospel in different languages so that peoples from many different lands could understand it in their most familiar tongues (Acts 2:1–13). Peter proclaimed God's message, explaining that the observed event had been foretold by the prophet Joel and that God would bring salvation to all who accepted the message (Acts 2:14–36). After hearing Peter's witness, the people cried, "What shall we do?" (Acts 2:37). Peter's answer was, "'Repent and be baptized, every one of you, in the name of Jesus Christ for the forgiveness of your sins. And you will receive the gift of the Holy Spirit'" (Acts 2:38).

Some confusion exists concerning this verse. Some have understood it to teach baptism as essential for salvation rather than a testimony of salvation. Understanding the verse hinges on the word, "for," which may be translated *for, unto, on the basis of, with respect to,* or even *as a result of.*[3] The word is used in Matthew 12:41 and Luke 11:32 with reference to the preaching of Jonah, saying that the people in Nineveh repented "at" the preaching of Jonah. Clearly, the meaning is not that they repented so that Jonah could preach but as a result of the preaching. Interpreting Acts 2:38 as meaning "repent and be baptized" *as a result of* or *on the basis of* the forgiveness of sins is linguistically sound and conforms to the broad teachings of the New Testament on the subjects of salvation and baptism.

Acts 8:26–38. The same teaching springs from the account of the deacon Philip and the treasury official from the land of Ethiopia (Acts 8:26–38). That the Ethiopian had been in Jerusalem for worship suggests he may well have been a proselyte or at least a God-fearer. (The term *God-fearer* refers to a person who was not a full-fledged Jew but who nevertheless worshiped the God of Israel.) The Ethiopian was reading Isaiah 53:7. He could not understand it, however, until Philip explained the Isaiah text and also told him the good news about Jesus (Acts 8:35).

Upon hearing the witness concerning Jesus, the Ethiopian cried out (8:36), "'Look, here is water, Why shouldn't I be baptized?'" The evangelist and the new believer descended from the chariot and went down

Ancient Baptismal Practices

Christianity was not the only religion to practice baptism in biblical times. Several different religious groups used baptism as a ritual relating to the removal of guilt and the beginning of a new life. Some of the mystery religions (called "mystery" religions because they used secret rites and methods) used baptism at times, even in blood. Around the time of Jesus, the Jews began using baptism for Gentile converts to Judaism.

The baptism of John the Baptist was similar to but different from that which early Christians used. John's baptism was one of repentance, calling people back to faithfulness and commitment to the law of God (Matt. 3:5–12; Luke 3:3). The baptism of John related to moral and ethical purification. Second, John's baptism looked forward to the coming of Messiah (Matt. 3:2; Mark 1:7–8).

Jesus followed John's baptism, thus showing the Lord's identification with the religious concerns of John and with sinful humanity (Matt 3:15; 2 Cor. 5:21). The Lord adapted baptism for his movement, commanding his followers to baptize those who became followers. Paul's understanding was that one was baptized into Christ, referring to relationship to Christ.

Baptism in the New Testament demonstrates a rich symbolism and a vital purpose. It became the first public act that identified believers with the death and resurrection of Christ. Baptism symbolized the inclusion of a person into the saving mission of Jesus.

into the water. Philip baptized the new convert (Acts 8:38). Verse 37, as it appears in the King James Version, is not adequately supported by the earlier manuscripts and is not in Lukan style. Therefore, most authorities consider the verse a later addition and not a part of the original, inspired text. Even without verse 37, the most likely understanding is that baptism follows and pictures salvation.

Acts 16:11–15. Two events in Acts 16, the conversion and baptism of Lydia and the jailer, took place in the city of Philippi. These events underline the proper sequence—salvation then baptism (Acts 16:11–15,25–34). Paul and his group had sailed from Troas, in the Roman province of Asia, to the island of Samothrace, and from there to Neapolis, the port city. Neapolis was about ten miles from Philippi in Macedonia, which was located in the area of modern Greece.

No record exists of Paul entering a synagogue in Philippi. Since ten adult men were required for establishing a synagogue, one may not have existed. Paul and his group went on the Sabbath to a place on the river, thinking a Jewish place of worship existed there. The apostle found there a group of worshiping women, including Lydia. She came from the city of Thyatira in the Roman province of Asia. Thyatira was well-known for its purple cloth. Lydia may have dealt in this cloth. More importantly, she was a "worshiper of God," perhaps already a proselyte (Acts 16:14). "The Lord opened her heart" and brought her to salvation (16:14). After her salvation, Lydia and her "household"—that is, family, slaves, and other dependents—were baptized (16:15). Clearly, salvation came first and then baptism.

Acts 16:25–34. The experience of the jailer in Philippi reinforces this teaching. After Paul cast the evil spirit from the slave girl and ruined the moneymaking scheme of some citizens of Philippi, these businessmen had Paul and Silas jailed (see Acts 16:16–24). Their prayers and hymns testified to their faith. The earthquake at midnight opened the doors and unlocked the shackles that held them. Thinking the prisoners had escaped, the jailer was in the process of falling on his sword when Paul stopped him. So impressed was the jailer that he called for the apostles and asked (Acts 16:29), "'What must I do to be saved?'" After salvation, he and his family were baptized. Once again, the meaning of baptism demands that saving faith precede it.

Baptism's meaning begins with the fact that only a believer, a saved person, should be baptized. This biblical truth rules out baptizing babies or others who cannot personally respond to Jesus in faith. The truth also denies any practice of being baptized for others—such as people who have already died. Only a person saved by faith in Jesus Christ can be properly baptized.

A second significant word, symbolic, also describes the meaning of baptism. Baptists regard baptism and the Lord's Supper as purely, totally, and only symbolic, with no power to save. Baptism, like the Lord's Supper, contains no magical meaning or power. Although meaningful religious rituals, these ordinances do not confer divine power or favor. The concept that some divine power resides in religious forms is called sacramentalism, and Baptists strongly resist any tendency toward such belief.

The Apostle Paul insisted that people are saved by grace through faith and not by works (Romans 3:21–31; Ephesians 2:8–10). The works to which he denied any saving power were religious rituals—such as were practiced in Jewish ceremonial law. Baptism symbolizes and pictures salvation. It does not give salvation; it is not required for salvation; and its absence does not withhold salvation.

Baptism symbolizes the total Christian experience. The one accepting baptism expresses his or her confession of faith in Christ, pictures in the act of baptism his or her burial or death to sin, and acknowledges his or her confidence in a resurrection to new life. The act of being baptized also expresses the believer's vital spiritual relationship with Christ. Only a saved person can join such a celebration (see Rom. 6:3–5). Baptist leader W. R. White wrote, "Baptists do not believe that baptism is essential to salvation, but they do believe that salvation is essential to baptism."[4]

The Mode of Baptism

How should baptism be practiced or administered? Is immersion in water really important or will some other mode equally express the meaning of baptism?

The basic meaning of the word *baptize* shows that Scriptural baptism requires immersion. Every lexicon (dictionary) of the Greek language defines the word *baptize* in terms such as dipping, submerging, immersing, or cleansing by submerging. The same teaching appears in the Septuagint (the Greek translation of the Old Testament) where Naaman "dipped himself in the Jordan" (2 Kings 5:14). The basic meaning of the word *baptize* is beyond dispute.

Immersion represents the New Testament mode for baptism. Only years after the apostolic period did another way of baptizing—by sprinkling or pouring—arise. The modification in mode of baptism arose out of a change in its meaning and significance—primarily as some groups came to consider baptism essential to salvation. The New Testament mode of baptism clearly is immersion in water.

Descriptions of baptism in biblical accounts support the teaching of immersion as the Scriptural mode of baptism. John was baptizing at Aenon, near Salim, "because there was plenty of water" (John 3:23).

For Baptists, Baptism Is:

- A symbolic act whereby a believer is immersed in water to picture salvation, new life, and commitment to Christ
- A public act of obedience by a believer
- A beautiful symbol of the totality of Christ's saving work in the believer
- A picture of the believer's death to sin and an expression of the believer's intention to walk in Christ's way
- An affirmation of the believer's faith in Christ's promised return
- An opening for the believer's entrance into church membership
- A testimony of the believer's trust in Christ

After Jesus' baptism, he "was coming up out of the water" (Mark 1:9–11). The man from Ethiopia and Philip went down to the water and "came up out of the water" (Acts 8:39). These and other verses strongly suggest immersion as the way baptism was done.

The very symbolism of the act requires immersion to express fully the meaning. Paul wrote, "having been buried with him in baptism, and raised with him through your faith in the power of God, who raised him from the dead" (Col. 2:12, see also Rom. 6:3–5). Only immersion completely symbolizes the believer's experience—picturing the believer's dying to sin, being raised to walk in newness of life, and expecting the Second Coming.

The Mandate for Baptism

Why is baptism important? If it does not give salvation and one can be saved without it, why go to the trouble of doing it? Three thoughts—*obedience, ordinance*, and *church membership*—clarify the mandate for baptism.

Baptism is an act of obedience to Christ. In the Great Commission (Matthew 28:19–20), Jesus instructed his followers to "make disciples" of all peoples in the world. One part of the process of making disciples involves "baptizing them" in the name of the Holy Trinity. Baptism expresses obedience on the part of the believer and on the part of the church.

Ethiopia

In biblical times, the designation of the nation Ethiopia was somewhat vague, but most likely the nation corresponds to the area of modern Nubia. The king in Ethiopia was thought to be too sacred a person to discharge secular business. So these functions were carried out by the queen mother, who generally bore the dynastic title, Candace.

An angel of the Lord guided Philip to a road in the desert that ran southwest from Jerusalem to Gaza, a Phoenician city about sixty miles from Jerusalem. On that road, Philip contacted the court official.

Baptists describe baptism with the term *ordinance*, meaning a practice that is commanded, decreed, mandated, or instructed by the Lord. Through history, Baptists have avoided the term *sacrament* because of the entanglement of this term with ritual acts that confer or give grace or forgiveness. The term *sacrament* may have slipped into Christian usage since the Latin word *sacramentum* signified the oath a Roman soldier took upon becoming a member of the legions. The ordinances may have been seen as the believer's declaration of his or her allegiance to Christ.[5] But the sense of sacrament as a dispenser or giver of grace and salvation has never been accepted by Baptists.

Baptists acknowledge only two ordinances—baptism and the Lord's Supper. Other rituals, such as foot washing (John 13:1–17), might very well be moving and deeply spiritual worship services. A service of foot washing is not, however, commanded by the Lord for his churches as are baptism and the Lord's Supper.

Church membership constitutes the third idea that describes the mandate for baptism. As the 1963 Baptist Faith and Message states, "Being a church ordinance, it is prerequisite to the privileges of church membership and to the Lord's Supper."[6] Baptism is not required for entrance into the Kingdom of God. It does, however, form the "door" to the local church and is necessary for membership in the local church.

Baptism is important; it constitutes a mandate from the Lord and a need in the Christian life. Its importance does not stem from any sense that the ritual brings or gives salvation, however. Baptism's importance consists of (1) demonstrating a believer's obedience to Christ; (2) offering a testimony of a believer's trust in Christ, (3) and providing the believer a means to become a part of the local church.

Baptism—A Personal Experience

The students at our Indonesian Baptist Theological Seminary and I had started a church in the central Java town of Salatiga. The church had grown under the leadership of a seminary student. He came to me one day and announced that twelve people were to be baptized at Salatiga the next Sunday.

"Praise God," I said.

Then came the student's question, "Will you come and baptize them?"

"Why don't you baptize them," I returned. "You are the pastor; you won them to Christ!"

"I can't do it," said the student. "I'm not ordained."

"What's that got to do with it?" I asked.

"Well," he said, "I'm *malu* [shy or embarrassed]."

"Ok," I answered. "If your church asks me I will come and baptize them if you will agree that the next time you will do it."

Then he told me that the baptismal service would be held in the public swimming pool. My Western mind thought, public swimming pool, Sunday, closed. When we reached the swimming pool Sunday afternoon, it was filled with swimmers. The pastor walked around the pool, calling, "Everyone out, we are having baptism." The swimmers didn't know what baptism was, but they got out and sat so quietly that I preached on the meaning of baptism.

After the baptism, walking back to the church building, I remarked to the church members that the service was exactly what baptism is. These twelve believers had given a public, open, courageous testimony of their faith in Christ—and everyone could witness it!

Then I did a no-no. I had to go out of the country and left money with the leaders of the church to build a baptistery at the church building. When I returned, there was the baptistery—right outside the building, with no roof or walls. They had made a window in the building so people inside could look out and see the baptistery.

Patiently, I asked why they had built the baptistery outside the building. "Well," they said, "You told us that baptism means an open, public, courageous testimony of faith in Christ. Had we put the baptistery inside the building the only ones who could witness it would be church members inside the building. This way, everyone up on the road can see the baptisms and receive the testimonies of those being baptized."

The members in Salatiga were correct! That is exactly what baptism is—an open, public, courageous testimony of one's placing one's faith in Christ, leaving the old life, and being made alive to new life. Baptism holds great importance both to Christians and the churches into which they are gathered.

QUESTIONS

1. How would you answer a person who says that baptism actually is not important to a Christian or to churches and the way it is done is even less important?

Obedience - Matthew 28-19-20 on the part of believer & the church
Jesus was baptized - setting the example Mark 1:9-11
Acts 8:39 Philip "went down to the water & "came up out of water

2. Do you think there is a danger is baptizing a person very soon after that person expresses faith in Christ? Is there a danger in waiting too long?

a reasonable amt of time - Why would the person want to wait?

3. Why is baptism important both to Christians and to churches?

It is a very important witness of following Jesus' example

4. A wealthy woman came to the pastor of a church and said, "It is time I was baptized. I want you, pastor, to baptize me in a private ceremony with only my husband present. I think I will feel much better once I have been baptized." What unbiblical understandings do you see in this story (a true event, by the way)?

I believe this event should be shared with others - witnessed by others as an acclimation of one's desire to show the world he or she is a Christian & declaring promise to follow Jesus - Seals the declaration

NOTES

1. Walter Thomas Conner, *Christian Doctrine* (Nashville, Tennessee: Broadman Press, 1937), 282.
2. Conner, *Christian Doctrine*, 260.
3. Herschel H. Hobbs, *The Baptist Faith and Message* (Nashville: Convention Press, 1971), 86.
4. W. R. White, *Baptist Distinctives* (Nashville: Convention Press, 1956), 31–32.
5. H. E. Dana, *A Manual of Ecclesiology,* 2d ed. (Kansas City, Kansas: Central Seminary Press, 1944), 281.
6. Article 7, "The Baptist Faith and Message," 1963. For a copy of "The Baptist Faith and Message," 1963, see http://texasbaptists.org/files/2010/08/1963BaptistFaithandMessage1.pdf. Accessed 12/8/2010.

LESSON FIVE

Congregational Church Government

BACKGROUND SCRIPTURES

Matthew 18:15–20; Acts 2:41–42,47; 5:11–14; 6:1–6; 11:1–18; 13:1–3; 14:23,27; 15:1–30; 16:4–5; 20:28; 1 Corinthians 5:1–5; 7:17; 16:1–3; 1 Timothy 4:14; 1 Peter 5:1–4

FOCAL TEXTS

Matthew 18:15–20; Acts 6:1–6; 13:1–3; 15:22; 1 Corinthians 5:1–5; 16:1–3

MAIN IDEA

"Baptists are democratic in their church government. Each local church is self-governing and independent in the management of its affairs."[1]

STUDY AIM

To explain how New Testament churches were organized and made decisions and what this teaches about church government today

QUICK READ

Baptists believe congregational church government best reflects New Testament practices, is demanded by biblical doctrines, and should be implemented in churches today. Baptists determine to resist all threats to its use and effectiveness.

I had completed a book on Baptist history in the Indonesian language. The book was ready for printing. The Indonesian seminary student who was drawing the picture for the book's cover was completing the picture. Everything was almost ready, but we still had not decided the book's exact title.

The student—in desperation, I think—indicated he could not finish the cover without a title. Again in desperation, he suggested, "What about calling it *The History of the Baptist Church*?"

Desperation, I suspect, drove me to respond, "Yes, let's just use that title!"

Another seminary student, who had heard the conversation, observed, "If what you taught us in the Baptist history class is correct, that would need to be *The Development of the Baptist Churches*, would it not?"

Of course the listening student was right. There is no "The Baptist Church." There are Baptist churches that often voluntarily join for cooperative efforts. Baptist historian Walter Shurden correctly notes that there is no "The Southern Baptist Church." One can properly speak of "The Methodist Church" or "The Presbyterian Church" but not of "The Baptist Church!"[2]

The Holy Spirit guided the early Christians to express their faith in Christ by banding together into spiritual fellowships that exhibited a church consciousness and corporate spiritual life (see Acts 2:1–4; 4:31; 8:14–17; 10:44). This corporate sense was rooted in the Jewish life in the synagogue. It came to fruit through their observance of the Greek concept of *ekklesia*, a word that refers to a community meeting for decision. Accepting this concept of the spiritual, corporate fellowship, Baptists have embraced congregational church government. Congregational church government both demands and allows democracy. Baptists believe New Testament churches were democratic bodies; they believe that churches today should be also.

Matthew 18:15-20 (NIV)

15"If your brother sins against you, go and show him his fault, just
between the two of you. If he listens to you, you have won your brother
over. 16But if he will not listen, take one or two others along, so that
'every matter may be established by the testimony of two or three witnesses.' 17If he refuses to listen to them, tell it to the church; and if he
refuses to listen even to the church, treat him as you would a pagan or
a tax collector.

18"I tell you the truth, whatever you bind on earth will be bound in
heaven, and whatever you loose on earth will be loosed in heaven.

19"Again, I tell you that if two of you on earth agree about anything
you ask for, it will be done for you by my Father in heaven. 20For where
two or three come together in my name, there am I with them."

Acts 6:1-6

1In those days when the number of disciples was increasing, the
Grecian Jews among them complained against the Hebraic Jews
because their widows were being overlooked in the daily distribution
of food. 2So the Twelve gathered all the disciples together and said, "It
would not be right for us to neglect the ministry of the word of God in
order to wait on tables. 3Brothers, choose seven men from among you
who are known to be full of the Spirit and wisdom. We will turn this
responsibility over to them 4and will give our attention to prayer and
the ministry of the word."

5This proposal pleased the whole group. They chose Stephen, a
man full of faith and of the Holy Spirit; also Philip, Procorus, Nicanor,
Timon, Parmenas, and Nicolas from Antioch, a convert to Judaism.
6They presented these men to the apostles, who prayed and laid their
hands on them.

Acts 13:1-3

[1]In the church at Antioch there were prophets and teachers:
Barnabas, Simeon called Niger, Lucius of Cyrene, Manaen (who had been
brought up with Herod the tetrarch) and Saul. [2]While they were worshiping the Lord and fasting, the Holy Spirit said, "Set apart for me Barnabas
and Saul for the work to which I have called them." [3]So after they had
fasted and prayed, they placed their hands on them and sent them off.

Acts 15:22

Then the apostles and elders, with the whole church, decided to choose some of their own men and send them to Antioch with Paul and Barnabas. They chose Judas (called Barsabbas) and Silas, two men who were leaders among the brothers.

1 Corinthians 5:1-5

[1]It is actually reported that there is sexual immorality among you,
and of a kind that does not occur even among pagans: A man has his
father's wife. [2]And you are proud! Shouldn't you rather have been
filled with grief and have put out of your fellowship the man who did
this? [3]Even though I am not physically present, I am with you in spirit.
And I have already passed judgment on the one who did this, just as if I
were present. [4]When you are assembled in the name of our Lord Jesus
and I am with you in spirit, and the power of our Lord Jesus is present,
[5]hand this man over to Satan, so that the sinful nature may be
destroyed and his spirit saved on the day of the Lord.

1 Corinthians 16:1-3

[1]Now about the collection for God's people: Do what I told the
Galatian churches to do. [2]On the first day of every week, each one of
you should set aside a sum of money in keeping with his income,
saving it up, so that when I come no collections will have to be made.
[3]Then, when I arrive, I will give letters of introduction to the men you
approve and send them with your gift to Jerusalem.

The Nature of Congregational Church Government

The New Testament does not spell out precisely the details of church government. We can cite texts from various parts of the Bible that seem to support each of the major options for church government. Among these options, Baptists follow the congregational pattern, which they feel best reflects apostolic church polity and remains most faithful to biblical teachings.

In congregational church government, church authority centers in local, sovereign, independent congregations. Local churches committed to the congregational church government pattern have both the right and the responsibility to care for their own affairs under the guidance of Jesus Christ. No bishop, no convention, no pastor, no influential group (either local or national), no civil authority, and no association should dictate either the doctrines or the practices of a local church. No organization or group in Baptist life is superior to or legislates for the local congregations. Baptist churches place authority in the membership of the local fellowship under the guidance of Christ and allow no outside force to dictate either belief or practice.

The following teachings provide biblical foundation for Baptists' conviction that congregational church government represents the New Testament pattern and the best polity for local churches:

1. *The New Testament churches were voluntary organisms.* These fellowships were composed of members who, because of their own spiritual experience and decision, voluntarily joined with one another for the purpose of carrying out the will of God and the mission of Jesus under the guidance of the Holy Spirit (Acts 2:41–42,47).

New Testament churches of necessity must be composed of born-again, baptized believers. Only believers should be members of a Baptist church. The voluntary and regenerate nature of Christians demands a participative pattern in church relationships. Congregational church government alone, of the various options available, provides this opportunity for participation.

2. *The New Testament churches were self-governing, spiritual democracies.* The word *democracy* comes from two Greek words that mean "rule of the people." Jesus encouraged his followers not to insist on the term "rabbi" for themselves but to recognize only Christ as their Master (teacher) and all believers as brothers (Matthew 23:8). Thus, in the churches of the New Testament, apostles could suggest solutions to problems, but all important matters were referred to the congregations for settlement (Acts 6:1–6; 1 Cor. 5:1–5; 2 Cor. 8:1–13).

This procedure clearly appeared in the appointment of workers to tend to the relief help for the "widows" (Acts 6:1–6). A problem arose over the neglect of the widows from the Greek-speaking group. This Greek-speaking group was possibly Jews of the dispersion from the Greco-Roman world, as over against the Hebraic Jews, who were probably natives of Palestine and spoke Aramaic rather than Greek.[3] The apostles suggested the number of men to serve in this role and their qualifications, but the actual choice was left to the congregation.

Interestingly, the names of all seven chosen are Greek. This fact suggests that they all, with the exception of Nicolaus, who was likely a Gentile proselyte, stemmed from the Greek-speaking contingent in the church. The congregational decision was attended by increased multiplication of disciples including a large number of Jewish priests (Acts 6:7).

The democratic ideal in the New Testament churches clearly surfaces in the accounts of the church at Antioch of Syria (Acts 13:1–3; 15:22). The Holy Spirit spoke to the church in Antioch, instructing that Barnabas and Saul be set apart for the missionary task. The entire church, not just leaders, took part in the commissioning (13:3). Later, after the council meeting in Jerusalem (15:1–21) had decided that Gentiles should not be required to follow Jewish customary regulations in order to become Christians, the apostles and elders "with the whole church" chose Judas (called Barsabbas) and Silas to accompany Paul and Barnabas to relate the council's advice to Antioch (15:22).

The teaching that the New Testament churches were self-governing, spiritual democracies also finds support in the fact that the apostles

The Congregational Pattern of Church Government

- Centers authority in church matters in the sovereign, independent body that has no direct, organic ties with any other church or governing body
- Allows no hierarchical power to dictate either faith or practice to the local churches
- Mirrors what seems to be the New Testament model
- Allows cooperation with other bodies so long as there are no entangling alliances
- Insists on the total freedom and responsibility of every member
- Follows democratic processes in its deliberations

advised and exhorted the churches but the congregations determined their own courses of action.[4] The sense of 1 Corinthians 16:1–3 is that Paul encouraged, but did not order, the Christians in Corinth to participate in the offering to the famine-stricken believers in Jerusalem. The same encouragement without coercion for giving appears in Paul's injunctions to the Corinthians in 2 Corinthians 8:1–13. Note especially verse 8. We can see a similar pattern in Paul's urging forgiveness to an erring but repentant brother (2 Cor. 2:5–8).

3. *The New Testament churches cared for their own memberships and members.* Church membership and church discipline rested in the hands of the local congregations. Evidently the New Testament churches had the authority to receive or reject people from their memberships.[5] Paul advised the church in Rome to accept without passing judgment on the weak person, that is, one unsure of certain disputable doctrines (Rom. 14:1–2). He suggested to the church in Corinth that the one who had caused distress (grief) by his behavior had already been sufficiently punished *by the church as a whole* (2 Cor. 2:5–8). The New English Bible translates 2 Corinthians 2:6 as follows: "The penalty on which the general meeting has agreed has met the offence well enough." Paul advised reinstating the erring member (2:7–8), but the actual discipline was the act of the entire church.

The accounts of church discipline in Matthew 18:15–20 and 1 Corinthians 5:1–5 further reveal the New Testament approach to church discipline. Jesus spoke of a believer who feels that another has wronged him or her (Matt. 18:15–20). The wronged believer should first go personally to the offender and try to work things out. Should this effort fail, the offended should take two or three others to hear the complaint. Should peace still be denied, the church should be asked to intercede. If the offender would not listen to the church, then the offender would be considered and treated as a "pagan or a tax-collector" (Matt. 18:17). The passage underlines the importance of church decision-making.

Paul expressed a similar view in 1 Corinthians 5:1–5. There Paul spoke of the sinful behavior of a member of the church in Corinth. Paul rejected the immoral behavior, but he said to the membership that they, not he, should have "put out of your fellowship the man who did this" (1 Cor. 5:2). Again, the final responsibility and authority resided in the congregation.

When we consider these various New Testament passages, we see the background for Baptists' belief in congregational church government. Nothing less than congregational church government reflects the pattern of church authority residing in the entire membership and not in some outside power or force.

4. The New Testament churches were fellowships of mutual care and responsibility. Mutual care, worship, witness, and support represent the essence of the nature of New Testament churches. The Jerusalem fellowship continued in worship, fellowship, mutual sharing, and evangelism (Acts 2:42–47). These Christians continued to share, to worship, and, in the face of great threats, to witness boldly about Jesus (Acts 4:13–31).

Peter's experience with Cornelius (Acts 10:1–48) led to criticism by some Jewish Christians. Peter reported to the entire group. Upon hearing what God had done, they laid aside their complaints and declared that "God has granted even the Gentiles repentance unto life" (Acts 11:18).

Clearly, the believers and the churches in the New Testament demonstrated both the freedom and responsibility to determine, under Christ and in compliance with Scripture, their own membership, beliefs, and practices. Baptists are convinced that the congregational pattern of church government remains most faithful to and reflective of the New Testament plan.

These teachings compel Baptists to affirm congregational church government. They maintain that the same form of church government revealed in the New Testament remains the best for churches today.

Other options for church government exist and are employed today. Baptists respect those who follow other practices and work with them wherever possible. They do not agree with their patterns of church government, however. Baptists are convinced that the congregational plan best represents the New Testament pattern, best interfaces with basic biblical doctrines, and most adequately allows for the Lord's work.

The Foundations of Baptist Belief in Congregational Church Government

Although support for other forms of church government can be found in biblical passages, Baptists see the bulk of Scriptural evidence upholding congregational government. Even more important to the Baptist view are Scriptural doctrines that serve as foundations for congregational government.

1. *The Priesthood of Every Believer*. This New Testament doctrine means that every believer is a priest! Speaking of all Christians, Peter declared that God's people are "a chosen people, a royal priesthood, a holy nation, a people belonging to God" (1 Peter 2:9). Every believer has the possibility of coming face-to-face with God, boldly, with no mediator other than Christ (1 Timothy 2:5; Hebrews 4:16). He or she can pray directly to God in Jesus' name (John 14:13–14), can confess his or her sins directly to God (1 John 1:9), and can read and interpret the

Scriptures as guided by the Holy Spirit (John 16:12–15). This priesthood of the believer involves both privilege and responsibility.

The priesthood of the believer means that all members serve as equals under God in the fellowship of a local church. Each believer, therefore, is obligated to serve as a priest on behalf of others. The doctrine of the priesthood of the believer constitutes a central affirmation of Baptists that must never be lost or its significance lowered.

In regard to congregational church government, this teaching means that every believer can seek and find God's will directly and therefore must be free to express his or her findings to the entire body. To ascertain God's directions, the church does well to hear the conclusions of every member and allow the full participation of the entire body of Christ. For these reasons, Baptists believe that authority in the church should be vested in the entire membership. Baptist leader W. R. White wrote, "The concept of the priesthood of every believer instead of a priestly class or caste makes democracy inevitable for the Lord's disciples."[6]

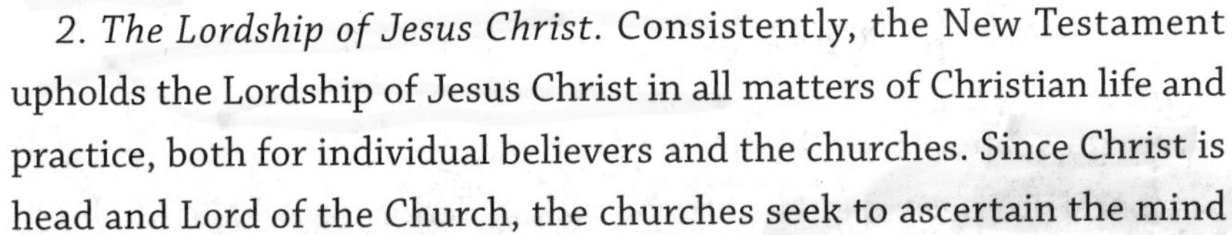

2. *The Lordship of Jesus Christ.* Consistently, the New Testament upholds the Lordship of Jesus Christ in all matters of Christian life and practice, both for individual believers and the churches. Since Christ is head and Lord of the Church, the churches seek to ascertain the mind

Options for Church Government

- *The hierarchical (autocratic) pattern* exalts a human leader to a dominant position and gives this leader almost total authority or power.
- *The episcopal pattern* centers authority in the bishop or bishops.
- *The connectional pattern* centers authority in the combined voice of all the local congregations that subscribe to a common and prescribed creed.
- *The congregational pattern* centers authority in church matters in the sovereign, independent body that has no organic ties with any other church or governing body.

of Christ in all matters of faith and practice (Ephesians 5:22–23). Freedom to respond to the Lordship of Christ in all circumstances is fundamental to the Christian faith, to human dignity, and to the proper functioning of Christ's churches. For this reason, the 1963 statement of "The Baptist Faith and Message" declares that "This church is an autonomous body, operating through democratic processes under the Lordship of Christ."[7]

Baptist understanding of the Lordship of Christ guides them directly to their stand on congregational church government. Every member has equal access to the Lord who is the head of the church (Colossians 1:18). No one person, no one group, no one power should take the place of Christ in the church.

3. *The Autonomy of the Local Church*. In order to remain an autonomous church, every congregation must be free from denominational, governmental, or other authoritarian pressures. Let us be clear about the meaning of church autonomy, however. As Baptist leader Charles Wade declares, "A church is not free to be or to do whatever it wants. It is called to be like Christ and do what Jesus would do."[8]

Local church autonomy means the church acts under compulsion and direction of Jesus Christ through the Holy Spirit rather than from outside pressure. Paul called on the church at Corinth to act in the "power of our Lord Jesus" (1 Cor. 5:4).

4. *The Church As the Body of Christ*. One picture or metaphor of the church is that of the body of Christ (Eph. 1:22–23; Rom. 12:4–5; 1 Cor. 12:12–31). Charles Wade calls this image the most dominant picture of the church in the New Testament.[9] The central theme in this metaphor is that of the many parts working together in unity and power to accomplish the overall purpose of the body. The concept of the church as the body of Christ points toward the understanding of the church as an organism, with every part important and necessary.

Since the church is a body, a living organism, every part must function for the whole to be strong and accomplish its task. Congregational church government provides a more certain avenue for such mutual

NOTES

1. Walter Thomas Conner, *Christian Doctrine* (Nashville, Tennessee: Broadman Press, 1937), 266.
2. Walter B. Shurden, *The Baptist Identity: Four Fragile Freedoms* (Macon, GA: Smyth & Helwys, 1993), 38–39.
3. Curtis Vaughan, *Acts: A Study Guide Commentary* (Grand Rapids: Zondervan, 1974), 44.
4. Herschel H. Hobbs, *What Baptists Believe* (Nashville: Convention Press, 1964), 79.
5. W. R. White, *Baptist Distinctives* (Nashville: Convention Press, 1946), 38.
6. White, *Baptist Distinctives*, 38.
7. Article 6, "The Baptist Faith and Message," 1963. For a copy of "The Baptist Faith and Message," 1963, see http://texasbaptists.org/files/2010/08/1963BaptistFaithandMessage1.pdf. Accessed 12/8/2010.
8. Charles R. Wade, with Lee and Carol Bowman, *The Jesus Principle: Building Churches in the Likeness of Christ* (Arlington, TX: Clear Stream Publishing Inc., 1998), 79.
9. Wade, *The Jesus Principle*, 74.
10. Shurden, *The Baptist Identity*, 38.
11. Shurden, *The Baptist Identity*, 38.

LESSON SIX

The Deity and Lordship of Jesus Christ

BACKGROUND SCRIPTURES

Psalm 2:7; 110:1; Isaiah 7:14; 53; Matthew 1:18–23; 3:17; 8:29; 11:25–30; 14:33; 16:13–16, 27; 17:1–8; 27:1–28:6, 19; Mark 1:1; 3:11; Luke 1:35; 4:41; 22:70; 24:46; John 1:1–18, 29; 5:31-47; 10:30–39; 11:25–27; 12:44-50; 14:7–11; 16:15–16, 28; 17:1–5, 21–22; 20:1–20, 28; Acts 1:9; 2:22–24; 7:55–56; 9:4–5, 20; Romans 1:1–6; 3:23-26; 5:6–21; 8:1–3, 34; 10:4; 1 Corinthians 1:30; 2:2; 8:6; 15:1–8, 24-28; 2 Corinthians 5:19–21; Galatians 4:4–5; Ephesians 1:18–23; 3:11; 4:7–10; Philippians 2:5–11; Colossians 1:13–22; 2:9; 1 Thessalonians 4:14–18; 1 Timothy 2:5–6; Titus 2:13–14; Hebrews 1:1–3; 4:14–15; 7:14–28; 9:12–15, 24–28; 12:2; 13:8; 1 Peter 2:21–25; 3:21–22; 1 John 1:7–9; 3:2; 4:14–15; 5:9; 2 John 7–9; Revelation 1:13–16; 5:1–14; 12:10–11; 13:8; 19:16

FOCAL TEXTS

Matthew 16:13–16; John 1:1–5, 14; 10:30–38; 20:28; Philippians 2:5–11; Colossians 2:9; Revelation 5:1–14

MAIN IDEA

"The Christ of the New Testament is not a man deified by his zealous disciples, but the eternal Son of God who voluntarily became man to redeem lost humanity."[1]

STUDY AIM

To state what the New Testament teaches about Jesus' deity and lordship

QUICK READ

Jesus Christ is God in human flesh. He is both fully God and fully human. As God, he is co-equal and co-eternal with God the Father and God the Holy Spirit.

An *iota* is the smallest letter in the Greek alphabet, but there was a time when the whole Roman Empire was divided over the question of just "one iota." About the time that Christianity was declared the official religion of the Roman Empire, the emperor Constantine called for a council of bishops to convene in the city of Nicea in the summer of 325 A.D. The purpose of the meeting was to settle a dispute that threatened the unity of the church and the empire.

A young priest from Egypt named Arius had begun to teach that Christ had been created by God and thus was not fully divine. For this heresy the Egyptian bishops "unfrocked" Arius. Some leaders of the church disagreed with the action. The dispute grew.

In an attempt to settle the question, Constantine convened the first great church council. The orthodox believers insisted that Christ is fully divine and of the same essence as God the Father. The term in the Greek language is *homo-ousian*—that is, the "same essence." Those following Arius contended that Christ was of a different essence from God, using the term *hetero-ousian*.

As many as 318 bishops attended the council, and some 300 of them agreed that Christ is of the same essence (*homo-ousian*). However, 17 of them refused to sign the document unless one subtle compromise was made. The letter *iota* had to be added to the defining word. The word would then become *homoi-ousian*. That word means "similar essence" instead of the "same essence." The decision of the council hinged on the one Greek letter, *iota*.

The majority refused to insert that little Greek letter and thus agree that Christ was less than fully God. Thus the council declared Arianism to be heresy. The Council at Nicea issued the following statement:

> We believe in one God, the Father All-mighty, maker of all things visible or invisible; and in one Lord Jesus Christ, the Son of God, begotten . . . not made, being of one essence [*homo-ousian*] with the Father . . . who for us . . . and our salvation came down and was made flesh, was made man, suffered, rose again the

> third day, ascended into heaven, and comes to judge the quick and the dead . . . .[2]

Church historian Philip Schaff said of Nicea, "It is the first and most venerable of the ecumenical synods, and next to the apostolic council at Jerusalem the most important and the most illustrious of all the councils of Christendom."[3]

Many other controversies about the nature and work of Christ have arisen across the centuries of Christian history. Even today the answer to the question that still distinguishes true Christianity is, "Who is Christ?"

We Baptists do not derive our doctrines from creeds or councils but from the Bible, which is the Word of God, truth without mixture of error. There is no more foundational doctrine for Baptists than the deity and lordship of Christ our Savior. In this study we will look at just a few of the many Scriptures that deal with the person and work of Christ.

Who Is Jesus? (Matthew 16:13-16)

In preparing his disciples for his impending crucifixion, Jesus asked what the latest public opinion polls said about him. While the religious leaders regarded Jesus as a blasphemer against God (Matthew 9:3), average people were complimentary of Jesus.

Some thought Jesus to be John the Baptist who had risen from the dead as Herod feared (Matt. 14:2). Others believed Jesus to be Elijah. It was prophesied in Malachi 4:5 that Elijah would precede and prepare the way for the Messiah. Another suggestion was that Jesus was Jeremiah who had returned.

In the next verse the Master pointedly changed the question. He asked, "But who do you say that I am?" (Matt. 16:15). Peter declared that Jesus was the long awaited Anointed One, the Christ who is the Son of the Living God. By this confession, Peter revealed that he understood that Jesus is God.

Matthew 16:13-16 (NASB)

13 Now when Jesus came into the district of Caesarea Philippi, He
was asking His disciples, "Who do people say that the Son of Man is?"
14 And they said, "Some say John the Baptist; and others, Elijah; but
still others, Jeremiah, or one of the prophets." 15 He said to them, "But
who do you say that I am?" 16 Simon Peter answered, "You are the
Christ, the Son of the living God."

John 1:1-5, 14

1 In the beginning was the Word, and the Word was with God, and the
Word was God. 2 He was in the beginning with God. 3 All things came
into being through Him, and apart from Him nothing came into being
that has come into being. 4 In Him was life, and the life was the Light of
men. 5 The Light shines in the darkness, and the darkness did not comprehend it.

• •

14 And the Word became flesh, and dwelt among us, and we saw His
glory, glory as of the only begotten from the Father, full of grace and
truth.

John 10:30-38

30 "I and the Father are one."
31 The Jews picked up stones again to stone Him. 32 Jesus answered
them, "I showed you many good works from the Father; for which of
them are you stoning Me?" 33 The Jews answered Him, "For a good
work we do not stone You, but for blasphemy; and because You, being
a man, make Yourself out to be God." 34 Jesus answered them, "Has it
not been written in your Law, 'I SAID, YOU ARE GODS'? 35 "If he called
them gods, to whom the word of God came (and the Scripture cannot
be broken), 36 do you say of Him, whom the Father sanctified and sent

into the world, 'You are blaspheming,' because I said, 'I am the Son of God'? [37]"If I do not do the works of My Father, do not believe Me; [38]but if I do them, though you do not believe Me, believe the works, so that you may know and understand that the Father is in Me, and I in the Father."

John 20:28

Thomas answered and said to Him, "My Lord and my God!"

Philippians 2:5-11

[5]Have this attitude in yourselves which was also in Christ Jesus, [6]who, although He existed in the form of God, did not regard equality with God a thing to be grasped, [7]but emptied Himself, taking the form of a bond-servant, and being made in the likeness of men. [8]Being found in appearance as a man, He humbled Himself by becoming obedient to the point of death, even death on a cross. [9]For this reason also, God highly exalted Him, and bestowed on Him the name which is above every name, [10]so that at the name of Jesus EVERY KNEE WILL BOW, of those who are in heaven and on earth and under the earth, [11]and that every tongue will confess that Jesus Christ is Lord, to the glory of God the Father.

Colossians 2:9

For in Him all the fullness of Deity dwells in bodily form . . . .

Revelation 5:1-14

[1]I saw in the right hand of Him who sat on the throne a book written inside and on the back, sealed up with seven seals. [2]And I saw a strong angel proclaiming with a loud voice, "Who is worthy to open the book and to break its seals?" [3]And no one in heaven or on the earth or

under the earth was able to open the book or to look into it. 4Then I
began to weep greatly because no one was found worthy to open the
book or to look into it; 5and one of the elders said to me, "Stop weeping; behold, the Lion that is from the tribe of Judah, the Root of David,
has overcome so as to open the book and its seven seals."

6And I saw between the throne (with the four living creatures) and
the elders a Lamb standing, as if slain, having seven horns and seven
eyes, which are the seven Spirits of God, sent out into all the earth.
7And He came and took the book out of the right hand of Him who sat
on the throne. 8When He had taken the book, the four living creatures
and the twenty-four elders fell down before the Lamb, each one holding a harp and golden bowls full of incense, which are the prayers of
the saints. 9And they sang a new song, saying,

"Worthy are You to take the book and to break its seals; for You
were slain, and purchased for God with Your blood men from every
tribe and tongue and people and nation.

10 "You have made them to be a kingdom and priests to our God;
and they will reign upon the earth."

11Then I looked, and I heard the voice of many angels around the
throne and the living creatures and the elders; and the number of
them was myriads of myriads, and thousands of thousands, 12saying
with a loud voice,

"Worthy is the Lamb that was slain to receive power and riches and
wisdom and might and honor and glory and blessing."

13And every created thing which is in heaven and on the earth and
under the earth and on the sea, and all things in them, I heard saying,

"To Him who sits on the throne, and to the Lamb, be blessing and
honor and glory and dominion forever and ever."

14And the four living creatures kept saying, "Amen." And the elders
fell down and worshiped.

Who Is Christ? (John 1:1–5, 14)

The first chapter of John begins with these words, "In the beginning was the Word, and the Word was with God, and the Word was God" (John 1:1). The Lord Jesus Christ is the "Word" in John 1:1. He is the first and last word from God. He is "the Alpha and the Omega" (Revelation 1:8). While God has spoken through the prophets, he has been most personally revealed in the Lord Jesus Christ (Hebrews 1:1–3).

As we study John 1:1–5, 14, let us consider first what these verses teach us about the deity of Christ. John 1:1–5 contains seven descriptions of Christ (the Word). These descriptions reveal that he is God.

- "In the beginning . . . the Word was God" (John 1:1). Christ is *co-eternal* with God. At the time of creation, the Word was already with God. Before anything was created, Christ was already in existence. Therefore, he is not a created being. He preceded creation.
- This phrase also reveals the *distinct personality* of Jesus Christ. He "was with God" (1:1). There is one God, and there are three distinct persons in God: Father, Son, and Holy Spirit. It is impossible for the finite mind to comprehend the doctrine of the "trinity" that is taught so clearly in Scripture. Many explanations have been given, but none are completely adequate.
- Christ is *co-equal* with God. Christ did not become God; he already was God. Christ is not inferior to God the Father. Any teaching that claims that the Lord Jesus Christ is less than God is unbiblical and untrue. The Word was not "a" God. Neither was the Word "the" God, which would eliminate the other persons in the Godhead. Nor was he merely "of" God, but in the beginning he was already in his nature and essence fully and completely God.
- Christ is *changeless*. "He was in the beginning with God" (John 1:2). "Jesus Christ the same yesterday, and to day, and for ever" (Hebrews 13:8, KJV).

- Christ is *creator*. "All things were made by him; and without him was not anything made that was made" (John 1:3, KJV; see also Colossians 1:15–17).
- Christ is the *life-source*. "In him was life" (John 1:4). First, Christ created the material universe, and then he brought living organisms into being.

  One of the legends making the rounds on the Internet describes a meeting of God and a scientist who had recently been successful in cloning an animal. In the story, the scientist challenged God, saying, "I can create human life." According to the story, God replied, "Go ahead and try." With that the scientist reached down and scooped up a handful of dirt. God supposedly replied, "Wait a minute. Get your own dirt."

  Not only is Christ the origin of all life, but he is the creator and sole proprietor of the new life that is eternal life. "I am . . . the life" (John 14:6).
- Christ is the *source of light* (see 1:4b–5). "God is Light, and in Him there is no darkness at all" (1 John 1:5). Jesus clearly said, "'I am the Light of the world; he who follows Me will not walk in the darkness, but will have the Light of life'" (John 8:12).

Consider now what John 1:14 teaches us about the humanity of Christ. Not only was Christ fully God, but he also became fully human and "dwelt" or "tabernacled" among us. The word translated "dwell" literally means "to tabernacle" or "to put up a tent."

The Lord Jesus Christ

The word "Lord" declares Jesus' divinity. The word "Jesus" designates his humanity. The word "Christ" describes his office as prophet, priest, and king. As prophet, he is the Word of God. As priest, he offered himself as the atoning sacrifice for sin. As king, he is sovereign over all creation.

Consider these five ways in which the Old Testament tabernacle symbolizes the first coming of Christ, when the Word became flesh.

(1) The tabernacle was intended to be temporary, as was the first coming of Christ.
(2) The tabernacle was to be used in the wilderness even as Christ endured the wilderness in his first coming.
(3) The tabernacle was very plain on the outside, but it was glorious on the inside, just as there was no outward beauty in Christ that we should desire him (Isaiah 53:2).
(4) The tabernacle was God's temporary dwelling place on earth even as the fullness of God dwelled in Christ bodily.
(5) The tabernacle was the place of sacrifice for sin even as Christ sacrificed himself in his own body on the cross (Hebrews 10:12).[4]

Christ Reveals His Deity (John 10:30-38)

Christ himself gave testimony to his deity. He said, "I and my father are one" (John 10:30, KJV). The religious leaders understood his meaning well, for they accused Jesus of claiming to be God.

Jesus did not often claim to be God because truth must be established in the mouth of two witnesses (Deuteronomy 19:15). In John 5:31–47 Jesus cited four independent witnesses who would testify that he is God.

(1) John the Baptist pointed to Jesus as the Lamb of God who would take away the sin of the world (John 5:33–35; see 1:29).
(2) The very works of Christ did bear witness that he is one with the Father (John 5:36).
(3) God the Father testified of Christ (John 5:37; see also Matthew 3:17).
(4) The Scriptures bear witness of Christ (John 5:39–47).

The Use of "Word"

The average Jewish person of Jesus' day spoke the Aramaic language. The translations of Old Testament passages into Aramaic were called "targums." In order to preserve the glory of the Almighty, the term "Word of God" was used whenever God acted with humans or in a human way. Here are just two examples from the targums. In Genesis 3:8–9 instead of "they heard the voice of the Lord God," the targums say that they heard the voice of "the word of the Lord God." Instead of "God called unto Adam," the targums say that "the word of the Lord called unto Adam." This term "the word of the Lord" occurred as many as 150 times in a single targum of the Pentateuch.[6]

To the Greeks, "logos," which means "word," was also a well-known term. Greek philosophers taught that the "logos" gave order and unity to the world. To the Greeks then, it is as if John were saying, I want to introduce your "logos" to you. He is the Christ.

Thomas Declares the Deity of Christ (John 20:28)

On the evening of resurrection day, ten of the apostles met in the upper room. Two were absent. Judas Iscariot had hanged himself, and Thomas was not there.

When the disciples assembled a week later, Thomas was present with them. Again Christ appeared in their midst and invited Thomas, "Reach here with your finger, and see My hands; and reach here your hand and put it into My side; and do not be unbelieving, but believing" (John 20:27).

There is no indication that Thomas touched the hands or the side of the Savior, but he openly confessed, "My Lord and my God!" (John 20:28). If Christ had not been God, he would have corrected Thomas. Christ accepted this justifiable praise.

Christ Is Equal with God (Philippians 2:5-11)

This passage in Philippians is one of the most glorious descriptions of the voluntary descent from heaven of the incarnate God in order to bear the sins of the world in his body on the cross. Of this passage F. B. Meyer says, "In the whole range of Scripture this paragraph stands in almost unapproachable and unexampled majesty. There is no passage where the extremes of our Savior's majesty and humility are brought into such abrupt connection."[5]

Christ was in his very nature all the fullness of God, but he did not consider that he should clutch and retain this exalted position. He was "equal with God" (Philippians 2:6, KJV). Even so he "emptied Himself," laid aside his garments of glory, and took the form of a servant (2:7). One would think that if the Son of God were to come to earth, he would come with all the trappings that would befit the office. He could have far superseded the triumphal entry of a Roman emperor. Instead he worked in a carpenter shop (Mark 6:3) and even washed the feet of his self-seeking disciples (John 13:5).

Jesus reached the depths of shameful treatment in the crucifixion, "even death on a cross" (Phil. 2:8). *The deepest humiliation ever endured produced the greatest work ever accomplished, making redemption available to the human race.* Therefore God has highly exalted the one who voluntarily humbled himself. God has caused the name "Jesus" to be exalted above every other name. One day every knee shall bow and every tongue shall confess that Jesus Christ is Lord. In this, God the Father will be glorified (see Phil. 2:9–10).

Christ Is the Fullness of God (Colossians 2:9)

The Book of Colossians was written to warn Christians about false logic and philosophy that produced theological and practical errors. False teachers taught that matter is the origin and vehicle of evil. This false doctrine produced the theological error that Christ could not have appeared in the flesh since flesh is evil. Many levels of intermediary beings between God and human beings were required and worshipped in this system. The practical error was that a rigid ascetic discipline was required to overcome the evil properties of the physical and material.

Both errors could be overcome with the understanding that in Christ dwells all the fullness of God in bodily form (Colossians 2:9). He is creator of all things in heaven and earth, "visible and invisible" (Col. 1:16). He is redeemer through "the blood of His cross" (1:20). All the fullness of God dwells in Christ (1:19).

A good test for any religion is how it regards Christ. Any religion that makes Christ in any way inferior to God the Father or requires the observance of rules and rituals for salvation is false.

True or False Religions?

If members of another religion were to come to your door and attempt to convince you to accept their doctrine, could you give a reason for your faith? Could you tell truth from error? How can you tell whether a religion claiming to be Christian is true or false? Here are two of the tests that can be applied.

1. What is its source of religious authority? Is it the Bible only, or does that religion have other revelations, sacred books, and other writings as sources of doctrine equal or superior to the Bible? If there is any authority other than the Bible as the source of its doctrine, then this religion is not the true Christian faith.

2. What is the Christology of the religious denomination? What do they believe about the nature of Christ? If they believe that Christ is less than coequal and co-eternal with God, or that Christ is not God incarnate in the flesh, then this is false Christianity.

This understanding is tremendously important because someday your children, your brother or sister, or your associate may become confused by the false claims of other religious groups. If a religion fails these tests at any point, then beware (see 1 John 2:22–23).

Christ Is Glorified in Heaven (Revelation 5:1-14)

In Revelation 5:1–14, there is a majestic picture of heaven. Not only is Christ, the Lamb of God, receiving praise from every creature, but he also is receiving praise co-equal with God upon the throne.

Your Lord and Your God?

The enemies of Christ said he was demented and demonic. The secular world may think of him as a great leader and religious martyr. Many religious people give intellectual assent that he is the Christ, the Son of the living God. Even that answer is inadequate without commitment to him as Lord. The saving answer is that of Thomas. Jesus is "*My* Lord and *my* God" (John 20:28, italics added for emphasis). Have you confessed Jesus as your Lord and your God?[7]

QUESTIONS

1. Why did Jesus not often claim to be God?

2. What is the difference between the confessions of Simon Peter and Thomas?

3. What experiences or circumstances led you to confess Christ as your Lord and your God?

NOTES

1. Walter Thomas Conner, *Christian Doctrine* (Nashville, Tennessee: Broadman Press, 1937), 64.
2. Cited in W. Durant, *Caesar and Christ* (New York: Simon and Schuster, 1944), 665.
3. P. Schaff, *History of the Christian Church*, vol. II (Grand Rapids, Michigan: W. B. Eerdmans, 1910), 630.
4. Adapted from A. W. Pink, *Exposition of the Gospel of John* (Grand Rapids, Michigan: Zondervan Publishing House, 1945), 34–37.
5. F.B. Meyer, *The Epistle to the Philippians* (Grand Rapids, Michigan: Baker Book House, 1952), 81.
6. A. Plummer, *The Gospel According to St. John* (Cambridge: The University Press, 1899), 61.
7. For additional assistance on the topic of this lesson, see *Bible Truths About God* by James Semple (Dallas, TX: BaptistWay Press, 2008); and *Jesus Is Lord!* by Howard K. Batson (Dallas, TX: BaptistWay Press, 2006). Call 1-866-249-1799 or see www.baptistwaypress.org.

LESSON SEVEN

Evangelism and Missions: The Great Commission

BACKGROUND SCRIPTURES

Genesis 12:1-3; Exodus 19:3-6; Isaiah 6:1-8; Matthew 9:37-38; 10:5-15; 13:8-30,37-43; 16:19; 22:9-10; 24:14; 28:18-20; Luke 10:1-18; 24:46-53; John 14:11-12; 15:7-8,16; 17:15; 20:21; Acts 1:8; 2; 8:26-40; 10:42-48; 13:2-3; Romans 10:1-15; Ephesians 3:1-11; 1 Thessalonians 1:8; 2 Timothy 4:5; Hebrews 2:1-3; 11:39–12:2; 1 Peter 2:4-10; Revelation 22:17

FOCAL TEXTS

Genesis 12:1-3; Exodus 19:5-6; Matthew 28:18-20; John 20:21; Acts 1:8; Romans 10:13-15

MAIN IDEA

"Missions/evangelism finds its ultimate source in the heart of God."[1]

STUDY AIM

To tell why evangelism and missions are essential tasks of churches and individual Christians

QUICK READ

Missions/evangelism is an essential task of Christ's church because God desires all people to be saved; salvation meets the ultimate human need; and Christ's commission obviously includes missions. Evangelism happens only in the Spirit's power.

Some years ago, my family visited Yellowstone National Park and watched as "Old Faithful" gushed water high into the air. We were impressed. I noted two cartoons on a wall in the area. Both showed people standing and watching "Old Faithful." In one cartoon, a watcher said, "Is that all it does?" In the second cartoon, a speaker said, "But what's it good for?"

Have you ever looked at the church (or a church) and asked, "Is that all it does?" Or have you inquired, "What's it really good for?" This study seeks to answer both questions—what do churches do and what are they good for!

Jesus called his church to carry forward his redemptive plan for all the people of the world. The task of the church includes proclaiming by word and deed the gospel of Jesus Christ, guiding believers into continuing growth and development in Christ, ministering to the needs of people in the communities, influencing the world toward right living, and preparing God's people for the Second Coming of the Lord Jesus Christ.

A prominent part of this overall task of the church relates to evangelism and missions, the effort designed to lead people to faith and salvation. While the full meaning of evangelism and missions includes everything the church does, in this study we will center on the mission of the church to bring people to saving faith in Jesus. No real difference exists between missions and evangelism. The two terms relate to the same task of bringing lost people to faith in Christ.

The Bible indicates that evangelism/missions constitutes an essential task both of the church and of individual Christians. Baptists affirm this task in "The Baptist Faith and Message": "It is the duty and privilege of every follower of Christ and every church of the Lord Jesus Christ to endeavor to make disciples of all nations."[2] Consider some reasons that missions/evangelism rests at the heart of the task of the church of Jesus Christ.

Genesis 12:1-3 (NIV)

1 The LORD had said to Abram, "Leave your country, your people and
your father's household and go to the land I will show you.
2 "I will make you into a great nation
    and I will bless you;
I will make your name great,
    and you will be a blessing.
3 I will bless those who bless you,
    and whoever curses you I will curse;
and all peoples on earth
    will be blessed through you."

Exodus 19:5-6

5 Now if you obey me fully and keep my covenant, then out of all
nations you will be my treasured possession. Although the whole earth
is mine, 6 you will be for me a kingdom of priests and a holy nation.'
These are the words you are to speak to the Israelites."

Matthew 28:18-20

18 Then Jesus came to them and said, "All authority in heaven and
on earth has been given to me. 19 Therefore go and make disciples of
all nations, baptizing them in the name of the Father and of the Son
and of the Holy Spirit, 20 and teaching them to obey everything I have
commanded you. And surely I am with you always, to the very end of
the age."

John 20:21

Again Jesus said, "Peace be with you! As the Father has sent me, I am sending you."

Acts 1:8

"But you will receive power when the Holy Spirit comes on you; and you will be my witnesses in Jerusalem, and in all Judea and Samaria, and to the ends of the earth."

Romans 10:13-15

13 for, "Everyone who calls on the name of the Lord will be saved."
14 How, then, can they call on the one they have not believed in? And how can they believe in the one of whom they have not heard? And
how can they hear without someone preaching to them?
15 And how
can they preach unless they are sent? As it is written, "How beautiful are the feet of those who bring good news!"

Missions/Evangelism Begins with the Loving Desire of God

(Genesis 12:1-3; Exodus 19:5-6)

We know that missions/evangelism constitutes an essential task of churches and Christians because the stimulus for the effort begins in God's loving desire to bring people to saving faith. Far from being a merely human endeavor, missions/evangelism springs from God's awesome desire to save sinful humanity and from God's direct call that his people be involved in this missionary effort (see Genesis 12:1–3; Exodus 19:5–6; Isaiah 49:6; Mark 10:45; John 3:16; Acts 1:8).

God announced his desire for all humanity and his intention that his people share the divine message of love with all humankind in his call of Abram (Abraham) in Genesis 12:1–3. Note the expression, "The LORD had said" (Gen. 12:1). This expression may indicate a renewal of the call first given in Haran as seen in Genesis 11:31–32.

The call to Abram required a radical separation from family, land, and natural roots in obedience to God. The word "make" indicates that God was forming a covenant with Abram (Gen. 12:2). If Abram remained obedient, this covenant promised a great nation (many, innumerable descendants), a blessing (God would make Abram and his people happy, safe, successful, and prosperous), and a great name (the family would be known over the entire world). The selection of Abram and his family was not for Abram's benefit. Rather, the reason for the selection was that in Abram and his descendants "all peoples on earth will be blessed through you" (Gen. 12:3).

God's call is always a call to share and bless, not to hold and be blessed. No person or group should consider the relationship with God only as a source of benefit. The blessings of God demand stewardship and responsibility. "We demonstrate the value of God's gifts more when we share them than when we possess them."[3] God's people must, therefore, be a missionary people. God calls and blesses his people *so that* they can realize God's mission to reach all peoples.

Few passages more stress the missionary/evangelistic message of the Bible than Exodus 19:3–6. There God declared that his people, Israel, were to be priests, that is, people who mediated between God and their fellow human beings to proclaim God's offer of salvation. The Lord reminded the people of how he had delivered them from Egypt. He had guided and protected them like an eagle guiding and protecting the fledgling that was learning to fly. God promised that if the people obeyed and followed him, he would make them his own "treasured possession . . . a kingdom of priests and a holy nation" among all the peoples of the earth (Exod. 19:3).

The entire nation of Israel was to become "priests" and serve as mediators between God and the nations—the other peoples of the world. This responsibility and opportunity now applies to the entire body of Christ's people. This great blessing given to God's people was—and is—never to be used exclusively for themselves. Christians today are God's people; they have experienced God's great and miraculous acts. They should, therefore, share God's love and salvation with all peoples and remain totally committed to him.

God has revealed his desire for all humankind throughout Scripture. In his message through Isaiah, God said, "'I will also make you a light for the Gentiles, that you may bring my salvation to the ends of the earth'" (Isaiah 49:6). Jesus enjoined his followers to pray that the Lord of the harvest would send out workers to the fields, fields that contain plentiful fruit (Matthew 9:37–38). The Lord sent out his followers to preach the message to the "lost sheep of Israel" (Matt. 10:5–15). He encouraged his followers by promising that the good soil would produce good fruit that would be harvested (Matt. 13:1–43). The Master further indicated the Father's great desire for lost humanity in the three wonderful parables of love for the lost—the lost sheep, the lost coin, and the lost son (Luke 15:1–32). John reflected this same divine desire in John 3:16. Paul mirrored God's desire in declaring that his heart's desire for the Israelites was "that they may be saved" (Romans 10:1).

Evangelism/missions remains a central and essential task of the church because the ultimate source for the effort springs directly from the revealed nature of God himself. God wants his lost children found and brought back to his fold.

Evangelism/Missions Meets the Ultimate Human Need (Romans 10:13-15)

Evangelism/missions is an essential task of the church because in these ministries, Christians bring sinful humanity to the one solution to their ultimate need. Jesus sent his followers to the "lost sheep of the house of Israel" (Matt. 10:5–15). The Lord intends that the message of his salvation be preached to all peoples before the end (Matt. 24:14). The apostle Paul showed this ultimate human need when he declared that all people have sinned and remain, in their unforgiven state, under the judgment of God (Rom. 3:21–31; 2 Cor. 5:11–21; Ephesians 2:1–10). Peter insisted that salvation was only in the name of Jesus (Acts 4:12). Sinful, unrepentant humans stand lost and condemned before God and have hope only in Christ.

Quotes on the Evangelistic/Missionary Task of the Church

"The church exists by mission just as fire exists by burning."

– **Emil Brunner**, *The Word and the World*, page 108.

"The rankest heresy of which a church can be guilty is to ignore or repudiate its missionary obligation. It is impossible for one to accept the divine authority of the New Testament and deny the missionary function of the church, unless he is blinded by ignorance and prejudice."

– **H. E. Dana**, *A Manual of Ecclesiology*, page 233.

"The church that is not missionary in spirit and practice does not deserve the ground upon which its building stands."

– **George W. Truett**, cited in Herschel Hobbs, *What Baptists Believe*, page 89.

Paul's heart's desire and prayer to God for his people, Israel, was "that they may be saved" (Rom. 10:1). The apostle's message in Romans 10:1–12 may be summed up in these three statements: (1) Although the Israelites were religious and sought strenuously to find a way to right-standing with God in human ritual, they remained lost because their quest was to no avail (Rom. 10:1–2). (2) Their failure to reach right standing with God resulted from the fact that they attempted to establish this position through their own, human actions (10:2–7). (3) A new and living way had been provided through Christ. Anyone who repented of his or her sin, confessed Jesus as Lord, and believed in his or her heart the truth of the gospel would be saved (10:8–12).

The people of Israel, though religious, stood in need of God's salvation. Salvation in Christ alone could meet the ultimate human need—that is, the need to overcome the sin barrier and find rightstanding with God. The church must accept, as an essential task, that of proclaiming this message of salvation and guiding lost and unsaved people into this new relationship with God in Christ.

Paul next asked how people could call upon him of whom they had not heard. Paul then declared to Christians and churches that their responsibility included the task of proclaiming Christ, by word and by deed, to the lost (10:13–15). Baptist pastor and scholar Herschel Hobbs wrote, " . . . the responsibility to tell the good news rested upon those who had heard it. It has been and always will be this way. Those who have received the gospel are to share it."[4]

An essential task of every Christian and every church is evangelism/missions. The urgent need of salvation among the peoples of the earth requires that Christ's churches proclaim the gospel and guide the lost to salvation. Apart from the message of salvation in Christ, there is no answer. Christians and churches must share the message!

William Carey (1761-1834)– The "Heart and Soul"[9] of Baptists' Initial Emphasis on Missions

In 1792, at the Baptist association meeting held in Nottingham, England, a young cobbler and preacher named William Carey preached what has been called the "Deathless Sermon." At that time, the antimissionary spirit of hyper-Calvinist theology dominated the thought of Baptists. Carey's text was Isaiah 54:2-3, and the theme of his message was "Expect great things from God; attempt great things for God." Carey's sermon called attention to the imperative of missions.

The sermon greatly impressed Carey's hearers. As is so often the case, however, it appeared that nothing would be done about it. At the business session the next day, many cautioned against taking immediate action.

Andrew Fuller, a greatly respected preacher, was sitting beside Carey. Carey turned and pleaded with him, "Is there nothing again going to be done, sir?" Fuller rose and spoke for missions. Fuller's prestige and his message drew support for Carey's cause. A motion was passed that "a plan be prepared . . . for propagating the Gospel . . . ."[10] Thus Baptists began their participation in the modern missionary movement.

Missions/Evangelism Responds Obediently to Christ's Commission (Matthew 28:18-20; John 20:21)

The church must respond to the task of evangelism/missions because this effort is clearly commissioned by Christ. After Jesus' resurrection, he commissioned his disciples to proclaim his message to all people. Jesus said he was sending his followers into the world on a redemptive mission as God had sent him (John 20:21). On the mountain in Galilee, the Master set out the Great Commission (Matt. 28:16–20). Jesus' words in the Great Commission contain (1) a great declaration; (2) a great imperative; (3) a great scope; (4) a great methodology; and (5) a great promise.

Jesus' great declaration stated that as risen and glorified Lord, he had received all power or authority in heaven and on earth (28:18). The church never needs to shy away from anything as it carries out the Great Commission, regardless of how difficult it might seem. The church can hold this assurance because the Lord of all authority demands the task and undergirds it! The Commission exists in light of this great declaration that Christ reigns supreme.[5]

The Great Commission contains Jesus' great imperative for witness and disciple-making among all the peoples of the world (Matt. 28:19). The main verb, an imperative, expresses the central command to "make disciples" of all the peoples in the world. Making disciples involves guiding lost souls to faith in Christ, incorporating them into God's family, and helping them to continue to grow in his way of life.

The great scope of the Commission indicates Jesus' desire to reach all the peoples of the world (28:19). Christ commanded that his followers make disciples among "all nations" (28:19), that is, among all the people groups of the world. Reaching every person in all the ethnolinguistic groups (peoples) in the world constitutes the overall purpose and primary command in the Great Commission.[6] The apostle John indicated that in his vision of God's eventual and eternal kingdom, he saw a "great multitude that no one could count, from every nation, tribe and people and language, standing before the throne and in front of the Lamb" (Rev. 7:9; see also 5:9). Here lies the great scope of the Commission.

Note three Greek words Jesus used in Matthew 28:19–20 to enunciate the great methodology for the Commission. These words revealed how the church could make all peoples his disciples. All three of the words are participles. The first Greek word means "going," which, although a participle, has a definite imperative force and can be translated "go." The term indicates that God's people do not have the option of passively sitting and waiting but must be actively and aggressively engaged in missionary effort.

The two other participles—"baptizing" and "teaching"—likewise express means for making disciples (Matt. 28:19–20). Baptism marks the beginning of the Christian life as the expression of salvation. By baptism, a person proclaims his or her allegiance to Christ and his kingdom. "Teaching them to obey everything I have commanded you" indicates training, not just in doctrine, but in the fullest expression of Christian life and integrity (28:20). The methods set out for the Great Commission include training believers to live out the full measure of what it means to be Christ's person.

The great promise in the Commission assures Christ's followers of his continued presence and power (28:20). The church has the assurance of Christ's presence and power no matter how difficult the task. "No task is too big, no burden too heavy, when Jesus himself is at work in the situation."[7] No place on earth is beyond the reach of God's love in Christ, and no Christian or church is alone while seeking to share the message and make disciples!

The Great Commission contains Christ's command to his people and therefore shows the essential nature of evangelism/mission to the church. Jesus commissions his churches first to mobilization, by going, then to evangelization, by making disciples, on to incorporation, by baptizing, and finally to indoctrination, guiding in Christian living by teaching them to obey all things. The church accepts the Great Commission as essential to its task. Baptist missionary and missions professor Bob Garrett wrote, "The church must take up the Great Commission, not just out of concern for the lost, or pity for those who are needy, but also because ringing in every disciple's ears is the command given by him to whom all authority is given in heaven and earth."[8]

Evangelism/Missions Operates in God's Promise of Divine Power (Acts 1:8)

Christians and churches never seek to carry out the essential task of missions/evangelism in human strength. Evangelism/missions, an essential task of the church, relies on the supernatural power of God for its attainment. Believers and churches feel divine compulsion to evangelize all peoples but never fear having to accomplish the effort apart from divine empowering.

Jesus instructed his disciples in Acts 1:8 that they would be his witnesses in Jerusalem (their immediate context), in Judea (their wider local place), in Samaria (their next neighbor), and then to the ends of the earth (the remotest parts of the world). The disciples were not, however, to become such witnesses until the event by which they would "receive power when the Holy Spirit comes on you" (Acts 1:8). This promised power came upon the disciples on the day of Pentecost (2:1–12).

After the remarkable event of the Spirit's coming upon the believers, many people heard the gospel in words they could fully understand. Upon further hearing the Word of God from Peter, about three thousand people turned in faith to Christ (2:14–41). These believers were then drawn into the Christian fellowship (the church), in which they continued to express their faith in Christ, their unity with one another, and their commitment to the task of evangelism and missions (2:42–47).

Missions/Evangelism—An Essential Task

Missions/evangelism constitutes an essential task of the church that must never be neglected or considered optional. This task is essential because missions/evangelism (1) begins with the loving desire of God for all humankind; (2) meets the ultimate need of people; (3) responds obediently to Christ's commission to his followers; and (4) operates in the promised, supernatural power of God.

Ultimately, missions/evangelism becomes reality as Christians apprehend the awesome desire of God for the salvation of all humankind. May God's people and God's churches be ever faithful to the essential task God has graciously given them. [11]

QUESTIONS

1. The church building had burned, and the members envisioned a difficult time in rebuilding. One member suggested that the money in the missions section of the budget be used locally until the building had been completed. What factors did this member overlook?

2. What assurances does the Bible provide for Christians and churches as they seek to promote evangelism/missions in their communities and in the world?

3. Suggest an outline for a message (lesson, devotional, sermon) on the Great Commission. What points would you want to cover in your presentation?

4. What is the meaning of the concept of proclaiming the gospel of Jesus Christ by word and by deed?

NOTES

1. Herschel H. Hobbs, *The Baptist Faith and Message* (Nashville, Tennessee: Convention Press, 1971), 108.
2. Article 11, "The Baptist Faith and Message," 1963. For a copy of "The Baptist Faith and Message" (1963), see http://texasbaptists.org/files/2010/08/1963BaptistFaithandMessage1.pdf. Accessed 12/8/2010.
3. Ebbie C. Smith, "The Call to Missions," *Adult Bible Teacher* (October, November, December 1989): 37.
4. Hobbs, *The Baptist Faith and Message*, 108.
5. Bob Garrett, "The Gospels and Acts: Jesus the Missionary and His Missionary Followers," in *Missiology: An Introduction to the Foundations, History, and Strategies of World Missions*, ed. John Mark Terry, Ebbie Smith, and Justice Anderson (Nashville: Broadman & Holman, 1998), 71.
6. Garrett, *Missiology*, 72.
7. Garrett, *Missiology*, 71.
8. Garrett, *Missiology*, 71.
9. Robert G. Torbet, *A History of the Baptists*, rev. ed. (Valley Forge: The Judson Press, 1963), 80.
10. Torbet, *A History of the Baptists*, 80–82.
11. For additional assistance on the theme of God's provision of salvation, see *This Magnificent Salvation* by Duane Brooks (Dallas, TX: BaptistWay Press, 2010). Call 1-866-249-1799 or see www.baptistwaypress.org.

LESSON EIGHT

Religious Freedom and Separation of Church and State

BACKGROUND SCRIPTURES

Genesis 1:27; 2:7; Matthew 6:6-7, 24; 16:26; 22:15-22; John 8:36; Acts 3:1–4:22; 5:17-29; Romans 6:1-2; 13:1-7; Galatians 5:1, 13; Philippians 3:20; 1 Timothy 2:1-3; James 4:12; 1 Peter 2:12-17; 3:8-17; 4:12-19

FOCAL TEXTS

Matthew 22:15-22; Acts 5:27-29; Romans 13:1-7; 1 Timothy 2:1-3; 1 Peter 2:13-17

MAIN IDEA

"The church should not seek to use the state for its purposes. The state should not commandeer the church for political ends. The state should not favor one religion above another."[1]

STUDY AIM

To summarize biblical teachings on religious liberty and the separation of church and state

QUICK READ

Religious freedom with its corollary of separation of church and state is a precious privilege that was dearly bought by our Baptist forebears and should be cherished and preserved.

The doctrine of religious liberty has been called the distinct contribution that America has made to the science of government. In George W. Truett's historic address, "Baptists and Religious Liberty," he cited the American historian Bancroft as having said, "Freedom of conscience, unlimited freedom of mind, was from the first the trophy of the Baptists."[2] Truett also cited English philosopher John Locke's statement, "The Baptists were the first propounders of absolute liberty, just and true liberty, equal and impartial liberty."[3]

Why did Baptists earnestly contend for the principle of religious freedom? For hundreds of years this small group of often-despised believers endured horrible and heart-breaking persecutions. Baptists saw the terrible results when a government-established church used the civil power to enforce religious edicts. Often Baptists had to stand alone while being persecuted by both Protestant and Catholic governments in Europe and America. If Baptists must stand alone today in defending religious freedom and the separation of the powers of the church and the state, it will not be the first time!

In 1920, Baptist preacher and leader George W. Truett could say that Baptists "have never been a party to oppression of conscience."[4] May God grant that it will always be said of the people called Baptists! In his memorable and watershed address on the steps of the U. S. Capitol, Truett went on to make this powerful statement:

> They [Baptists] have forever been the unwavering champions of liberty, both religious and civil. Their contention now is, and has been, and, please God, must ever be, that it is the natural and fundamental and indefeasible right of every human being to worship God or not, according to the dictates of conscience, and, as long as this does not infringe upon the rights of others, they are to be held accountable alone to God for all religious beliefs and practices. . . . It is the consistent and insistent contention of our Baptist people, always and everywhere, that religion must be voluntary and uncoerced, and that it is not the prerogative of

> any power, whether civil or ecclesiastical to compel men to conform to any religious creed or form of worship, or to pay taxes for the support of a religious organization to which they do not belong and whose creed they do not believe. God wants free worshipers and no other kind.[5]

The fundamental principles of Baptist theology supporting the doctrine of religious liberty include the following:

1. The Lordship of Jesus Christ over all creation, the church, and the individual lives of Christians
2. The Bible as the only rule of faith and practice, in which the will of Christ is revealed
3. The priesthood of believers (1 Peter 2:9), including individual accountability before God, personal ability to read and interpret Scripture under the guidance of the Holy Spirit, and individual responsibility for witnessing in the name of Jesus Christ, who is the only provision for salvation of the human race
4. The church as a spiritual body with Jesus Christ as Head, the Word of God as the only authority, and with each church member being of equal standing before God

In this Bible study we will examine some of the Scriptural principles that are the foundation for this exceedingly precious Baptist doctrine of religious freedom and the separation of the powers of the church and the state.

Matthew 22:15-22 (NASB)

15 Then the Pharisees went and plotted together how they might
trap Him in what He said. 16 And they sent their disciples to Him, along
with the Herodians, saying, "Teacher, we know that You are truthful
and teach the way of God in truth, and defer to no one; for You are not
partial to any. 17 "Tell us then, what do You think? Is it lawful to give a
poll-tax to Caesar, or not?" 18 But Jesus perceived their malice, and
said, "Why are you testing Me, you hypocrites? 19 "Show Me the coin
used for the poll-tax." And they brought Him a denarius. 20 And He said
to them, "Whose likeness and inscription is this?" 21 They said to Him,
"Caesar's." Then He said to them, "Then render to Caesar the things
that are Caesar's; and to God the things that are God's." 22 And hearing
this, they were amazed, and leaving Him, they went away.

Acts 5:27-29

27 When they had brought them, they stood them before the
Council. The high priest questioned them, 28 saying, "We gave you
strict orders not to continue teaching in this name, and yet, you have
filled Jerusalem with your teaching and intend to bring this man's
blood upon us." 29 But Peter and the apostles answered, "We must
obey God rather than men."

Romans 13:1-7

1 Every person is to be in subjection to the governing authorities. For
there is no authority except from God, and those which exist are established by God. 2 Therefore whoever resists authority has opposed the
ordinance of God; and they who have opposed will receive condemna-
tion upon themselves. 3 For rulers are not a cause of fear for good
behavior, but for evil. Do you want to have no fear of authority? Do
what is good and you will have praise from the same; 4 for it is a minister of God to you for good. But if you do what is evil, be afraid; for it
does not bear the sword for nothing; for it is a minister of God, an

avenger who brings wrath on the one who practices evil. [5]Therefore it
is necessary to be in subjection, not only because of wrath, but also for
conscience' sake. [6]For because of this you also pay taxes, for rulers are
servants of God, devoting themselves to this very thing. [7]Render to all
what is due them: tax to whom tax is due; custom to whom custom;
fear to whom fear; honor to whom honor.

1 Timothy 2:1-3

[1]First of all, then, I urge that entreaties and prayers, petitions and
thanksgivings, be made on behalf of all men, [2]for kings and all who are
in authority, so that we may lead a tranquil and quiet life in all godli-
ness and dignity. [3]This is good and acceptable in the sight of God our
Savior.

1 Peter 2:13-17

[13]Submit yourselves for the Lord's sake to every human institution,
whether to a king as the one in authority, [14]or to governors as sent by
him for the punishment of evildoers and the praise of those who do
right. [15]For such is the will of God that by doing right you may silence
the ignorance of foolish men. [16]Act as free men, and do not use your
freedom as a covering for evil, but use it as bondslaves of God. [17]Honor
all people, love the brotherhood, fear God, honor the king.

The Principle of the Separation of Church and State
(Matthew 22:15–22)

Two of the political/religious parties of Jesus' day were the Pharisees and the Herodians. They were rival parties, but they were united in their opposition to Jesus. The Pharisees were very much opposed to the Roman occupation of the Jewish nation. On the other hand, the Herodians were followers of the Herod family, who accommodated themselves to Roman rule.

Apparently the two parties had a running debate on the propriety of paying taxes to Rome. In an attempt to trap Jesus, they brought their dispute to him. With flattering words, they attempted to entice him

The Struggle for Religious Liberty in New England

Isaac Backus (1724–1806) led the efforts of Baptists in New England to secure religious liberty. One of the examples of persecution cited by Backus involved his own mother. In her own words in a letter, we have a moving description of her experience. By reason of conscience, Mrs. Backus and other members of the church refused to pay the religious tax to support the clergy of the state church, and they were placed in jail.

Norwich, November 4, 1752

> Your Brother Samuel lay in prison 20 days. October 15, the collectors came to our house, and took me away to prison about 9:00 o'clock in a dark rainy night. Brothers Hill and Sabin were brought there the next night. We lay in prison 13 days, and then set at liberty by what means I know not. . . . O the condescension of heaven! though I was bound when I was cast into this furnace, yet was I loosed, and found Jesus in the midst of the furnace with me. . . . Now the prison looked like a palace to me. I could bless God for all the laughs and scoffs made at me. . . . Then I could forgive as I would desire to be forgiven, and love my neighbor as myself. . . . These from your loving mother,
>
> **–Elizabeth Backus**[16]

onto the horns of a dilemma. Their question was, "Is it lawful to give tribute unto Caesar, or not?" (Matthew 22:17, KJV).

If Jesus answered "Yes," he would be alienated from the majority of the population. They despised Roman taxes. If he said "No," he could be charged with sedition by the Romans for encouraging the people not to pay their taxes. The Pharisees and the Herodians thought that they had Jesus in an impossible situation, but he confounded their efforts with an object lesson.

Jesus seldom answered questions with a direct "yes" or "no." For example, in this instance, he called for the coin that was used to pay the "tribute," meaning the tax. This Greek word for "tribute" is *kensos*. In Latin the word would be *census*. This "tribute" (KJV) or "poll-tax" (NASB) was an annual tax on every man and woman. The people hated this tax especially. It was very hard on the poor, being a full day's pay for a working man (two days' pay for a married couple). Furthermore, it was seen as a humiliating symbol of Jewish slavery to Rome.

Jesus asked whose image and writing appeared on the coin. The co-conspirators gave the patently obvious answer, "Caesar." They must have been wondering, *Where is he going with this?*

Jesus answered the question so simply that even his enemies marveled at his words. The intended debate ended suddenly, and the inquisitors quietly melted into the astonished crowd.

The answer was a profound and a radically new thought: "Then render to Caesar the things that are Caesar's; and to God the things that are God's" (Matt. 22:21).

Applications of the Principle

(Acts 5:27-29; Romans 13:1-7; 1 Timothy 2:1-3; 1 Peter 2:13-17)

Perhaps Jesus' statement in Matthew 22:21 was the first enunciation of the principle of the separation of civil and spiritual authority. The thought is introduced through the symbolism of two images: the image of Caesar on the coin of the realm and the image of God in the creation of humanity. The applications and ramifications of this revelation are many.

1. *God created people, male and female, in his own image.* Therefore, humanity has been "endowed with certain 'unalienable' rights," as worded in the Declaration of Independence of the United States. Created in the image of God, each person is of infinite value and worth. Furthermore, each person is answerable only to the Creator in matters of spiritual conscience.

An early English Baptist leader, Thomas Helwys, published a book in 1612 explaining the Baptist position and calling for freedom of religion. Helwys sent an autographed copy to King James I (of "King James Bible" fame) with this inscription, "The King is a mortall man and not God, therefore hath no power over y immortall soules of his subjects to make lawes and ordinances for them and to set spirituall Lords over them."[6] Baptist historian Robert G. Torbet called Helwys' book, "The first claim for freedom of worship to be published in the English language."[7]

For this brave testimony of Baptist convictions, the king had Helwys placed in Newgate prison until his death about 1616.[8] He was but one of thousands who sealed with his life what he had spoken with his lips.

2. *The civil government has neither the right nor the capability to legislate or dictate religious doctrine or practice, except in such instances as when other people's freedom is being denied or their safety is being endangered.* When both the civil and religious authorities commanded the apostles not to teach in the name of Jesus, "then Peter and the other apostles answered and said, We ought to obey God rather than men" (Acts 5:29, KJV).

Simon Peter proceeded to preach Jesus to the religious council in Jerusalem. When he accused the religious leaders of killing Jesus and hanging him "on a tree" (Acts 5:30), the council began to lay plans to kill the apostles also.

Persecution is the ugly fruit that comes from the union of religion and civil government. Even "the land of the free" has a record of religious persecution that is largely unknown. Our remarkable religious heritage must be taught in our Baptist churches if we are to treasure and

The Struggle for Religious Liberty in Virginia

John Leland (1754-1841) led the struggle for religious freedom in Virginia and the South. He is credited with having influenced James Madison to introduce the Bill of Rights as amendments to the Federal Constitution. He wrote the following to answer the question, "Are the rights of conscience alienable, or inalienable?"

> . . . Does a man upon entering into social contact surrender his conscience to that society. . . . I judge not, for the following reasons: *First.* Every man must give an account of himself to God, and therefor every man ought to be at liberty to serve God in a way that he can best reconcile to his conscience. *Second.* . . . It would be sinful for a man to surrender that to man, which is to be kept sacred for God. *Third.* But supposing it was right for a man to bind his own conscience, yet surely it is very iniquitous to bind the conscience of his children. . . . *Fourth.* Finally, Religion is a matter between God and individuals; the religious opinions of men not being the objects of civil government, nor in any way under its control.[17]

maintain the religious liberties that have been bought with painful price.

Between 1768 and 1777, no less than thirty Baptist preachers in Virginia were fined, whipped, and imprisoned for nothing more than preaching the gospel and calling for the conversion of sinners. Lewis Craig may have been the first Virginia Baptist preacher to have been indicted in a court of law for public preaching. At his arraignment Craig said, "I thank you, gentlemen of the Grand Jury, for the honor you have done me. While I was wicked and injurious, you took no notice of me; but since I have altered my course of life and endeavored to reform my neighbors, you concern yourselves much about me."[9]

Sitting on that grand jury was John Waller. He was known as "Swearing Jack" before his conversion. As a result of Craig's testimony, Waller soon professed Christ and joined the Baptists. On June 4, 1768, John Waller, Lewis Craig, James Childs, and others were arrested. They were brought before the court and charged as follows: "May it please your worships, these men are great disturbers of the peace; they cannot meet a man upon the road, but they must ram a text of Scripture down his throat."[10] After forty-three days in jail, the prisoners were discharged. However, the persecutors found that the imprisonment of the preachers actually resulted in the furtherance of their cause. They preached regularly through the bars of the jail to larger crowds than they had in their churches.

3. Christians are to obey the law of government (Romans 13:1–7). Consider what these verses tell us about church and state and their relationship.

- Government authority is ordained by God (Rom. 13:1).
- To resist government authority is to resist the ordinance of God (Rom. 13:2), unless the will of God and government are in opposition (Acts 5:29).
- Government should restrain evil and promote good (Rom.13:3).
- Government should administer temporal justice (Rom. 13:4; see 1 Peter 2:14).
- Christians should pay taxes for the support of civil government (Rom. 13:6).
- Christians should pay proper respect to government authority (13:7).

Other New Testament Scriptures provide additional insights.

- Christians should pray for the leaders of government (1 Timothy 2:1–2).
- Government should promote domestic tranquility (1 Tim. 2:2).
- Good citizenship pleases God (1 Tim. 2:3).
- Christians are to submit themselves "to every ordinance of man for the Lord's sake" (1 Peter 2:13, KJV).
- Good citizenship bears a positive witness before the world (1 Pet. 2:15).
- Christians should exercise liberty as servants of God and not as an excuse for evil (1 Pet. 2:16).

The Struggle for Religious Liberty in Texas

One reason Texas Baptists have always been strong advocates of religious freedom and the separation of church and state is because Texas was once under the domination of a state-supported church. When Moses Austin asked to be allowed to settle 300 families in Texas in 1820, all colonists were required to be Roman Catholics or agree to convert to that church before they could settle. Even after the Mexican Revolution of 1820 achieved independence from Spain, the Roman Catholic Church continued as the official state religion. Only priests were allowed to conduct funerals or perform weddings.

Joseph L. Bays, Kentucky Baptist preacher and friend of Daniel Boone, joined the colonists of Moses and Stephen F. Austin. Bays preached his first sermon in Texas in 1820 at the cabin of Joseph Hinds, about eighteen miles from San Augustine. The Bays family became a part of the original 300 settlers of the Austin colony.

Bays was arrested in 1823 while preaching in San Felipe. While he was being taken to San Antonio for trial, Bays overcame his guard and escaped. He later went to San Antonio, not to stand trial, but to preach. Bays became a close friend of Sam Houston and fought in the Battle of San Jacinto in 1836.[18]

4. *The power of the civil government to tax should not be used to support religion or religious institutions.* The Bible teaches that church ministries ought to be supported by the voluntary offerings of its adherents and sympathizers. God desires a willing heart. "Take from among you a contribution to the Lord; whoever is of a willing heart, let him bring it" (Exodus 35:5). "Each one must do just as he has purposed in his heart, not grudgingly or under compulsion, for God loves a cheerful giver" (2 Corinthians 9:7).

When it was proposed to the Virginia legislature in colonial times that government money should be used to support the teachers of the Christian religion, James Madison led the opposition. He said, " . . . The Christian religion itself . . . disavows a dependence on the powers of this world . . . this religion both existed and flourished, not only without the support of human laws, but in spite of every opposition from them."[11]

Benjamin Franklin wrote in a letter, "When a religion is good, I can see that it will support itself; and when it cannot support itself, and God does not take care to support it, so that its professors are obliged to call for the help of the civil power, it is a sign, I apprehend, of its being a bad one."[12]

5. All people should be free to worship God according to the directions of their own conscience and to practice and propagate their religious convictions. We do well to remember that on spiritual matters, each of us is accountable to God (Rom. 14:12).

Indeed, Christians are advised to examine themselves to see whether they be in the faith and to prove for themselves that the Lord Jesus Christ is within them (2 Cor. 13:5). In the practice of religious life, neither Daniel nor his fellow Hebrews would be governed by the authority of a temporal king. As a result Daniel was cast into the lions' den, and Shadrach, Meshach, and Abednego were cast into a fiery furnace (Daniel 6:16; 3:14–18).

In 1651 pastor John Clarke, along with two Baptist laymen, Obadiah Holmes and John Randell, went up from Newport, Rhode Island, to Lynn, Massachusetts, to visit an aged and blind Baptist friend, William

Texas' Declaration of Independence

Richard Ellis, a Baptist, presided at the convention when Texas declared independence on March 2, 1836, and again on March 17 when the first Texas constitution was adopted. Baptist historian Robert A. Baker writes,

> One of the injustices named by the Convention as the basis for the Declaration reads as follows: "It denies us the right of worshiping the Allmighty (sic) according to the dictates of our own conscience, by the support of a national religion calculated to promote the temporal interests of its human functionaries rather than the glory of the true and living God."[19]

Wisdom on Church and State

"Neither church nor state should exercise authority over the other. History records that a free church in a free state proves a blessing to both."[20]

Witters. It took two days to walk the eighty miles. On Sunday they held a private religious service in Witters' home. In the midst of the service two constables broke into the house and arrested the three visitors in the act of worship. This was a serious offence. It was a violation of the law for anyone to hold divine services without the consent of the government-established Congregational Church of the Massachusetts Bay Colony.

At their trial, they were accused, among other things, that they did "Baptize such as were Baptized before . . . And also did deny the lawfullness of Baptizing of Infants."[13] Puritan John Cotton, determined to have a theocratic state, accused the three of being soul murderers because they denied the saving power of infant baptism.

The three men were given the choice of a whipping or a fine. The fines of two of the men were paid, but Obadiah Holmes refused to allow his fine to be paid. After several weeks in jail, Holmes was taken to Boston Commons where his hands were tied to a stake. He was stripped to the waist, and the flogger used a whip of three hard leather lashes, stopping three times to spit on his hands, and laying on the whip with all his might.[14]

During the whipping Holmes prayed that the Lord would not lay this sin to their charge. He continued to preach all the way through the punishment. When the ordeal was over, he said to the magistrates, "You have struck me as with roses."[15] Holmes was so injured by the severity of the whipping that he was unable to leave Boston for several weeks. He could rest at night only by crouching on his elbows and knees. He carried the scars of the beating to his grave as a badge of honor for his devotion.

Preserving Religious Freedom

Religious freedom is a right that was achieved only after years of struggle. It cost our Baptist forebears persecution, whippings, imprisonment, sufferings, and painful horrible death.

No matter what course others may take, we should preserve the right to witness to the saving grace of Jesus Christ our Savior and to worship him according to the pattern of Scripture. We should not use the sword of secular power in spiritual matters. Rather we should use the sword of the Spirit only. We should not coerce any person to conform to religion. We should protect the religious freedom of minorities since we were once a despised and persecuted sect. In most of the world today, Baptists are still a small minority, and we must hold these principles dear for their sakes also.[21]

QUESTIONS

1. What are four fundamental principles of religious freedom?

2. What difficult issues regarding religious liberty do we face today?

3. How can Baptists respond to challenges to religious liberty in light of biblical teachings?

4. Why should Christians exercise good citizenship?

NOTES

1. Herschel H. Hobbs, *The Baptist Faith and Message* (Nashville, Tennessee: Convention Press, 1971), 142.
2. George W. Truett in an address made on May 16, 1920, on the steps of the U. S. Capitol Building. The full text of George W. Truett's sermon, "Baptists and Religious Liberty," can be accessed on the internet at this address: www.bjconline.org. See "Sermons" under "Resources." Accessed 12/3/2010.
3. Truett, "Baptists and Religious Liberty," 1920.
4. Truett, "Baptists and Religious Liberty," 1920.
5. Truett, "Baptists and Religious Liberty," 1920.
6. Cited in Robert G. Torbet, *A History of the Baptists*, rev. ed. (Philadelphia: The Judson Press, 1963), 38.
7. Torbet, *A History of the Baptists*, 38. Thomas Helwys' book was titled *A Short Declaration of the Mystery of Iniquity*.
8. Torbet, *A History of the Baptists*, 39.
9. Harry Leon McBeth, *The Baptist Heritage* (Nashville, Tennessee: Broadman Press, 1987), 270.
10. McBeth, *A Source Book for Baptist Heritage* (Nashville, Tennessee: Broadman Press, 1990), 183.
11. A. P. Stokes and L. Pfeffer, *Church and State in the United States* (New York: Kohn, Harper and Row Publishers, 1964), 57
12. Stokes and Pfeffer, *Church and State in the United States*, 41.
13. McBeth, *A Source Book for Baptist Heritage*, 93.
14. O. K. Armstrong & M. M. Armstrong, *The Indomitable Baptists* (Garden City, N.J.: Doubleday and Company, Inc., 1967), 60–62.
15. McBeth, *The Baptist Heritage*, 140.
16. McBeth, *A Source Book for Baptist Heritage,* 173.
17. McBeth, *A Source Book for Baptist Heritage,* 179.
18. McBeth, Texas Baptists: *A Sesquicentennial History* (Dallas, Texas: BAPTISTWAY PRESS®, 1998), 14.
19. Robert A. Baker, *The Blossoming Desert* (Waco, Texas: Word Books, 1970), 23.
20. Hobbs, *The Baptist Faith and Message*, 143.
21. For additional assistance on the theme of religious liberty and separation of church and state, see *Baptists and Religious Liberty: The Freedom Road* by William M. Pinson, Jr. (Dallas, TX: BaptistWay Press, 2008). Call 1-866-249-1799 or see www.baptistwaypress.org.

LESSON NINE

Salvation Only by Grace Through Faith

BACKGROUND SCRIPTURES

Exodus 6:2-8; Matthew 1:21; 4:17; 16:21-26; Luke 1:68-69; 2:28-32; John 1:11-14,29; 3:3-21,36; 5:24; 10:9; Acts 2:21; 4:12; 15:11; 16:25-34; 20:32; Romans 1:16-18; 3:23-25; 4:3-13; 5:8-10; 10:9-13; Galatians 2:20; 3:13; 6:15; Ephesians 1:7; 2:8-22; Hebrews 5:8-9; 9:24-28; 1 John 2:1-2; Revelation 3:20

FOCAL TEXTS

Acts 16:25-34; Romans 1:16-18; Galatians 2:20; Ephesians 2:8-10

MAIN IDEA

"Salvation by grace means salvation as a free gift on God's part. . . . Receiving salvation as an unmerited gift on God's part is faith."[1]

STUDY AIM

To explain the way of salvation

QUICK READ

Two facets of God's grace are the grace of salvation and the grace of daily living. God saves us, not just from hell, but *to* a specific lifestyle

"'Believe on the Lord Jesus, and you will be saved, you and your household'" (16:31). Such a plain, straightforward way of introducing someone to God. No frills, no barriers, just faith.

What barriers do we put in the way of people seeking the Lord? What barriers do we place in our own path as we seek to follow Christ? One thing we can know with certainty—God's grace surmounts and destroys all barriers.

A Tower Experience (Romans 1:16-18)

Martin Luther (1483–1546) found no peace, no matter how many hours he spent in confession, no matter how much he beat himself, no matter how strongly he longed for relationship with God. Even as a monk and a priest, peace eluded Luther's grasp. He yearned for acceptance by God. One day, as he sat in a tower room preparing a seminary lecture on Romans 1:16–18, the gospel smacked him right between the eyes. God transferred Luther's focus from the wrath of God consuming all sinners to God's grace saving through faith.

The Protestant Reformation latched onto this insight, and as Baptists developed in the early 1600s, they affirmed Luther's emphasis that salvation is *sola gratias*—solely of grace. We don't gain salvation by being baptized as infants or by being born in America. We don't earn salvation by growing up in a Baptist church or by going to a Baptist school. The true gospel "is the power of God for salvation to everyone who has faith . . ." (Romans 1:16). Salvation comes by the Lord's grace to those who believe.

In our age of tolerance, we easily forget that people need God's grace. Romans 1:18 reminds us that God's wrath is real. People need to know that eternal consequences flow from their actions and attitudes. We ignore opportunities to share the gospel because we don't want to be labeled as fanatics. We remain silent in the face of immorality or sin because we don't want to appear judgmental. We cling to the gift of God's grace for ourselves, hope others find it, too, and yet do little to share that word of grace. How sad. Luther's insight caused him to

Lottie Moon

Lottie Moon (1840-1912) lived the gospel daily. Although she made mistakes like all of us, she modeled Christ's love to the Chinese with whom she worked. Adopting their dress, eating their food, and mastering their language, she became a "little Christ" for the people of Ping Tu for several decades. God's grace poured into folks in Ping Tu because Lottie Moon accepted God's power to live a Christian life, and because they responded in faith to the gospel. Illness plagued her. Fatigue made her feel inadequate for the task. The lack of trained missionary personnel made her work overwhelming. Yet, in it all, she persevered in sharing the gospel by word and deed.

Unable to address men directly because of cultural norms, when she spoke to women inside a house, she raised her voice and articulated each word so that the men gathered outside near the windows heard the gospel clearly. From baking cookies for the town's children, to offering aid to the poor and spiritual guidance to new Christians, Charlotte Diggs Moon lived the gospel, a life of good works.

explode into his religious world with the radical claim that God's grace is sufficient. What will our insight into God's grace cause us to do?

God reminds us of Paul and Silas in prison, and God will grant us the courage to explain the gospel to a person in spiritual need. As we live in God's grace, the Lord guides us to take loving stands on important moral issues in our world. By ones and twos, by families and congregations, we can make a difference in the spiritual and moral lives of those around us. As members of the body of Christ, we gain strength to accomplish godly purposes, and wisdom to live as Christians. But we must be willing to share God's simple message—"'Believe on the Lord Jesus'" (Acts 16:31).

God's Grace in Daily Life (Galatians 2:20; Ephesians 2:8-10)

From the early 1600s when Baptists began writing confessions of faith to let the world know what a particular community of faith believed,

Baptists have asserted that salvation comes by grace through faith. This idea shaped the Baptist understanding of baptism, the Lord's Supper, the function of the church, and the need to share the gospel. Salvation by grace defines who we are as Baptists.

God lays claim to our lives. In Galatians 2:20, Paul explained the place of the Lord's grace in our lives: ". . . it is no longer I who live, but it is Christ who lives in me. And the life I now live in the flesh I live by faith in the Son of God, who loved me and gave himself for me." If we take this doctrine seriously, we should live our lives as "little Christs" wherever we are. "Christ in us" means we share our knowledge of God's gift of salvation with a world that desperately needs that knowledge. We cannot create faith, and we cannot create grace. We can, however, create an understanding of God's desire for relationship with those we know, and we can live out God's grace in our world. The Baptist doctrine of salvation by grace through faith means we share the gospel each moment by how we live, how we present "Christ in us." Let us live a deliberate, consistent, and grace-filled gospel before the world.

God's gracious gift of salvation is free, but it is also costly! Christ demands our all. As we come to the Lord, we live daily in faith. Too, as God's grace embraces our lives, we embrace our world with faith, love, and grace. In a real sense, we are pathways for God's grace into the world. We extend God's promises to people who need those promises. Christ lives in us to sustain us and through us to sustain the world. What a wonderful way to experience God!

In Ephesians 2:8–10, Paul reminds us that salvation is God's grace-gift. Verse 10 also reminds us that this gift lays claim to our lives. God calls us to live godly lives. Salvation, as we already have noted, is a process that includes regeneration (saved), sanctification (being saved), and glorification (will be saved). The words in parentheses in the previous sentence refer to what we might call the "tenses" of the Christian life. Regeneration speaks of *having been saved*, sanctification of *being saved*, and glorification of *will be saved*, referring to the fullness of salvation that is yet to come. Walking with God daily is as much a grace-gift part of salvation as being saved from eternal damnation. In some ways, we find it more difficult to live a godly life than to accept Christ by faith. Sharing our faith and living as God would have us to live come as part of the process, however. Do we take the "daily" part of salvation seriously enough?

Baptists take the gospel very seriously. As stated by Paul in Romans 1:18, the unworthy will fall under God's wrath, and we believe all humans fit that description. Without Christ, no one can be a child of God or accept God's grace. We support missions and evangelism to bring the knowledge of Christ to the world. Yet, we find it easier to give money to missions or to pay a preacher than to live a Christian life that presents the gospel to the world, in word and deed.

"For we are what he [God] has made us, created in Christ Jesus for good works, which God prepared beforehand to be our way of life" (Eph. 2:10). "Our way of life" is to do "good works." What a challenge! Being Christ in the world is a difficult task. But Paul assured us, from his life story and from his writing, that God's grace proves sufficient for our daily lives. When was the last time we began our days with a "thank you" for the grace to get through the next twenty-four hours as a "little Christ" in the world? How often do we experience God's power in daily life? What effort do we put forth to live out our faith in God's grace

Living a "Christ" Life

1. Set aside a time each day to spend at least ten minutes in prayer.
2. Ask God to guide each decision you make, each word you speak, and each gesture you make during the day.
3. Be silent for five minutes, allowing God time to speak to you.
4. As you face tough situations during the day, silently ask for God's grace to surround the issue.
5. Before going to bed, thank God for evidence of God's grace during the day.

through our personal relationships, within our families, and in our work habits?

Paul promised us, and as Baptists we take this promise seriously, that God intends us to walk with the Lord each moment. Stumbling over spiritual obstacles, erecting ungodly barriers, we forget that the Lord knows what we face and provides more than enough grace to meet our needs.

God made us for good works, to be "little Christs" in the world, and told us exactly what doing good works means. (See Romans 12:1–2, for example.) We need to participate deliberately in God's plan each day. Saved from the punishment of sin, we must live saved from the power of sin, and we will be saved from the presence of sin. The gospel is the message we are to share with the world.

Too, we are to live our daily lives as members of a community of faith, accountable to one another and to God for our attitudes, beliefs, and lives. By accepting wise counsel, godly advice, and loving inspiration, we benefit from God's grace. The promise of salvation includes membership in a church family. God provides a community of believers to provide encouragement, to help us make tough decisions, and to enable us to work through grief and distress. We struggle side-by-side with other Christians, learning how to be God's children and how to share that knowledge with the world. As Baptists, we believe that God's grace empowers us to live Christ-like lives, supported by a community of faith. Praise God, from whom all blessings flow![2]

QUESTIONS

1. When did you last share the gospel verbally? How did it feel?

2. Within you, what barriers exist to sharing the gospel with co-workers or family?

3. How might God overcome those barriers?

4. Looking at the last year, what experiences of God's grace can you point to?

5. Who in your church shared God's grace with you?

6. With whom have you shared God's grace?

NOTES

1. Walter Thomas Conner, *Christian Doctrine* (Nashville, Tennessee: Broadman Press, 1937), 197.
2. For additional assistance on the biblical theme of salvation, see *This Magnificent Salvation* by Duane Brooks (Dallas, TX: BaptistWay Press, 2010). Call 1-866-249-1799 or see www.baptistwaypress.org.

LESSON TEN

The Security of the Believer

BACKGROUND SCRIPTURES

John 5:24; 10:27-30; 17:6, 12, 17-18; Acts 20:32; Romans 5:9-10; 8:28-39; Ephesians 1:4-23; 2:1-10; Colossians 1:12-14; 2 Thessalonians 2:13-15; 2 Timothy 1:12; 2:19; 1 Peter 1:2-5, 13; 2:4-10; 1 John 3:2

FOCAL TEXTS

John 10:27-29; Romans 8:31-39; 1 Peter 1:3-5

MAIN IDEA

"One who is truly regenerated will continue in faith and will be finally delivered from sin."[1]

STUDY AIM

To summarize the New Testament teachings on Christian perseverance and its implications for our lives

QUICK READ

Believers are saved by the grace of God and kept by the power of God.

The eternal security of the believer in Christ is one of the great doctrines in the Bible, but it also is one of the least understood. Of all Baptist beliefs this is probably the most controversial. After more than fifty years in the ministry, I have heard more people say that they could never become Baptists because of this one belief than any other teaching. This doctrine is also known as "the perseverance of the saints," or more popularly it is stated as "once saved, always saved."

Why do so many people find this doctrine difficult to understand or accept? Sincere people raise questions like the following: *What about those who were once professing believers but now are living wicked, ungodly lives? Wouldn't that doctrine be an encouragement to sin? Besides, doesn't it say somewhere in the Bible that you have to work out your own salvation and that you can fall from grace?*

Such objections deserve serious consideration, but first let's look at the teachings of Scripture on the subject. Then we will attempt to answer the objections.

Biblical Evidence for Eternal Security

John 10:27–29 gives three very important facts about the eternal security of the believer in Christ.

1. His sheep are a purchased possession (John 10:27).

Jesus used the sheep/shepherd analogy to teach that sheep belong to and are purchased by the shepherd. No flock of sheep ever got together and pooled their wool into a mutual fund to purchase a shepherd. Rather the shepherd always purchases the sheep. Jesus said, "I am the good shepherd; the good shepherd lays down His life for the sheep" (John 10:11). Again, "I lay down My life for the sheep" (John 10:15). Pastors are urged "to shepherd the church of God which He purchased with His own blood" (Acts 20:28).

It would be a mistake to believe that Christians are purchasing a Savior on the installment plan, and that salvation will be repossessed if the weekly payments are not made. Christians are not purchasing

John 10:27-29 (NASB)

27 "My sheep hear My voice, and I know them, and they follow Me; 28 and I give eternal life to them, and they will never perish; and no one will snatch them out of My hand. 29 "My Father, who has given them to Me, is greater than all; and no one is able to snatch them out of the Father's hand."

Romans 8:31-39

31 What then shall we say to these things? If God is for us, who is against us? 32 He who did not spare His own Son, but delivered Him over for us all, how will He not also with Him freely give us all things? 33 Who will bring a charge against God's elect? God is the one who justifies; 34 who is the one who condemns? Christ Jesus is He who died, yes, rather who was raised, who is at the right hand of God, who also intercedes for us. 35 Who will separate us from the love of Christ? Will tribulation, or distress, or persecution, or famine, or nakedness, or peril, or sword? 36 Just as it is written,

"For Your sake we are being put to death all day long;
We were considered as sheep to be slaughtered."

37 But in all these things we overwhelmingly conquer through Him who loved us. 38 For I am convinced that neither death, nor life, nor angels, nor principalities, nor things present, nor things to come, nor powers, 39 nor height, nor depth, nor any other created thing, will be able to separate us from the love of God, which is in Christ Jesus our Lord.

1 Peter 1:3-5

3 Blessed be the God and Father of our Lord Jesus Christ, who according to His great mercy has caused us to be born again to a living hope through the resurrection of Jesus Christ from the dead, 4 to obtain an inheritance which is imperishable and undefiled and will not fade away, reserved in heaven for you, 5 who are protected by the power of God through faith for a salvation ready to be revealed in the last time.

Christ, but he has already purchased us. A proof that the sheep have been purchased by the Shepherd is that they hear his voice and are following him (John 10:27).

2. His sheep receive eternal life as a gift (John 10:28).

The Good Shepherd said, "I give unto them eternal life . . . " (10:28, KJV). Eternal life is a gift from God. It is not of works lest any person should boast (see Ephesians 2:8–9).

One of the most basic of all biblical doctrines is that salvation comes by the grace of God and not by the work of human beings. If it were possible, what could cause people to lose eternal life after they had received it? The only reason would be that they failed to maintain their good works. If that were true, then salvation would depend on their good works.

The Bible clearly states, "I do not frustrate the grace of God: for if righteousness come by the law, then Christ is dead in vain" (Galatians 2:21, KJV). If we attempt to substitute our works for his grace, then we are frustrating the grace that God desires to give us. If we could be saved by keeping the works of the law, there would be no reason for Christ to

"I Don't Know Whether I Am Saved or Not"

Across the years, many people have said to me, "I don't know whether I am saved or not." I have always said to them that the matter can be settled if in repentance and faith they will call on the name of the Lord. I suggest that they pray something like this, *Lord, I don't know whether I was saved before or not, but I do know that I want to give my life to you now. Please forgive me, and I am giving you my whole life.* Then I suggest, "You live with that decision for a little while. You may realize that you really were a Christian but lacked assurance. If you decide that this is the first time that you have really given your life to Christ, then you need to confess him publicly and follow him in believer's baptism." It is a sobering fact that most of the people who prayed under those conditions, later came to be baptized. We certainly ought to examine our hearts to see whether we are in the faith (2 Corinthians 13:5).

have died upon the cross. If there were any other way for the human race to be redeemed, Christ would not have suffered and died for our sins. The doctrine of eternal security is inseparably related to the basic biblical doctrine of salvation by grace. You can't have one without the other.

But some have said, *It will take all that God and I can do together to get me to heaven. It will take both grace and works.* This feeling is not uncommon, but the Bible clearly states that grace and works cannot be mixed to produce salvation. "And if by grace, then is it no more of works: otherwise grace is no more grace. But if it be of works, then is it no more grace: otherwise work is no more work" (Romans 11:6, KJV). Salvation is either a gift of grace or a product of our works. It cannot be both. Salvation is a gift of grace.

3. His sheep are kept by the power of God (John 10:28–29).

The Lord Jesus said, "No one will snatch them out of My hand" (10:28). He also said, "No one is able to snatch them out of the Father's hand" (10:29). Furthermore, Scripture states, "you were sealed in Him with the Holy Spirit of promise" (Eph. 1:13)." So the Bible teaches that the sheep are kept by the power of the Son and of the Father and are sealed by the Holy Spirit. Believers are not kept by their own strength, but by the power of the triune God.

This emphasis was also the personal testimony of Paul when he wrote to Timothy, "For I know whom I have believed, and am persuaded that he is able to keep that which I have committed unto him against that day" (2 Timothy 1:12, KJV). Paul did not say, *I am able to keep that which I have committed unto him.* He clearly understood that *Christ* is able to keep us.

Simon Peter also gave the same testimony concerning the incorruptible inheritance that is reserved in heaven for us, "Who are kept by the power of God through faith unto salvation ready to be revealed in the last time" (1 Peter 1:5, KJV). Peter also declared that we are kept by the power of God and not by our own will power.

meaning. If we have truly been saved, then our natures have been changed, and it grieves us when we sin and fall short of the glory of God.

The doctrine of the eternal security of the believer is no excuse for living contentedly in sin. If people can live wickedly all during the week and then show up in church on Sunday and be perfectly contented in the worship of a holy God, then they should surely examine themselves to see if they are truly in the faith.

A third question may be asked: *But what about the verse that says, "Work out your own salvation." Doesn't that mean that we must continue to work for our salvation?*

That verse is found in Philippians 2:12: "So then, my beloved, just as you have always obeyed, not as in my presence only, but now much more in my absence, work out your salvation with fear and trembling."

One of the important principles of biblical interpretation is to examine the context in which a verse is found. Otherwise, some strange doctrines have been concocted by stringing isolated verses together. The very next verse explains, "For it is God who is at work in you both to will and to work for His good pleasure" (Phil. 2:13). It is God who is working in us, and we are not earning our salvation by our good works.

A fourth objection comes in a question like this: *Isn't there a verse that says you can "fall from grace"?* A verse containing that thought is found in the Book of Galatians. Remember first that Galatians was written for

Kept by the Power of God

All true believers endure to the end. Those whom God has accepted in Christ, and sanctified by His Spirit, will never fall away from the state of grace, but shall persevere to the end. Believers may fall into sin through neglect and temptation, whereby they grieve the Spirit, impair their graces and comforts, bring reproach on the cause of Christ, and temporal judgments on themselves, yet they shall be kept by the power of God through faith unto salvation.

—Article 5, "The Baptist Faith and Message," 1963[2]

the purpose of teaching that salvation comes by God's grace and not by our works. The entire verse reads like this: "You have been severed from Christ, you who are seeking to be justified by law; you have fallen from grace" (Galatians 5:4).

"Fallen from grace" does not mean that they had lost their salvation. Paul wrote to the Galatians as believers and repeatedly called them "brethren" (for examples, see 4:32, immediately before this passage, and 5:11, immediately after). In Galatians 5:4, Paul was reminding them that they had been saved by grace. Thus it would be futile to attempt to live the Christian life by the works of keeping rules and regulations. The verse does not say that such persons have lost their salvation. Just as we have been saved by faith, we must live by faith (Gal. 3:11). Otherwise, we would lose the powerful effect Christ has in our lives.

Fifth, *but isn't there a verse in the Bible that talks about those who "fall away"?* This question likely refers to a very solemn passage of Scripture found in Hebrews. "For it is impossible for those who were once enlightened, and have tasted of the heavenly gift, and were made partakers of the Holy Ghost, And have tasted the good word of God, and the powers of the world to come, If they shall fall away, to renew them again unto repentance; seeing they crucify to themselves the Son of God afresh, and put him to an open shame" (Hebrews 6:4–6, KJV).

If this passage means that it is possible for a person to fall away after having been saved, then it must also teach that it is impossible for them to ever be renewed again unto repentance. That would mean that if you ever fell away once, then you could never be saved again. There are not many people who deny the validity of the eternal security of the believer who would be willing to accept that consequence.

Although this passage is difficult to interpret, many scholars believe that it may mean one of three things. Citing the use of the word "tasted," some would say that these persons had only "tasted" of the heavenly gift and had never really received it. They had come close to receiving Christ but had finally rejected the gospel and would never again be renewed unto repentance. Others believe that it means that a Christian can lose his or her opportunity for service and be placed on the shelf, never again to be used in the service of God. A third possible interpretation is that the writer suggests a hypothetical case, which is used to prove the impossibility of losing one's salvation.

Why This Doctrine Is Important

The doctrine of the security of the believer is tremendously important. Consider several reasons.

First, *it determines our view of salvation.* Is a person saved by works or by the grace of God? There really are only two kinds of religions in the world: the gospel of grace and all the others that rely on some system of works or achievement. If salvation depends on Jesus plus any thing else, it is not the gospel.

Second, *it determines our relationship to God.* Is God a Father who loves and keeps his children, or are we merely hired hands in God's employ? Our motivation for serving the Lord should not be our fear of the loss of our salvation but our love for him and our desire to please him.

Third, *it influences the work of the church.* If you can't be sure of your own salvation, much less the salvation of others that you bring to Christ, then the urgency of evangelism is diminished.

QUESTIONS

1. Why do people have such difficulty in accepting the doctrine of the eternal security of the believer?

2. What reasons did Jesus give in John 10:27–29 that his sheep are eternally secure?

3. What does 1 John 2:19 say about people who leave the Christian faith?

4. What do you think the term "fall away" means in Hebrews 6:6?

5. Why should the doctrine of the eternal security of the believer be an encouragement to live the Christian life?

6. What would you say to someone who is doubting his or her salvation?

NOTES

1. W. T. Conner, *The Gospel of Redemption* (Nashville, Tennessee: Broadman Press, 1945), 247.
2. For a copy of "The Baptist Faith and Message" (1963), see http://texasbaptists.org/files/2010/08/1963BaptistFaithandMessage1.pdf. Accessed 12/8/2010.

LESSON ELEVEN

Soul Competency and the Priesthood of the Believer

BACKGROUND SCRIPTURES

Genesis 1:26–27; 2:7; Exodus 19:1–6; Psalm 8; 42:1–2; Jeremiah 31:29–34; Ezekiel 18:1–4; Matthew 16:13–17; John 3:1–16; 8:36; 14:12; Acts 4:12; 1 Corinthians 3:21,23; Galatians 5:1,13; Ephesians 2:11–21; Hebrews 4:14-16; 8:8-13; 1 Peter 2:4-10; Revelation 5:1-10

FOCAL TEXTS

Genesis 1:26–27; Jeremiah 31:29–34; Matthew 16:16–17; John 3:16; 1 Peter 2:4–10

MAIN IDEA

"There should be no institution, human person, rite, or system which stands between the individual person and God. . . . All have equal access to the Father's table, the Father's ear, and the Father's heart."[1]

STUDY AIM

To identify implications of soul competency and the priesthood of the believer

QUICK READ

Baptists believe in the priesthood of the believer and the soul competency of a believer. We believe we relate to God without human mediators, both as individuals and as a body of believers.

Religious freedom is a precious liberty. Baptists have battled legislatures, congresses, local authorities, and each other for the right of all people to worship, or not worship, God in their own way. The demand for religious liberty comes from the Baptist doctrines of soul competency and the priesthood of a believer or believers.

From Thomas Helwys to Roger Williams to George Truett, mainstream Baptist leaders have contended that each person bears responsibility for his or her relationship with God. An individual has the God-given competency to respond to God or not. An individual has the right and responsibility to interpret Scripture and apply biblical teachings to life. No authority has the power to coerce belief.

For generations Baptist laypeople and theologians, ministers and Sunday School teachers, have asserted these twin doctrines of right and responsibility. Some folks have even died to make the point that God gives every woman and man the competency to encounter the Lord, and that each believer has the responsibility to act as a priest before the Lord.

In the Beginning . . . (Genesis 1:26-27)

During the sixth creative event, according to Genesis 1:26–27, God made humans in the divine image. Then God gave the females and males "dominion" over everything else. What a sweeping statement and great responsibility!

Each time I teach Hebrew Bible to college freshmen, I ask the question, "How are we in God's image?" Sometimes they respond that we look like God, but I remind them that God is Spirit, and that the Hebrews condemned images and forbade making idols. With a bit of prompting, the students come up with some ways we reflect God's being. Consider these:

- Humans are rational beings. We can think, identify our emotions, make decisions, and accept responsibility.

Genesis 1:26-27 (NRSV)

[26]Then God said, "Let us make humankind in our image, according
to our likeness; and let them have dominion over the fish of the sea,
and over the birds of the air, and over the cattle, and over all the wild
animals of the earth, and over every creeping thing that creeps upon
the earth."

[27]So God created humankind in his image,
in the image of God he created them;
male and female he created them.

Jeremiah 31:29-34

[29]In those days they shall no longer say:
"The parents have eaten sour grapes,
and the children's teeth are set on edge."

[30]But all shall die for their own sins; the teeth of everyone who eats
sour grapes shall be set on edge.

[31]The days are surely coming, says the LORD, when I will make a new
covenant with the house of Israel and the house of Judah. [32]It will not
be like the covenant that I made with their ancestors when I took them
by the hand to bring them out of the land of Egypt—a covenant that
they broke, though I was their husband, says the LORD. [33]But this is the
covenant that I will make with the house of Israel after those days,
says the LORD: I will put my law within them, and I will write it on their
hearts; and I will be their God, and they shall be my people. [34]No
longer shall they teach one another, or say to each other, "Know the
LORD," FOR they shall all know me, from the least of them to the greatest, says the LORD; for I will forgive their iniquity, and remember their
sin no more.

Matthew 16:16-17

[16]Simon Peter answered, "You are the Messiah, the Son of the living
God." [17]And Jesus answered him, "Blessed are you, Simon son of

Jonah! For flesh and blood has not revealed this to you, but my Father in heaven.

John 3:16

"For God so loved the world that he gave his only Son, so that everyone who believes in him may not perish but may have eternal life."

1 Peter 2:4-10

4Come to him, a living stone, though rejected by mortals yet chosen
and precious in God's sight, and 5like living stones, let yourselves be
built into a spiritual house, to be a holy priesthood, to offer spiritual
sacrifices acceptable to God through Jesus Christ. 6For it stands in
scripture:

"See, I am laying in Zion a stone,
a cornerstone chosen and precious;
and whoever believes in him will not be put to shame."

7To you then who believe, he is precious; but for those who do not
believe,

"The stone that the builders rejected
has become the very head of the corner,"

8and

"A stone that makes them stumble,
and a rock that makes them fall."

They stumble because they disobey the word, as they were destined to do.

9But you are a chosen race, a royal priesthood, a holy nation, God's own people, in order that you may proclaim the mighty acts of him who called you out of darkness into his marvelous light.

10Once you were not a people,
but now you are God's people;
once you had not received mercy,
but now you have received mercy.

- Women and men are religious beings. No matter what civilization an anthropologist finds or an archeologist digs up, that people group has a religion of some sort. They practice a religion.
- People are moral beings, recognizing good and evil. Cultures define "good" and "evil" differently, but all people have a concern for morality, however they define the details. Created in God's image, we think, make decisions, have religious yearnings, and have a sense of morality.

God gave us the capacity to make religious decisions, to recognize God's handiwork. God made us accountable for these abilities. God gave us soul competency because the Lord wanted uncoerced relationships to grow between ourselves and God.

Jesus modeled this doctrine for us. At no time in his ministry did he resort to force to make a point or coercion to create a positive response. In fact, when the disciples wanted to destroy an unfriendly village (Luke 9:51–56) and Peter cut off Malchus's ear (Matthew 26:47–55; John 18:10), Jesus rebuked the use of force to gain any spiritual end. True belief shines when people exercise their soul competency, when they use their God-given capacity to choose to follow God, not when someone suffers punishment if they don't conform religiously to a norm set by an authority. We have soul competency. God made us in the divine image, making us responsible for our decisions about relating to the Lord. No one can force true belief.

God Made a Promise . . . (Jeremiah 31:29-34)

The children of Israel lived with despair after the Babylonians took them into Exile and destroyed Jerusalem and the temple in 587 BC. Demoralized by their plight, the Hebrews asked tough questions. Has God deserted us? Can we worship God in this foreign place? Why did this happen?

God raised up prophets to help the Israelites answer these questions. One such prophet was Jeremiah of Anathoth. Jeremiah worked for more than forty years as a prophet in Judah. From the time of good King Josiah, through three Babylonian invasions, through an assassination attempt, Jeremiah wrestled with these questions. Through his writings, Jeremiah helped the Hebrews in Babylonia deal with their new life, and he affirmed God's presence with and care for the exiles. He affirmed that God had not deserted them, that they could worship God in Babylonia without the temple, and that their sin caused the destruction of Judah.

God gave Jeremiah a new insight into the way God wanted to relate to people. In Jeremiah 31:29–34, the prophet presented the New Covenant. Unlike the Mosaic Covenant, which the Law fleshed out for daily life and which focused on the creation of a Hebrew political state, the New Covenant emphasized the individual nature of religious commitment to God.

Thomas Helwys

In the early 1600s Baptist preacher Thomas Helwys wrote a pamphlet titled *The Mystery of Iniquity*. In it he called for complete religious freedom in Great Britain. He presented a simple argument. Each person will stand before God and be judged alone. So, each individual must have the freedom to make spiritual decisions without coercion, because they will be judged for their choices. King James I sent Helwys to jail. The Baptist preacher died there.

What was most important to Helwys was not that he wrote the first plea for complete religious freedom published in England or that he served as pastor of the first Baptist church on English soil. What was most important to Helwys was that each person must relate to God individually in choosing to be a Christian, interpreting Scripture, and living a godly life under the direction of the Holy Spirit. Helwys paid dearly for his affirmation of the Baptist doctrine of soul competency and the priesthood of believers, but he considered it a price worth paying.

In verses 29–30, Jeremiah took the exiles to task for blaming their ancestors for their suffering. In traditional Hebrew life, the decisions of the head of the tribe affected all people in the clan. This corporate identity shifted with Jeremiah's firm insistence that each person is accountable to God for his or her own life. Community responsibility remained strong for the Hebrews, but spiritual life begins within the individual's decision regarding God. A parent can not choose God for a child, and neither can a child choose God for a parent. Each person, exercising soul competency, must choose or reject God by his or her own will.

With the New Covenant, God makes no promise regarding the creation of a political state. Rather, the promise concerns the spiritual state of each person. The Lord will inscribe the divine law on the hearts of believers, and they will know God. External sources can help clarify, explain, and teach, but it is in the personal relationship that God comes to a believer. Jeremiah does not minimize the importance of external influences in helping chart a person's spiritual growth. Rather the prophet stresses that the ultimate relationship is between God and the heart of a believer whose soul is competent to choose the Lord.

Fulfilled by Jesus . . . (Matthew 16:16-17; John 3:16)

Every major religion has priests. No matter what the religion, a priest has two functions: to lead in worship and to mediate between God and the world. The priest takes the world's needs to God and brings God's word to the world. Priests may function somewhat differently from religion to religion, but priests hold a special place in all religions.

Baptists teach that believers are priests. Each one has the responsibility to relate to God, to understand the Bible, and to interact with the Holy Spirit. We teach that God reveals God's self to each believer and that a Christian has the responsibility to respond to God's direction.

Matthew 16:16–17 illustrates this belief. Jesus withdrew from Jewish territory to rest and teach his closest followers on several occasions. One

They also recite the Old Testament prophecies in Psalm 118:22; Isaiah 8:14; 28:16. God constructs the church from the individual building blocks of believers' lives. For persecuted believers, these words brought peace and hope, encouragement and comfort.

I always get excited when I have a chance to write or preach on 1 Peter 2:9–10, because these verses tie so wonderfully to God's promises from the Old Testament. In Exodus 19:5–6, God laid out the basic elements of the Mosaic Covenant for the Hebrew people. God made three promises to the Hebrews if they would obey the word of the Lord. If a Hebrew would keep God's commandments to show her or his love for the Lord, in return God would show divine love by keeping the three promises—to make of the Hebrew people a special treasure, a royal priesthood, and a holy nation.

Although we will focus on the "royal priesthood" promise, let's look quickly at the other two promises mentioned in both 1 Peter 2:9 and Exodus 19:5–6. God's chosen people, God's special treasure, alludes to a fact of ancient oriental life. A ruler owned everything in the realm—air, land, people, commerce. The ruler held it all for the next generation's use. The ruler, however, would have a "special treasure" that belonged to the monarch alone. The ruler could do with this "special treasure" whatever he or she wanted. Similarly, God created everything and owned all that existed, but the Hebrews constituted God's "special treasure."

God also promised to make the Hebrews a "holy nation" (1 Pet. 2:9; Exod. 19:5). To that end, God gave the Law so the Hebrews would know how to live. Being "holy" meant living a separated, pure life devoted to good. The rules found in the Old Testament provided guidelines for how to be a holy nation, how to separate themselves from their unbelieving neighbors. First Peter draws this theme from Exodus 19 and claims the church is God's holy nation now. Set apart by lifestyle and a desire for goodness and wholeness, believers live within God's commands given through the life and teaching of Jesus. To love God with everything and to love others as ourselves (Matthew 22:34–40)—these characteristics should define the "holy nation" of the church.

God promised in 1 Peter 2:9 (see Exod. 19:6) to make believers a "royal priesthood." For Baptists, the Lord fulfilled this promise by creating a community of faith. The church is the "new Israel" (see Galatians 6:16). Our doctrine affirms that as a community of faith we learn from each other, pray for each other, and mediate God to the world.

First Peter 2:9–10 teaches that the Christ-event fulfilled God's promise by making the church a priesthood of believers. Note the plural—*believers*. We are not lone rangers, on our own in the big, bad world. We are a people who have both individually and corporately related to God as priests. Thus, the body of Christ, through the priesthood of believers, mediates the world to God and God to the world. As good Baptists, we talk about this act with words like "evangelism" and "missions" rather than "mediation." But the intent is the same. By mediating God to the world, we seek to bring people to a point of exercising their soul competency to choose Christ. We also seek to mediate the needs of the world to God through prayer and responsible citizenship.

Are the concepts of priesthood of the believer and priesthood of the believers in conflict? No! One complements the other. As cooperating Baptists, we mediate God to the world through evangelism and missions, but as individual believers, we stand responsible before the Lord for our individual lives and actions in the church, in the home, and in the workplace. We mediate God to the world through how we live our lives and how we witness to the Lord. First Peter 2:4–10 contends that we are individuals responsible to and relating to God, but we also form a body of believers with responsibilities before the Lord. The two forms of priesthood complement one another, strengthen each other, and support the basic Baptist and Christian belief that God saves.

QUESTIONS

1. How does the priesthood of the believer work out in your life?

2. Does anyone, according to this Baptist doctrine, have the right to tell you what to believe or how to interpret the Bible?

3. How does your church function as a priesthood of believers?

4. What are some implications of the doctrine of soul competency for American politics?

NOTES

1. Herschel H. Hobbs and E.Y. Mullins, *The Axioms of Religion*, rev. ed. (Nashville, Tennessee: Broadman Press, 1978), 75.

LESSON TWELVE

Symbolic Understanding of Baptism and the Lord's Supper

BACKGROUND SCRIPTURES

Matthew 3:13-17; 26:26-30; 28:18-20; Mark 1:9-11; 14:22-26; Luke 3:21-22; 22:14-20; John 3:23; Acts 2:41-42; 8:35-39; 16:30-33; 20:7; Romans 6:1-7; 1 Corinthians 10:16,21; 11:23-29; Colossians 2:12

FOCAL TEXTS

Mark 1:9-11; Romans 6:1-7; 1 Corinthians 11:23-29

MAIN IDEA

"Christ instituted two ceremonial ordinances and committed them to his people for perpetual observance—baptism and the Lord's Supper. These two ceremonies are pictorial representations of the fundamental facts of the gospel and of our salvation through the gospel."[1]

STUDY AIM

To describe the Scriptural view of the nature of baptism and the Lord's Supper

QUICK READ

The two ordinances, baptism and the Lord's Supper, tie Baptists together by reminding them of the commitments they have made to God and to one another

When I returned to America after two years in Vietnam as a Missionary Journeyman, I wept the first time I heard the national anthem, and I got a lump in my throat the first time I saw the American flag flying in the breeze. The flag and the anthem are just symbols. But what power they possess!

Symbols play vital roles in our lives. Yet sometimes we forget how symbols shape our thoughts and actions. Never underestimate the power of a symbol, whether a symbol of national identity or of Baptist identity.

Baptists believe that the ordinances of the Lord's Supper and baptism are symbolic. As we consider this lesson, let us remember that Baptist doctrines fit together. Because we believe in salvation by grace, we also believe that baptism and the Lord's Supper do not save a person. No act you or I do saves us from our sin. But baptism and communion are powerful symbols of our faith, and we should take them seriously. Each ordinance says something about our covenant with Christ and with the church.

Baptism, a Symbol of Commitment (Mark 1:9-11)

We do well to look to the life of Jesus to begin understanding this doctrine. In Mark 1:9–11, the author recorded Jesus' baptism by John, his cousin. John, already acknowledged as a prophet, baptized folks in the Jordan River when they publicly repented of their sin and renewed their covenant with God. Baptism for Jews symbolized repentance and becoming part of the community of faith (see small article, "The Background of Baptism"). John offered serious people the opportunity to make a public statement about their relationship with God, a relationship that already existed.

When Jesus chose to be baptized, he made an important public statement. He did not need to repent of sin, because Jesus did not sin (Hebrews 4:15). Jesus identified with our human dilemma and made a

Mark 1:9–11 (NRSV)

9 In those days Jesus came from Nazareth of Galilee and was baptized by John in the Jordan. 10 And just as he was coming up out of the water, he saw the heavens torn apart and the Spirit descending like a dove on him. 11 And a voice came from heaven, "You are my Son, the Beloved; with you I am well pleased."

Romans 6:1–7

1 What then are we to say? Should we continue in sin in order that grace may abound? 2 By no means! How can we who died to sin go on living in it? 3 Do you not know that all of us who have been baptized into Christ Jesus were baptized into his death? 4 Therefore we have been buried with him by baptism into death, so that, just as Christ was raised from the dead by the glory of the Father, so we too might walk in newness of life.

5 For if we have been united with him in a death like his, we will certainly be united with him in a resurrection like his. 6 We know that our old self was crucified with him so that the body of sin might be destroyed, and we might no longer be enslaved to sin. 7 For whoever has died is freed from sin.

1 Corinthians 11:23–29

23 For I received from the Lord what I also handed on to you, that the Lord Jesus on the night when he was betrayed took a loaf of bread, 24 and when he had given thanks, he broke it and said, "This is my body that is for you. Do this in remembrance of me." 25 In the same way he took the cup also, after supper, saying, "This cup is the new covenant in my blood. Do this, as often as you drink it, in remembrance of me." 26 For as often as you eat this bread and drink the cup, you proclaim the Lord's death until he comes.

27 Whoever, therefore, eats the bread or drinks the cup of the Lord in an unworthy manner will be answerable for the body and blood of the Lord. 28 Examine yourselves, and only then eat of the bread and drink of the cup. 29 For all who eat and drink without discerning the body, eat and drink judgment against themselves.

covenant with us and with God by his baptism. In Mark's account, the Holy Spirit descended on Jesus and a voice from heaven said, "You are my Son, the Beloved; with you I am well pleased" (Mark 1:11). For Jesus, baptism signified a covenant made and a relationship established between himself and humanity. He did not need salvation, but he did want to identify publicly with those committed to God.

Jesus accepted his role in the salvation process at his baptism. The voice from heaven put together parts of a psalm about the coming Messiah, the Promised One of Israel (Psalm 2:7), and the Servant (Isaiah 42:1) who would suffer and die for the salvation of the people. At his baptism, Jesus accepted the mantle of Messiah and Suffering Servant, two ideas that didn't flow together naturally within Judaism. Identifying with a sinning race and accepting his call, Jesus established the powerful nature of baptism as a symbol of commitment to God. Although not necessary for salvation, baptism became an important ritual of commitment to the way of God, and for humans, of turning from their old life to a new life with Christ.

Jews of Jesus' day believed in the symbolic nature of baptism. For the Jews, baptism was a symbol of entering the faith or of repentance and cleansing. However, at the time when Baptists began emerging from the Reformation in the 1600s, the general understanding of Christian baptism was that the act of baptism was part of salvation. A priest baptized babies to free them from the burden of original sin. Even in the Reformation traditions of Martin Luther and John Calvin, baptism remained more than symbol, and infants continued to be baptized into the church.

In the early 1600s, Baptists wrestled with who should be baptized and why. Baptists concluded that baptism symbolized a commitment to Christ already made and salvation already accepted. Thus, early Baptists baptized only adults who could make such a decision for Christ by themselves. In fact, as the new denomination grew, other Christians called the denomination "Baptist" because of Baptists' practice of adult believers' baptism and rejection of infant baptism. The process of understanding the role of baptism took decades. By 1644, however, when the First London Confession was written by Baptists in that city, it clearly presented the symbolic nature of baptism:

> That Baptisme is an Ordinance of the new Testament given by Christ, to be dispensed onely upon persons professing faith, or that are Disciples, or taught, who upon profession of faith, ought to be baptized.[2]

Baptists today practice immersion when baptizing. At the beginning of the denomination's history, though, its leaders were not unanimous about the form of baptism. Accepting baptism as a symbol, Thomas Helwys, the pastor of the first Baptist church in England, felt okay with using affusion (flicking water from one's fingertips over the believer's head). Early Particular Baptists, those who believed Jesus died only for those "elected" to salvation, sprinkled believers. Particular Baptists adopted immersion as the correct form of baptism in the 1640s.

Immersion eventually became the standard form of baptism because the Greek verb *baptizo*, from which our word "baptize" comes, means "to immerse" (see small article, "The Background of Baptism"). As people who take Scripture seriously, Baptists identified immersion as the appropriate way to baptize people, because that is what the Bible says.

Death, Burial, and Resurrection (Romans 6:1-7)

Some folks think if an act is symbolic, it has no importance. Wrong! Baptism and the Lord's Supper are symbols, but they remain critically important to the identity of Baptists and of Christians generally. Paul thought they held great importance for the early church and for all believers.

Paul wrote the Letter to the Romans to introduce himself to that church. He had not visited the congregation. He knew, though, of their work in the Imperial City, and they knew of his work in the provinces.

The Background of Baptism

When the translators of the King James Version of the Bible came to the Greek verb *baptizo*, they had trouble. The verb means "to dip, to plunge, to immerse under water." Because the Church of England sprinkled as the rite of entry into the church, the scholars faced a problem—how to translate the verb. They solved the problem by not translating the word *baptizo*. The scholars simply brought the verb into the English language as *baptize*.

The biblical form of baptism parallels the form one experienced to become an adult convert to Judaism. Being immersed to become a Jew symbolized death to the old life and cleansing for the new life. To become a Jew, a person underwent several immersions over a period of time, but the early Christians adopted one immersion as sufficient.

The symbolism in Judaism carried over to Christianity—death, burial, and resurrection; cleansing from sin to a pure life. For the Hebrews and for Baptists, baptism is not magical and carries no power of its own, but it symbolizes a very important reality.

Paul intended to ask for the Romans' help to make a missionary journey to Spain. To enlist their aid, he wrote the Letter of Romans to explain his beliefs and commitments. He included theological insights he felt critical to the Christian faith. Of all his letters, the one to the Roman church presents most fully what Paul believed and taught. To this book we turn to gain insight into Paul's position on the importance of baptism, looking particularly at Romans 6:1–7.

As discussed in the lesson on salvation by grace, Baptists believe that the process of salvation includes salvation from the punishment for sin (regeneration), current salvation from the power of sin (sanctification), and future salvation from the presence of sin (glorification). In Romans 6:1–7, Paul talked about these three facets of salvation and tied each one to baptism, not just baptism with water, but baptism into the life of Christ.

Dealing with the important topic of freedom from sin, Paul used powerful imagery to explain how a Christian relates to the salvation event and process. We as baptized believers share in Christ's death, burial, and resurrection. Paul explained how baptism symbolizes burial of our old selves with Christ's burial and our emergence into "newness of life" as we came out of the water (Romans 6:4). For Paul, the act of baptism meant our identification with Christ publicly, with the sorrow of his death, but also with the power of his resurrection. What hope Paul extended to us as he struggled to understand and communicate the meaning of the Christ-event!

Paul piled on promise after promise symbolized by baptism. We share Christ's death; we share Christ's burial; we share Christ's resurrection; we share the glory of Christ. No longer bound by sin, we live a new life, one powered by our commitment to God. But we also live this life in community with other believers. Baptism is a public event, a public commitment to the Lordship of Christ, a public identification with the community of faith. Paul taught that with this one act of baptism, the purpose and power of the Incarnation became clear to everyone viewing the baptism or participating in the act itself.

My church celebrates baptisms at the beginning of Sunday morning worship, and our ministers take turns officiating. One Sunday, when the youth minister baptized a couple of young people, she said something that struck me. I hadn't thought about the promise the church makes to the person being baptized. As Susan lowered and raised each young person, she reminded the congregation that as these new church members made promises to us about their commitment to Christ, we made a promise to them to help nurture and "grow" them in the faith. For the first time in a long time, the power of the symbol held me—death, burial, resurrection in Christ, *and* a commitment to the body of Christ.

Paul wrote to the church at Rome, not just to individuals who happened to hear the letter read at a worship service. For Baptists, the public act of baptism of believers by immersion signifies the commitment already made by the individual. It also symbolizes the covenant made by the congregation with the new member and with God. Jesus

Case Study

You have a good Christian friend visiting from out of town. This friend goes to church with you on the Sunday that your congregation celebrates the Lord's Supper. Your friend is a Methodist and wants to participate in the Lord's Supper. What do you tell your friend? What do *you* think about the issue?

person to celebrate the Lord's Supper and find it meaningful, but the presence of like-minded sisters and brothers in Christ makes the celebration much more powerful. Whether grape juice or wine, whether bread or crackers, the symbol of communion gains strength when shared within the body of Christ.

Some Baptists disagree about who should participate in the celebration of communion in the local church. Some folks think anyone confessing Christ as Lord qualifies for the celebration. Others think only Baptists should participate in the Lord's Supper. Still others include only members of that local Baptist church in the celebration. Historically, Baptists were all over the map on this issue. English Baptists argued in the 1700s over whether they should include John Bunyan's church in their fellowship, because he served communion to any Christian. In America, the Landmark movement leaders of the 1800s protested that only local church members should take communion.

According to Baptist doctrine, each congregation must decide whom to include and whom to exclude when celebrating the Lord's Supper. I would suppose, however, that when we get to heaven, God will have no restrictions on which of the residents of heaven can come to the heavenly table.

Taking the Symbols Seriously

Baptism and the Lord's Supper are two powerful symbols of our individual and corporate relationship with God. All of us need to take these celebrations more seriously and more thoughtfully. As Baptists we affirm their importance. As Baptists, let us take our own affirmation to heart and take these two ordinances more seriously.

QUESTIONS

1. What is most meaningful to you about baptism?

Going down in the water - washing away past sins, coming back out of water - forgiven & a "newness of life" starting over - promising loyalty as a believer in Christ

2. What is most meaningful to you about the Lord's Supper?

acknowledging humbling grateful
renewal of my faith in Jesus -
my loyalty to the Father
my gratefulness of His sacrafice -
Community of believers

3. What might your church do to enhance the meaningfulness of the celebration of the two ordinances?

Baptism

"Sins washed away - forgiveness of God - rededication and renewal - newness of life."

4. Do you feel uncomfortable when attending another church that does communion or baptism differently? Why?

no - because I recognize the real meaning and in fact - I'm encouraged in participating with another community of believers knowing that all have the same Christian beliefs just we are individuals made by God and placed in different places of worship -

NOTES

1. Walter Thomas Conner, *Christian Doctrine* (Nashville, Tennessee: Broadman Press, 1937), 273.
2. William L. Lumpkin, *Baptist Confessions of Faith*, rev. ed. (Valley Forge: Judson Press, 1969), 167.

LESSON THIRTEEN

Voluntary Cooperation Among Churches

BACKGROUND SCRIPTURES

Acts 15; Galatians 2; 2 Corinthians 8–9

FOCAL TEXTS

Acts 15:1-2, 22-32; Galatians 2:1-10; 2 Corinthians 8:1-8, 16–9:6

MAIN IDEA

"That the churches in the New Testament were local autonomous bodies under the lordship of Christ is quite clear. At the same time there is the pattern of voluntary cooperation between churches in matters of mutual interest and concern."[1]

STUDY AIM

To describe the New Testament pattern Baptists follow in relationships with fellow churches

QUICK READ

While Baptist churches are independent, autonomous, and diverse in membership and ministry, we have a great desire to cooperate together to advance the cause of Christ.

Two bedrock convictions of Baptists are the priesthood of every believer and the autonomy and independence of every New Testament church. For centuries Baptists have rejected the priestly system and the hierarchical and presbyterial forms of church government.

Baptists have believed in the direct access of each believer to the throne of mercy to find grace and help in time of need without any human intermediary. They further have believed that the only "head" of any church is none other than Jesus Christ. No local church is answerable to any other body on earth and should not be ruled by any internal or external hierarchy or presbytery.

Some Baptists have misunderstood this to mean that they are forbidden to work together with any other group but their own local churches. Too, most Baptists like to work together with others of like faith and order. They prefer cooperation but absolutely reject coercion in any form.

Cooperative Missions (Acts 15:1-2, 22-33)

This passage describes the first meeting of more than one local church to discuss subjects of spiritual concern. The matters considered are not as relevant to this particular study as the manner in which the issues were settled.

Acts 13—14 recounts the bold mission adventure and exciting results of the first missionary journey of Paul and Barnabas. When they returned to Antioch they gathered the church together and gave a report of how God "had opened a door of faith to the Gentiles" (Acts 12:27). Everyone in the church must have been thrilled and excited.

But some men came down from Judea and began teaching that a person cannot be saved without following the Jewish ritual of circumcision (Acts 15:1). Paul and Barnabas disagreed vehemently with this return to legalism. They debated the visiting Judaizers (15:2). The Judaizers were people of Jewish background within the Christian church who believed that Gentiles first had to become Jews and keep the Jewish laws and rituals before they could become Christians. To deal with the

Acts 15:1-2, 22-32 (NASB)

1 Some men came down from Judea and began teaching the brethren, "Unless you are circumcised according to the custom of Moses,
you cannot be saved." 2 And when Paul and Barnabas had great dis-
sension and debate with them, the brethren determined that Paul and
Barnabas and some others of them should go up to Jerusalem to the
apostles and elders concerning this issue.

• •

22 Then it seemed good to the apostles and the elders, with the
whole church, to choose men from among them to send to Antioch
with Paul and Barnabas—Judas called Barsabbas, and Silas, leading
men among the brethren, 23 and they sent this letter by them,
"The apostles and the brethren who are elders, to the brethren in
Antioch and Syria and Cilicia who are from the Gentiles, greetings.
24 "Since we have heard that some of our number to whom we gave no
instruction have disturbed you with their words, unsettling your souls,
25 it seemed good to us, having become of one mind, to select men to
send to you with our beloved Barnabas and Paul, 26 men who have
risked their lives for the name of our Lord Jesus Christ. 27 "Therefore
we have sent Judas and Silas, who themselves will also report the
same things by word of mouth. 28 "For it seemed good to the Holy
Spirit and to us to lay upon you no greater burden than these essen-
tials: 29 that you abstain from things sacrificed to idols and from blood
and from things strangled and from fornication; if you keep yourselves
free from such things, you will do well. Farewell."
30 So when they were sent away, they went down to Antioch; and
having gathered the congregation together, they delivered the letter.
31 When they had read it, they rejoiced because of its encouragement.
32 Judas and Silas, also being prophets themselves, encouraged and
strengthened the brethren with a lengthy message.

Galatians 2:1-10

1Then after an interval of fourteen years I went up again to
Jerusalem with Barnabas, taking Titus along also. 2It was because of a
revelation that I went up; and I submitted to them the gospel which I
preach among the Gentiles, but I did so in private to those who were of
reputation, for fear that I might be running, or had run, in vain. 3But
not even Titus, who was with me, though he was a Greek, was com-
pelled to be circumcised. 4But it was because of the false brethren
secretly brought in, who had sneaked in to spy out our liberty which
we have in Christ Jesus, in order to bring us into bondage. 5But we did
not yield in subjection to them for even an hour, so that the truth of
the gospel would remain with you. 6But from those who were of high
reputation (what they were makes no difference to me; God shows no
partiality)—well, those who were of reputation contributed nothing to
me. 7But on the contrary, seeing that I had been entrusted with the
gospel to the uncircumcised, just as Peter had been to the circumcised
8(for He who effectually worked for Peter in his apostleship to the circumcised effectually worked for me also to the Gentiles), 9and
recognizing the grace that had been given to me, James and Cephas
and John, who were reputed to be pillars, gave to me and Barnabas
the right hand of fellowship, so that we might go to the Gentiles and
they to the circumcised. 10They only asked us to remember the poor—
the very thing I also was eager to do.

2 Corinthians 8:1-8, 16-24

1Now, brethren, we wish to make known to you the grace of God
which has been given in the churches of Macedonia, 2that in a great
ordeal of affliction their abundance of joy and their deep poverty overflowed in the wealth of their liberality. 3For I testify that according to
their ability, and beyond their ability, they gave of their own accord,
4begging us with much urging for the favor of participation in the support of the saints, 5and this, not as we had expected, but they first
gave themselves to the Lord and to us by the will of God. 6So we urged
Titus that as he had previously made a beginning, so he would also
complete in you this gracious work as well.

[7]But just as you abound in everything, in faith and utterance and
knowledge and in all earnestness and in the love we inspired in you,
see that you abound in this gracious work also. [8]I am not speaking this
as a command, but as proving through the earnestness of others the
sincerity of your love also.

• •

[16]But thanks be to God who puts the same earnestness on your
behalf in the heart of Titus. [17]For he not only accepted our appeal, but
being himself very earnest, he has gone to you of his own accord. [18]We
have sent along with him the brother whose fame in the things of the
gospel has spread through all the churches; [19]and not only this, but he
has also been appointed by the churches to travel with us in this gracious work, which is being administered by us for the glory of the Lord
Himself, and to show our readiness, [20]taking precaution so that no one
will discredit us in our administration of this generous gift; [21]for we
have regard for what is honorable, not only in the sight of the Lord,
but also in the sight of men. [22]We have sent with them our brother,
whom we have often tested and found diligent in many things, but now
even more diligent because of his great confidence in you. [23]As for
Titus, he is my partner and fellow worker among you; as for our brethren, they are messengers of the churches, a glory to Christ.
[24]Therefore openly before the churches, show them the proof of your
love and of our reason for boasting about you.

2 Corinthians 9:1-6

[1]For it is superfluous for me to write to you about this ministry to the
saints; [2]for I know your readiness, of which I boast about you to the
Macedonians, namely, that Achaia has been prepared since last year,
and your zeal has stirred up most of them. [3]But I have sent the brethren,
in order that our boasting about you may not be made empty in this
case, so that, as I was saying, you may be prepared; [4]otherwise if any
Macedonians come with me and find you unprepared, we—not to speak
of you—will be put to shame by this confidence. [5]So I thought it necessary to urge the brethren that they would go on ahead to you and

arrange beforehand your previously promised bountiful gift, so that the same would be ready as a bountiful gift and not affected by covetousness.

[6]Now this I say, he who sows sparingly will also reap sparingly, and he who sows bountifully will also reap bountifully.

disturbance brought about by the Judaizers, the church members decided that Paul and Barnabas should go to Jerusalem and settle the issue (15:3).

The church at Antioch had not sought permission from the church at Jerusalem to send Paul and Barnabas on their missionary journey. So it is obvious that they did not assume that the church in Jerusalem was in authority over them. However, they had a desire to confer with the Jerusalem church to prevent a schism in the ranks and to share the obvious movement of God among the Gentiles.

Although the churches were separate and autonomous, they desired to have strong ties of fellowship. Anyone who knows anything about the life of Paul would know that he most assuredly did not go to Jerusalem to "get permission" for Gentiles to be saved!

After the two missionaries arrived in Jerusalem, it became known that some of the Pharisees who had become followers of Christ did not believe Gentiles could be saved without first becoming Jewish proselytes (15:5). Steeped in Judaistic legalism, it was difficult for them to understand that salvation was by grace and available to Jew and Gentile alike.

Paul and Barnabas seem to have kept a low profile in the discussions. Simon Peter recounted again his experience with the household of Cornelius (Acts 10). On that occasion the Gentiles were so obviously saved that no one could deny it. He further made the point that there was only one pattern of salvation and not two. Peter clearly maintained that all must be saved through the grace of the Lord Jesus Christ (15:11). Then Paul and Barnabas gave an account of the mighty acts of God that had been done among the Gentiles (15:12).

Evidently James, half-brother of the Lord, as pastor of the church served as moderator of the meeting. When the discussion was over, James cited several Old Testament prophecies that Gentiles would seek the Lord (15:15–18). He then gave his own personal "judgment" on the subject along with a few words of advice (15:19–21). His conclusion was that the Gentiles who were turning to God should not be troubled, but that the Gentile converts should be sensitive to the feelings of the Jewish people.

When James said, "It is my judgment" (15:19), he did not mean that he was a judge issuing his verdict. Rather he meant that he was sharing his best judgment on the matter with the assembled group for their response. The apostles, elders, and the whole church participated in the decision. Some of the leaders were chosen to hand-deliver a letter to the church at Antioch from the council that had convened in Jerusalem (15:22). Judas, called Barsabbas, and Silas were selected to represent the Jerusalem brethren at Antioch.

The text of the letter is contained in Acts 15:23–29. The letter begins with a greeting not only to the church in Antioch but also to the Gentile Christians in Syria and Cilicia (15:23). The official letter from no less than the apostles and the brethren disavowed the mission of the men who had disturbed the new Gentile Christians. The church had neither sent nor instructed them (15:24).

The unified opinion of the group was mentioned so that the churches at Antioch would be encouraged to know that the matter was settled and that there was no disagreement among them. Both Barnabas and Paul were called "our beloved" and were affirmed and admired for having "risked their lives" for the name of our Lord Jesus Christ (15:25–26).

The purpose of the mission of Judas and Silas was to report by word of mouth the same things that were written on the paper, and no doubt, to answer any questions. Plain words written on cold parchment could be misunderstood. It was good for someone to go along and share the demeanor, tone of voice, and gentle spirit that was intended (15:27). The leadership of the Holy Spirit is acknowledged as the foundation of the response that is being made to the Gentile Christians (15:28).

Because of the *diaspora* (the spread of the Jewish people beyond the land of Israel), there were Jews and synagogues scattered all over the Roman world (15:21). The Gentile Christians were asked to abstain from things sacrificed to idols, from blood, from things strangled, and from fornication, which was so rampant in pagan worship (15:29). Gentile Christians should be sensitive to the deep-seated customs and high moral standards of the Jews. At the same time, Jewish Christians should not burden Gentiles with rituals and regulations.

When the group arrived in Antioch, the whole congregation gathered together to hear the reading of the letter (15:30). When they heard it, there was great rejoicing, and they were all encouraged by it (15:31).

Judas and Silas were also prophets (preachers) and "encouraged" (or "exhorted," KJV) and strengthened the brethren "with a lengthy message"—just like preachers (15:32)! Under the inspiration of the occasion the two preachers were exhorting and strengthening these Gentile Christians in the faith.

Cooperation

Christ's people should, as occasion requires, organize such associations and conventions as may best secure cooperation for the great objects of the Kingdom of God. Such organizations have no authority over one another or over the churches. They are voluntary and advisory bodies designed to elicit, combine, and direct the energies of our people in the most effective manner. Members of New Testament churches should cooperate with one another in carrying forward the missionary, educational, and benevolent ministries for the extension of Christ's Kingdom. Christian unity in the New Testament sense is spiritual harmony and voluntary cooperation for common ends by various groups of Christ's people. Cooperation is desirable between the various Christian denominations, when the end to be attained is itself justified, and when such cooperation involves no violation of conscience or compromise of loyalty to Christ and His Word as revealed in the New Testament.

–Article 14, "The Baptist Faith and Message," 1963[5]

Bible commentator W. Graham Scroggie has a wonderful comment on Acts 15:

> We should learn from this conference that it is well for brethren to confer, and endeavor to see one another's view-point, and well is it, also, that we should be willing, in the interests of Christian concord to yield something, whenever we can do so without the sacrifice of principle. . . . It is not to be expected that all Christians will ever see alike on all matters, nor is it desirable, but it is always possible while holding our particular view, to have the fullest fellowship for those from whom we differ. . . . Christianity is a religion of freedom and not of bondage, of peace and not of strife, of love and not of ill will.[2]

Voluntary Cooperation (Galatians 2:1–10)

The Letter to the Galatians provides another illustration of the voluntary cooperation of autonomous churches. Galatians was written by the Apostle Paul to encourage the Gentile Christians who had been confused by the efforts of the Judaizers. The Judaizers had given the message to the Galatian Christians that Gentiles had to keep the Jewish laws and rituals to become Christians. The previous passage in Acts 15 describes the events that took place at the Jerusalem conference. This passage shows the "damage control" that Paul attempted to do among the Gentile churches as the conflict continued.

Paul stoutly maintained that he had received the gospel through a revelation of Jesus Christ, not from the apostles in Jerusalem (Galatians 1:11–12, 15–17). He said, "We did not yield in subjection to them for even an hour, so that the truth of the gospel would remain with you" (Gal. 2:5). Paul and Barnabas presented their gospel message to people known as the "pillars" of the church—James (the half-brother of Jesus), Peter, and John (2:2, 9). They then gave Paul and Barnabas the "right hand of fellowship" (2:9).

Paul said that they were specifically asked to remember the poor, which he was very eager to do (2:10). Indeed, Paul had already been part of a delegation some years before who had taken a special offering for hunger relief from the church in Antioch to the Christians in Judea (Act 11:27–30).

In this account some very important issues concerning cooperative efforts among New Testament Christians are clarified.

- Cooperation was voluntary. Not even the "mother church" in Jerusalem, not Peter and John, and not even James, the half-brother of the Lord himself, exercised hierarchical powers over Paul or the mission efforts of the church in Antioch.
- Paul voluntarily submitted himself to his fellow Christians in the interest of maintaining the fellowship of the Christian community. Greek scholar A. T. Robertson called the right hand of fellowship the "dramatic and concluding act of the pact for cooperation and coordinate, independent spheres of activity. The compromisors and the Judaizers were brushed to one side when these five men shook hands as equals in the work of Christ's Kingdom."[3]
- The word translated "fellowship" (Gal. 2:9) is the Greek word *koinonia*. The word refers to "partnership." The Christian community has a partnership together in the gospel enterprise. By such joint efforts churches are able to do together far more than any one of them could ever do alone. This "gospel partnership" extended at least to missions, ministries, and hunger relief in the New Testament. Pulling together the smallest churches can do more for the cause of Christ than a mega-church can do alone. From many tiny raindrops, a great river flows.

Cooperative Giving (2 Corinthians 8:1-8, 16–9:6)

In this passage Paul commended the Macedonian churches for their generosity in giving an offering to help the churches in Jerusalem. He also explained to the church at Corinth the financial safeguards that had been put into place. Further, he strongly encouraged the Corinthian church to give the offering previously promised.

Paul pointed to several reasons for the church at Corinth to give to the offering in cooperation with fellow believers. He first emphasized the greatest example of sacrificial giving, the Lord Jesus: " . . . Though He was rich, yet for your sake He became poor, so that you through His poverty might become rich" (2 Corinthians 8:9).

Paul also referred to the example of the Macedonian churches. The Macedonian churches would include Thessalonica, Berea, and Philippi. Paul may well have been at Philippi as he wrote this letter. The spirit and conduct of these churches continue to be a source of inspiration to us today. Although they were in "a great ordeal of affliction," they possessed an "abundance of joy" (2 Cor. 8:2). In spite of the "deep poverty" they were experiencing, they "overflowed in the wealth of their liberality" (8:2). How could these churches have given in such a manner? Giving is more a matter of the heart than the pocket book. The secret was that they had first given themselves to the Lord (8:5).

Apparently Paul had been reluctant to receive an offering from Macedonia, given the dire circumstances of those churches. He wrote, however, that they were "begging us with much urging for the favor of participation in the support of the saints" (8:4). Perhaps the contemporary

"Particular Baptists of the Old School"

The "Particular Baptists of the Old School" convened at Black Rock, Maryland, September 28, 1832. They unanimously approved a committee report that stated their objections to some "modern inventions."

Among these "modern inventions" were Sunday Schools, colleges and theological schools, cooperation in mission work, and meetings aimed at winning the lost. Little wonder that this group has long ago passed out of existence.

spirit of our age today is illustrated by a question asked on a television program that used to be on the air. The program was called *Greed*, and the recurring thematic question was, "Do you have a need for greed?" Christians have exactly the opposite need. We have a need to give joyfully for the furtherance of the gospel.

Note the word "participation" in verse 4. The Greek word for "participation" in this verse is, again, a form of the word *koinonia*. As indicated in discussing Galatians 2:9, a basic meaning of this word is "partnership." Just because the Macedonian Christians were poor, they did not want to be denied the privilege of investing in the gospel partnership. No wonder Paul could write to the Philippian Christians, "I thank my God in all my remembrance of you . . . thankful for your partnership in the gospel from the first day until now" (Philippians 1:3, 5 RSV[4]). Partners have both responsibilities and rewards. Spiritual investments in time will yield dividends for all eternity (see Phil. 4:17).

Note that Paul was sensitive to the need for strict accountability for the use of the funds that had been given so sacrificially. Representatives of each participating church were sent to see that the offerings were used for their intended purpose (2 Cor. 8:20–23).

Generosity in cooperative mission giving is encouraged. The offering was so large that it evidently required an entire year to get it all together (2 Cor. 9:2). All giving to the Lord should be done cheerfully and generously, not grudgingly (9:6–7). Any farmer who is stingy with his seed by

The "Voluntary Principle"

"Churches may sometimes best carry out their mission by a combination of efforts. . . . Mission boards, associations, and conventions of all kinds represent such co-operative effort on the part of individual Christians and churches.

"In all such movements it should be remembered that the voluntary principle should be maintained for both the individual and the church, and the independence of the local churches should be strictly safeguarded."[6]

seeing how little he can sow and how much he can keep back will have a very small harvest. The farmer "who sows bountifully shall also reap bountifully" (9:6).

Our Work Together

Just as there are many different kinds of people in the body of Christ, there are also many different kinds of Baptist churches. The members of the churches are gifted in many different ways to profit the whole body (see 1 Corinthians 12:4–7).

For the very same reason, all kinds of Baptist churches are needed to reach an increasing diversity of peoples and to provide an increased variety of ministries. Diversity is good. We should neither expect nor desire that all churches will be exactly alike. One of the first principles of voluntary cooperation among the churches is that diversity is desirable.

Another important principle is that because we have one Head over all the churches, we ought to have unity in the midst of our diversity. We should celebrate our diversity but also preserve diligently our unity. We do not all have to be alike as long as we have "one Lord, one faith, one baptism, one God and Father of all who is over all and through all and in all" (Ephesians 4:5–6). We Baptists (and all Christians) are entreated "to walk in a manner worthy of the calling with which you have been called, with all humility and gentleness, with patience, showing tolerance for one another in love, being diligent to preserve the unity of the Spirit in the bond of peace" (Eph. 4:1–3).

We can do many times more together than we ever could separately. The impact of the whole is greater than the sum of its parts! By joining hearts and hands we can provide more ministries, hospitals, universities, children's homes, ministerial education, mission support, church encouragement, and assistance than separate churches could ever supply. A rope of a thousand strands is stronger than a thousand single strands.

The motivation for this voluntary cooperation is that we love and serve the same Lord. How can people who are so diverse, so fiercely independent, so completely democratic, cooperate without coercion in such an effective way? This is one of the wonders of the entire religious world. Maybe we are like the ant, "which, having no chief, officer or ruler, prepares her food in the summer and gathers her provision in the harvest" (Proverbs 6:7–8). Individually we may be like the tiny ant, but collectively working together, each one doing his or her part, we can exert a powerful influence in the world for good and for God.

QUESTIONS

1. Why is diversity desirable among Baptist churches?

2. What did Jesus do to become the greatest of all examples of Christian giving?

3. Why is the tiny ant a good example of voluntary cooperation?

4. What did Paul do to ensure accountability for the offerings given?

5. Why do you think most Baptists want to voluntarily cooperate together?

NOTES

1. Herschel H. Hobbs and E.Y. Mullins, *The Axioms of Religion*, rev. ed. (Nashville, Tennessee: Broadman Press, 1978), 107.
2. W. G. Scroggie, *The Acts of the Apostles* (Grand Rapids, Michigan: Zondervan Publishing House, 1976), 116–117.
3. A. T. Robertson, *Word Pictures in the New Testament*, vol. 4 (Nashville, Tennessee: Broadman Press, 1931), 286.
4. Scripture marked RSV is from the Holy Bible, Revised Standard Version, copyright 1946, 1952, Division of Christian Education of the National Council of the Churches of Christ in the United States of America.
5. For a copy of "The Baptist Faith and Message" (1963), see http://texasbaptists.org/files/2010/08/1963BaptistFaithandMessage1.pdf. Accessed 12/8/2010.
6. W. T. Conner, *Christian Doctrine* (Nashville, Tennessee: Broadman Press, 1937), 270.

Praise for STILLWATER

"A deeply moving coming-of-age novel about family secrets, mental health, and the importance of girlhood friendships."

TERI CASE, award-winning author

"When I first read *Stillwater*, Mary Jo Hazard's inaugural novel, I was hypnotized by her compelling prose and immersed in the mysteries of a small town that felt eerily all too familiar. You will speed through this gem and ask for more when the last page is consumed. Hazard has done a masterful job!"

DR. H, M.D., associate professor of clinical medicine at UCLA, and TV personality

"In this bittersweet coming-of-age story, Mary Jo Hazard cracks open issues of divorce, suicide, and mental health in a time when they were taboo topics. Through rich historical details and the feisty and loveable trio of Grace, Maggie, and Louanne, Hazard shows us the power of friendship and takes us into a world where the colorful characters aren't always who they seem."

LISA MANTERFIELD, award-winning author of *The Smallest Thing*

STILLWATER

STILLWATER

a novel

Mary Jo Hazard
M.A., M.F.T.

www.mascotbooks.com

STILLWATER

For more information, please contact:
Mascot Books
620 Herndon Parkway #320
Herndon, VA 20170
info@mascotbooks.com

Library of Congress Control Number: 2018910671

CPSIA Code: PRV0220A
ISBN-13: 978-1-68401-928-1

Printed in the United States

For my father

STILLWATER RUNS DEEP...

*"Be aware of the danger—
but recognize the opportunity."*

John F. Kennedy

CHAPTER 1

WHEN I WAS TWELVE years old, a madman tried to kill me. I lost someone special that summer—and my innocence too.

The summer of 1956 started with a bang. Maggie and I were taking our English final when a line of severe thunderstorms rolled through the Hudson River Valley.

"Oh my God," I mouthed to Maggie as a sharp crack of thunder made the whole class jump.

"Maybe Sister will call off the test," she whispered, covering her mouth with her hand.

Maybe my room will clean itself so I won't have to.

Huge lightning bolts flashed close to the school, and a branch on the maple tree in the playground crashed to the pavement. Most of the class leaped out of their seats and ran over to the windows. But not Maggie and me.

"No one gave you permission to get up," Sister John the Baptist yelled over the noise of the storm. "Get back in your seats this minute, before I flunk the lot of you." She gave a disgusted snort and looked down at the papers she was grading.

Sister J the B could put a damper on anything—even a thunderstorm.

I finished the test, double-checked my answers, and looked out the window. The storm had really picked up.

"What're we going to do?" Maggie asked after we handed in our papers. "We can't wait outside at the bus stop. Seriously, lightning freaks me out."

It definitely freaked me out because we had a whole hour to kill before the Stillwater bus came. Usually when that happened, we'd walk over to Tiny's Diner and waste an hour having french fries and cherry cokes, but the storm was getting worse, and going to the diner seemed like a bad idea.

"Let's just wait here," I said, motioning toward the gym.

"Good idea," Maggie said.

We ducked into the gym and watched the walkers from the window. Most of them were dressed for the weather. They had on yellow slickers and brown rubbers, and they gripped their umbrellas like Mary Poppins waiting for liftoff.

"How come we didn't get the memo it was going to storm?" Maggie said, raising her eyebrows and making a weird face. "We didn't even bring jackets—let alone bumbershoots."

The funniest teacher in the school, Sister Mary Perdita, flew past, holding her big black umbrella with both hands, veil flapping up and down, rosary beads beating against her black woolen skirt. I waved, and she nodded.

Mr. Kutter, the janitor, walked up behind us with his floor polisher and a bucket of paste wax. "Ain't that nun a sight?"

Without waiting for a response, he continued. "Good thing you girls ain't out there. Lightning's fierce." He shook his head and sniffed. "Old friend of mine got struck by lightning a ways back. Damn fool took cover under a tree and got fried—didn't even have time to bend over and kiss his you-know-what goodbye."

Maggie raised her eyebrows and looked at me.

"My father was killed in an accident," I said, giving Maggie my "It's okay to talk about death" look. "He was at work."

"Sorry to hear that, little lady," Mr. Kutter said. "What kind of accident?"

"I'm not sure," I said, feeling embarrassed. My mother told me he died in an accident on the loading dock, but she kept the details to herself—almost like she was hiding something. I'd asked her so many times, but she'd tear up and only say, "He's in a better place, Grace, and he's happy."

Mr. Kutter swept his hair out of his eyes with the back of his hand. His hair was dark and greasy, and it curled over his collar. My grandfather would have said that he looked like he was down on his luck. My mother would have said he looked like ten cents worth of God-help-us.

The janitor had thick eyebrows, and he squinted when he looked at you—the way people did when they needed glasses—and he had a weird habit of running the tip of his tongue over his bushy mustache. His plaid shirt was unbuttoned, and his undershirt had a couple of small holes in the front. His stomach rolled over his snakeskin belt when he bent down to put some wax on the floor. A black comb—with several missing teeth—stuck out of his back pocket, and his work boots were caked with mud.

"I hope nobody gets killed this afternoon," Maggie said, peering out the window. "Mr. Kutter, everyone's gone, even Sister

Mary Perdita. Can Grace and I wait here until the bus comes? There's so much lightning."

"Sure," he said, still staring at me. "Gonna take me that long to polish the floor."

His eyes moved slowly down my body and back up to my face. A shiver ran down my spine; I tensed my shoulders and looked away. Mr. Johnny, our old janitor, was never creepy like that. I reached into my book bag for my library book, climbed up a few rows of the old wooden bleachers, and sat down with my book bag between my feet.

I wished Mr. Johnny hadn't had a heart attack over Christmas break. He'd been at Saint Mark's School since I was a kindergartner, but when he got sick, the doctor made him retire. Mr. Kutter was Mr. Johnny's replacement, and I didn't know him very well.

Mr. Kutter put some of the Johnson paste wax on the floor and plugged the polisher into the wall. I covered my nose with one hand and tried not to breathe in the smell. The janitor noticed and smirked. I looked down at my book and tried to concentrate.

A flash of lightning lit up the auditorium, followed by a deep clap of thunder. The wind picked up, and the rain pelted down and drummed on the roof.

"Listen to that rain," Maggie said.

I looked out the window. "That's not just rain; it's hailing."

"We're going to be stuck here all night," Maggie yelled over the noise of the storm and the floor polisher. "The storm's getting worse."

"I wish it would stop," I yelled back. "The wax stinks, and it's so hot in here."

"Hey," Mr. Kutter said, turning the polisher off. "You girls hot?"

"I'm boiling," Maggie said, fanning herself. "My uniform's sticking to me."

"Mine too," I said, pushing my knee socks down.

Mr. Kutter slapped himself on the forehead. "The furnace, dammit! Forgot to shut it off."

"Why is the furnace on, Mr. Kutter?" I said, wrinkling my brow. "It's summer."

"The heater's brand new," he said, straightening his shoulders. "I had to run a cycle to make sure it works."

"You better shut it off," Maggie said. "If it gets any hotter you might burn the school down."

"That ain't a problem." Mr. Kutter started across the gym toward the basement door and then turned back toward us.

"You girls ever see a furnace?" His tongue slid slowly over his top lip, and he rested his hands on his belt buckle. "This one's really big. Really big."

"No, never seen a furnace," Maggie said, shaking her head.

"Me neither, but that's okay," I said, rolling my eyes. "We're good."

"No, you girls gotta see this thing. You know where it is—in the basement right next to your lunchroom."

Maggie gave me a look, and I knew that we were both thinking the same thing. Why would anyone in her right mind want to see a furnace?

"You got time. Your bus ain't coming for a half hour." The janitor looked at his watch. "And we got ourselves a problem." Narrowing his eyes, he continued. "I can't leave you two in the gym alone. You gotta come with me."

Before I could say, "I don't want to, I'll wait here," the library book slid off my lap and crashed through the bleachers onto the floor.

"Darn it," I said, getting up.

"Whoops," Mr. Kutter said, crawling under the bleachers. "I'll get it, little lady."

Maybe he wasn't so bad after all.

I picked up my book bag, clambered down from the bleachers, and walked over to him.

"Leave your stuff here while we go downstairs," he said, handing the book to me. "Nobody's in the school but us."

"Thanks," I said, glancing at Maggie.

She shrugged. We were good Catholic schoolgirls, trained to obey adults and never, ever question authority figures. We left our things on the bottom bleacher and followed Mr. Kutter down the steep metal steps into the basement.

CHAPTER 2

MR. KUTTER HIT THE light switch in the hall and stopped outside the boiler room. He motioned for us to go in ahead of him. As soon as I stepped into the room, the smell of rotten eggs hit me.

"Oh my God, this place stinks," Maggie said, covering her mouth. "I can hardly breathe."

"Maggie's right," I said, feeling sick to my stomach. "Mr. Kutter, can you turn the furnace off fast so we can get out of here?"

"You little girlies hold your horses."

The only light in the room came from one dim bulb that was hanging from a frayed cord taped to a pipe on the ceiling. The janitor stayed behind us, blocking the doorway.

I blinked a few times until my eyes got accustomed to the weak light. Old rags were piled up in the far corner, and cleaning supplies lined the wooden shelves on the back wall. Cigarette butts littered the filthy floor. Several cartons of Pall Malls, the kind my mother smoked, were piled in the dirty sink next to an empty bottle of whiskey, and a box of Cut-Rite wax paper sat on the counter next to a stack of *Stag* magazines.

"That's her," Mr. Kutter said, pushing past us and pointing at the metal tank in the middle of the room. Sweat trickled down his forehead as he reached over and touched the furnace, tapping it with the tips of his dirty fingers. "Cost a lot of money. She heats up like you know what."

Maggie poked me in the ribs. "Okay, Mr. Kutter. We see it, but it stinks really bad, and I'm suffocating. Can we go upstairs now?" Her voice was hopeful, as if she really thought the janitor would let us leave.

He ignored her and unbolted the furnace door. Hot air shot into the small space, driving Maggie and me back against the wall. The flames hissed and flared up; weird shadows wove their way up and down the walls and swirled slowly across the ceiling. Maybe this was what Sister Christina had meant when she said that our class smelled like sin, and if we didn't clean up our act, we were going to be punished in hell for all eternity.

Mr. Kutter's dark eyes looked different in the firelight. He flicked his tongue slowly over his top lip and rested both hands on his belt buckle. Dark shadows moved over his face, and his breathing quickened. There was something very strange and frightening about him. I wanted to look away, but I was afraid to. My back felt like it was crawling with spiders. In spite of the heat, I felt cold, and I pressed myself against the wall by the furnace, trying to disappear.

"Not something you see every day." Mr. Kutter furrowed his eyebrows and laughed an awful laugh. "Right, little girlies?" He slammed the furnace door.

The sound reverberated through the small space. I covered

my ears and tried to think of a furnace compliment. I didn't know why, but something told me we had to get out of there fast.

Maggie elbowed her way past me; I lost my balance, and my hand hit the hot metal furnace. "Ow! Ow! Ow!" I said, stuffing my hand in my mouth. "That thing is really hot."

"Oh, Grace, I didn't…"

"Little girls. You gotta watch yourselves down here," Mr. Kutter said slowly in a voice so low I could barely hear him, one far too close to me.

He put his arm around me, squeezed me up against him, and whispered in my ear, "There's some nice, soft butter in the lunchroom. I could rub it all over that burn of yours—make it stop hurting real quick."

Mr. Kutter's breath smelled so bad I could hardly stand it. My skin crawled. The hairs on the back of my neck stood up, and I jerked away from him. My first impulse was to scream, but I knew it wouldn't do any good—nobody was around to hear me.

"No, no. It's okay," I said, trying to fight down the terror rising in my chest. "I'll fix it when I get home."

A monstrous clap of thunder shook the old building almost off its foundation, and the bulb went out, plunging the room into darkness—the only light was the eerie red glow from the furnace. Another clap of thunder rocked the school, Mr. Kutter's laugh echoed through the room, and the lights flickered enough for me to see the way out.

Holy Mary, mother of God, get me out of here, and I'll never sin again!

"Hurry, Maggie," I gasped, running out of the room and up the basement steps.

Mr. Kutter's deep voice followed us up the stairs. "You girls, wait…"

We snatched our book bags off the bleachers. My library book fell, and I didn't stop to pick it up. Maggie beat me to the door but not by much. Saint Mark's Church, with its tall gray steeple, towered over us, and the bell tolled three times. The worst of the storm was over; the fresh air and drizzle felt good on my face. I ran as fast as I could across the slippery church parking lot to the bus stop.

"What the heck was that about?" Maggie said, panting. Rain dripped down her brown bangs into her face. She bent over, trying to catch her breath, and wiped the water from her eyes. "We shouldn't have gone down there. Mr. Kutter is such a creep."

"He said we had to," I reminded her, gingerly touching the blister on my palm. "But I'm never going anywhere near him again."

"Don't tell anybody—especially your mother," Maggie said, grabbing my shoulders and sticking her face an inch away from mine. "Listen, Grace, we'll get in big trouble if anyone finds out, especially my father. They'll think we did something to make Mr. Kutter act like that."

CHAPTER 3

AFTER DINNER THAT NIGHT, I took a long shower and scrubbed myself twice with Ivory soap, but my skin still smelled like rotten eggs. My mother's Chanel No. 5 was on the counter, so I squirted myself with it several times before I put on my pajamas, but that rotten-egg smell stayed in my nose. I couldn't get rid of it.

I lay down on my bed and thumbed through my religion textbook while my mother put my younger brother to bed. My father used to call her his wild Irish rose. Back then, her long brown hair fell in waves over her shoulders, her eyes were dark blue, and her complexion was the same creamy color as the strand of pearls my father had given her on their wedding day. After he died, she cut her hair into a short bob and tucked the pearls in her top dresser drawer under her nighties. She never wore them again.

My grandfather, Doc, lived in the apartment below us. He wasn't a doctor—he was a retired accountant—but people called him Doc because he was wise and made everyone feel better. I don't know what Denny and I would've done if he hadn't been there after my father died. Doc played with us, read to us, and made us bread-and-butter sandwiches with sugar on top. He taught us how to play poker, and sometimes he let us win. He blew perfect smoke rings, taught us right from wrong, and never laughed at our mistakes. He loved to go to Yankees games in New York City with his friend Sulley, and that's why he wasn't home tonight.

My mother walked into my room and sniffed a few times. "Did you use my perfume, Grace?"

"What?" I answered, pretending I didn't hear her.

"Yes, you did," she said, kissing me on top of the head. "I told you before; don't use it unless you ask me. Chanel No. 5 costs a lot of money."

"Sorry."

She lay down on my bed beside me, closed her eyes, and folded her hands on her chest. "Denny's finally asleep," she said, "and I'm exhausted."

Denny was my eight-year-old brother. He had the longest bedtime routine in the history of the world, and it didn't help that my mother babied him.

"I thought you were going to quiz me for my religion test," I said, thinking she had all the time in the world for Denny, but what about me?

"Don't get upset, Grace," she said, picking up my religion book. "Where should I start?"

"Last chapter summary—morality."

"Hmm, pretty heavy stuff," she said, leafing through the pages. "Okay, what is morality?"

"Morality is—wait. I know it," I said, trying to picture the paragraph in my mind—I was a visual learner.

"Take your time; think about it," my mother said, checking out her nail polish.

"Morality is, um…it's the distinction between right and wrong," I said, finally seeing it clearly. "It's the determination of what should be done and what shouldn't be."

"What else? What does it deal with?"

"What does it deal with?" I thought some more. "Morality deals with behaviors as well as motives."

My mother's eyes zeroed in on the bandage on my hand. "What happened?"

"Nothing," I said, turning my hand over.

"Well you did something. That's a big Band-Aid."

"It's okay," I said quickly. "I burned it on the furnace at school, but don't worry. I popped the blister with a needle and put Unguentine on it."

"The furnace in the school basement, Grace?" My mother sat up. "What on earth were you doing down there?"

I explained how Mr. Kutter had wanted us to see his new furnace and watched her expression change—from happy-let-me-help-you-with-your-homework mom to why-does-this-kid-always-do-this mom.

"He took you and Maggie down to the basement?" She threw her hands up in the air and mumbled, "Dear Lord."

"We weren't there that long." My mother was a worrier, and since she was already having a cow, there was no way I was going to tell her how weird Mr. Kutter acted. Maggie was so, so right; I shouldn't have said anything.

"Mom," I said, trying my best to make her understand, "Mr. Kutter said he was responsible for us, and he couldn't leave us in the gym alone."

"What?"

"That's what he said."

"Grace." Mom sighed. "You're learning about motives. Bad things could have happened."

She pulled the Band-Aid half off of my hand so she could see my blister. "It doesn't look infected."

"Ow! That hurts," I said, pulling my hand back.

"What did Maggie's mother say?"

"Nothing," I said, gently smoothing the Band-Aid over my hand. "Maggie didn't tell her."

"Well, Grace, she has to know," she said, glaring at me. "And you girls should know better than to go down to the basement with the janitor."

My mother was the one who always told me to obey my elders, and now she was telling me not to?

She glanced at the door. "Listen for your brother in case he wakes up. I'm going over to talk to Ruth."

"Mom! Don't tell Maggie's mother. My burn doesn't hurt," I begged, grabbing her arm. There's no reason—"

"Grace, stop it," my mother said, jerking her arm away and walking right out of the room.

I sank back on the bed. Maggie was going to be so mad—she was going to murder me. I closed my eyes and thought about how I could get out of this.

Fifteen long minutes later, the phone rang. I shot out of bed and ran into the living room to answer it before Denny woke up.

"I can't believe you told your mother," Maggie's voice whispered over the phone.

"Maggs, I'm—"

"Shut up. I've got to talk fast. Mom just walked your mother to the car. Grace, they called Sister John the Baptist. She wants to see us in the morning. We're in big trouble. Why—"

The phone went dead.

CHAPTER 4

I DRAGGED MYSELF BACK to the bedroom and fell face-first on my bed. What the heck was wrong with my mother? So what if Mr. Kutter wanted to show us his stupid furnace—it was new, and he wanted to show it off. What difference did it make? Okay, I didn't like it when Mr. Kutter put his arm around me, but he wouldn't have done that if I hadn't gotten hurt. My mother hadn't even known about that, and she'd flipped out. I never should have told her anything.

I wished Doc was home instead of in New York watching the Yankees. He never went nuts like my mother; he listened.

I rolled over and pulled the pillow over my head. In my mind, I started singing "Ninety-Nine Bottles of Beer on the Wall" as loud as I could to drown out my thoughts. At around seventy-five bottles, my mother walked into my room.

"Grace, are you awake?"

"Yes," I said, gritting my teeth. I sat up and pulled my grandmother's old quilt around my shoulders. My mother brushed my hair back with her fingers and sat down beside me. I pulled away and sank back into the soft pillows.

"There's no reason to be so upset," my mother said in her nice voice. "Sister John the Baptist told me she'd take care of everything tomorrow."

My mother didn't believe that Sister John the Baptist was a mean person. Every kid in the school, including me, was afraid of her, and for good reason. For example, last month some boys in my class had started calling me "Subs." Even Allen Montgomery—a boy who rode on my bus, liked me, and wanted desperately to copy my math homework—called me that.

Finally, I got fed up. The next time Allen asked me if he could copy my homework, I said maybe—if he gave me two packs of M&M's and told me what "Subs" meant. He had a D in math, and if he missed another assignment, he'd get an F, so it didn't take him more than a minute to pull out two packs of peanut M&M's and mumble, "It means 'Stuck-up Bryant stinks.'"

Maggie came over to my house after school, and we filled two of my brother's squirt guns with equal parts Chanel No. 5 and water.

The next day was First Friday, and the whole school had to go to Mass. The nuns said that if you were a Catholic and made nine First Fridays in a row, you automatically went to heaven when you died. Personally, I didn't believe it, but I'd made them about five times, so I had all my bases covered just in case.

We lined up in rows by class in the schoolyard and waited for the signal from Sister John the Baptist to walk over to the church. Bobby Farrell pointed at me and smirked. "How's it going, Subs?" Maggie and I pulled the squirt guns out of our blazer pockets and let him have it.

"See who stinks now, Farrell," I said, squirting away. "How do you like it?"

Everyone laughed except Sister John the Baptist and Bobby Farrell, who screamed like a girl. Sister John the Baptist said we could've blinded him with the perfume, and if we ever brought squirt guns to school again, we'd be expelled. She made us sit in the back of her class for five days and copy the entire dictionary.

The only kid in the whole school Sister John the Baptist liked was Joanne Connolly, and that was because her older brother had stepped into a nest of copperhead snakes when he was in basic training camp for the marines in South Carolina.

Sister had all the kids in school pray for him because everyone knew kids' prayers meant more than adults' prayers because kids were innocent. In spite of the innocent prayers, he died, but Joanne's family made a big donation to the school in his name. And just like that, Joanne was Sister John the Baptist's pet.

"Mom, I knew Sister would blame us," I said, trying to make her see. "Remember those thunderstorms this afternoon? It rained really hard. The thunder and the lightning were awful. We asked Mr. Kutter if we could wait inside for our bus. He let us because, and you might not believe this, lightning killed one of his friends a long time ago. He wanted us to be safe."

"I know you were frightened, but you should have asked Sister for help—not Mr. Kutter."

My mother always had perfect solutions for problems after they happened and expected me to know just what to do in the moment.

"Grace, for the love of God, just tell her what you told me."

"Mom?" A picture of Sister John the Baptist popped into my mind, and I squirmed under the covers. I saw her in that long black habit squinting at me from behind her Heinrich Himmler glasses, her lips in a tight line, and the bristly hairs over them glistening with sweat. "Was she mad? She's really mean sometimes."

"It's angry, not mad—only dogs get mad. Why would Sister John the Baptist be angry?" Mom said. "She's the school principal. Her job is to take care of the students and make sure they're safe." She yawned and looked at her watch. "Now go to sleep, Grace; it's late."

CHAPTER 5

MAGGIE AND I PACED back and forth in the schoolyard, waiting for the bell to ring. Ominous gray clouds filled the sky—a clear sign that more thunderstorms threatened. The wind blew my hair every which way, my shoes squished when I walked, and my stomach ached. I pictured Sister John the Baptist ordering, "Bring me the head of Grace Bryant," and Mr. Kutter grinning as he handed it to her on a silver platter.

Maggie kept repeating, "I don't know why you told your mother. Sister is never going to understand what happened. We are in so much trouble. I told you to keep your mouth shut."

I turned away, but I was worried too.

We didn't have long to wait. Sister John the Baptist called us into her office first thing. "Come in and close the door," she said, glaring at us from behind her dark wooden desk covered with file folders, papers, and a three-foot-tall statue of Saint Joseph.

We knew that look.

"I hope you girls know what you did."

What?

Sister banged a book on her desk, not once but twice. My library book—the one that I'd left in the gym yesterday. Her rosary beads rattled on her habit. I jumped and crossed my arms.

"Did you know Mr. Kutter has a wife and six children and lives in the projects? The poor man could lose his job over your accusations."

I looked at Maggie.

Accusations?

She shook her head.

Sister started talking louder and louder. Even though the door was closed, I'm sure the class across the hall heard every word she said. My head pounded, and I grabbed onto the edge of her desk.

"How could you possibly accuse the man of something like that? I know what kind of girls you are," she said, shaking her bony finger at us. "Stay away from Mr. Kutter. You understand me? Now get back to class. I'm disgusted with the pair of you. Grace, you're going to hell just like your father."

I froze.

She stood up and shouted. "I don't care how bad a storm is—don't you ever stay in the school waiting for your bus again. If you get struck by lightning, you have no one to blame but yourselves."

I bit my bottom lip and looked at Maggie.

"I hope you're happy," she said, walking away.

"Maggs," I called after her. "Wait. We didn't do anything."

But it didn't matter. The rest of the week, the nuns ignored us, and it was obvious most of the kids knew we were in trouble. I pretended not to notice, but they whispered to each other and giggled when they passed me in the halls, but Mr. Kutter ignored us too, so it was okay.

My mother asked me if Sister John the Baptist talked to us. I said yes, but I didn't tell her what Sister said. Maggie kept quiet too. We didn't want things getting any worse.

CHAPTER 6

I MADE IT THROUGH the last week of school by thinking about the fun Maggie and I were going to have when our best friend, Louanne, got here. She'd moved away four years ago, but when she came back and stayed at her grandmother's house every summer, it was like she'd never left. Doc used to call us the Maguire Sisters because the three of us were always together, but we called ourselves the three musketeers—one for all and all for one.

Maggie was still mad at me, and she insisted she wasn't going over to Louanne's when I was there. She said that I got her in so much trouble with her father over Mr. Kutter that she never wanted to see me again. It didn't matter how many times I said I was sorry—she just brushed me off.

I'd set my portable clock radio for seven o'clock, but I shouldn't have bothered because the doorbell rang a little after six o'clock and woke me up.

"Maggie," I heard Doc say. "What are you doing here this early?"

"I'm meeting Grace," Maggie said. "Isn't she up?"

"Let's see," my grandfather said, tapping on my bedroom door. "Grace, there's an early bird out here looking for you. Are you awake?"

"I am now," I said, throwing on some clothes.

Doc gave me a "What's going on?" look when I walked into the living room. I shrugged, and he headed back toward the kitchen.

"Are we still in a fight?" I said. "It's too early to fight."

She flushed and turned away. "I just had to get out of my house."

Maggie had shown up like this a few times. Sometimes her eyes were red like she'd been crying, but today she just looked like I felt—tired.

"I thought you were mad and didn't want to see me ever again," I said.

"No," she said, shaking her head. "Not anymore."

"Why?" I said, waiting for her to apologize. "Why did you change your mind?"

"Uh, we ran out of Rice Krispies."

"Really?" I said, rolling my eyes. "You came over for Rice Krispies?"

She looked down at the floor. "Please."

I figured she wanted to be friends again but just didn't know how to tell me. So since I was pretty easygoing, I smiled and pointed toward the kitchen. Doc was sitting at the table drinking coffee and reading his racing form. He looked up when we came in, but he was into the horses and didn't say anything.

My mother walked in when we were almost finished eating. She was wearing a frilly white blouse, a little low-cut if you asked me, and new blue pedal pushers. For years after my father died, she hadn't cared a thing about what she wore, but now she went on shopping sprees almost every weekend. And she started piling on the makeup—especially the blue eye shadow.

Forget Maggie; I have my own problems, I thought.

"Have fun at Louanne's," my mother said, pouring herself a glass of juice. "If there's the slightest problem, come home."

Maggie and I exchanged glances. My mother—the worrier.

"Louanne's aunt and grandmother will be there."

"I'm not worried about Michelle and Mrs. Dodd," my mother said, putting her hand on my shoulder. "I'm worried about Tony. Remember?"

I remembered.

Tony Dodd was Mrs. Dodd's son, Aunt Michelle's brother, and Stillwater's boogeyman. People said that he was perfectly normal until he turned sixteen, and then, depending on who was telling the story, he became a paranoid schizophrenic—or he came down with a high fever that destroyed his brain. It didn't matter which story you believed; even a lot of adults were afraid of him.

My mother had known Aunt Michelle and her brother Tony since they were children. They'd grown up together. My mother didn't worry about Tony; she worried about me annoying him, which was silly because I'm not the annoying kind. Even if I was, he slept all day.

My grandfather looked up from his newspaper. "Like I tell you every year, Grace, Tony's just a poor fish with mental problems. Don't bother him, and everything will be fine. He's a good egg." Doc was no psychiatrist, but he was smart, and even though he was old, I trusted his advice.

It's true that Uncle Tony had a dark side—every so often he'd go bananas. When that happened, Aunt Michelle would call her boyfriend, Vinnie the butcher. Vinnie would lock his shop and run over to try and calm Uncle Tony down. If he couldn't, Aunt Michelle would call O'Malley the cop.

O'Malley would hurry over—a portable flashing light stuck somewhere on the top of his white Pontiac sedan—with the siren blaring. The ambulance would arrive right after him, and the attendants would wrestle Uncle Tony into a straitjacket. Off they'd roar to the state hospital in Utica, more than three hundred miles away. When they let Uncle Tony out, he'd be okay for a while.

"Grace," my mother said, sighing heavily. "Did you hear what Doc and I just said?"

"Yes," I answered, jumping up to put my cereal bowl in the sink. "Come on, Maggie, let's cut out."

We raced down the street to the Dodds'. They lived on Hudson Avenue, only seven houses down from us. All the houses on our side of the street had been built on the banks of the Hudson River. Small businesses lined the other side, like the candy store that sold more beer and cigarettes than candy, the malt shop, Black's Grocery Store, the convent, and the corner store.

Maggie's heart wasn't in the race. I beat her by a mile and rang the doorbell before her feet even touched the porch steps. Something smelled like cinnamon. Aunt Michelle was the best baker in town. She baked the entire time Louanne visited—cinnamon buns in the morning, chocolate cookies after lunch, and brownies most evenings. I was so jealous; my mother never baked. She bought.

Louanne threw open the door and screamed. We screamed back and grabbed her like we were afraid she was going to disappear. I stepped back to look at her. She seemed a little different this year, not just taller—maybe more sure of herself. It wasn't her Bermuda shorts or matching fingernail and toenail polish;

it was kind of the way she carried herself. Maybe she thought we looked different too, but if she did, she didn't say anything.

We sat down at the kitchen table, and Louanne caught us up on things in her world while we inhaled Aunt Michelle's cinnamon rolls. Lou told us about her tonsillectomy—her throat hurt a lot after—but the pain was worth it because her mother let her eat all the ice cream she wanted for one whole week.

And even more exciting, Lou confided, looking around to make sure no one but us could hear her, she'd had her period last month. To celebrate, her mother bought her three new training bras. She pulled up her pink tee shirt and showed us the white lace one she was wearing.

"Neat," I said, wishing I had one.

"It's not the pointed bra I'll get when I graduate from the trainers," she said with authority. "But it's a start—like a dress rehearsal. Did you two know that men like the pointy look better? I read it in *Cosmo*."

Maggie snorted, and milk shot out of her nose. She grabbed a paper napkin from the wicker holder on the table and wiped her face. "Oh my God! I am so not looking forward to that."

"Well, Mar-gar-et," Louanne said, batting her long eyelashes. "It's only a matter of time before you get your friend and some boobies too."

"Louanne, what is wrong with you? You're disgusting," Maggie said, wiping the milk off of her face. She threw her dirty napkin on her plate. "Nothing is private with you. You're just like Grace."

"What's not private with Grace?" Louanne said, taking the rubber band off of her ponytail and shaking her hair out. "Spill; clue me in."

I clenched my jaw and waited.

Aunt Michelle walked into the kitchen, and her eyes widened as she took in Louanne's bright fuchsia lips. "Honey," she said, cocking her head to the side, "that's a beautiful color, but don't you dare wear any lipstick outside this house. If your mother could see you, she'd have a heart attack."

"My mother's a thousand miles away, and I know exactly what she'd say—no respectable young lady wears makeup until she's sixteen!" Louanne stood up and pushed her chair back from the table. "Let's go up in the attic and dress up. We can wear all the makeup we want up there."

"Thanks, Aunt Michelle," I said, getting up. "Those rolls were really good."

"Why, Grace, you're so welcome," she said, smiling. "It's my pleasure. I love baking for you girls."

I hurried upstairs after Louanne and Maggie and followed them down the hall. We passed the room Lou stayed in when she was visiting. Her old teddy bear, Sir Lawrence Olivier, was lying on the bed; she never went anywhere without him. I bent down to tie my shoe and plowed into Maggie.

"What's wrong with you?" I said. "Don't do that."

Maggie moved her index finger across her neck like she was slitting her throat. "Dum de dum dum," she whispered, pointing down the hall. "We're dead."

"Stay Out!!!" was painted on Uncle Tony's door in gigantic red letters. The paint had dripped down the door like blood oozing out of a fresh wound. He'd taped some papers to the door under the sign, and below them he'd taped a brown manila envelope with an American flag sticking out of the top.

"Creepy," I whispered, as a chill went through my body. "What the heck?"

"It wasn't here last year, Louanne," Maggie said. "Right?"

"No, Uncle Tony has started using his door as a bulletin board," Lou said shrugging. "Aunt Michelle said his doctors want him to express himself in writing."

My father used to paste notes on our kitchen wall. When my mother found them, she'd rip them into little pieces and throw them in the trash.

"My brother has a 'No girls allowed' sign on his door," Maggie said, "but this is nuts."

"It scared me when I saw it the first time," Louanne admitted. "It takes some getting used to."

"Are you sure his doctors are right?" Maggie asked. "Seriously, this looks like the room of a murderer."

"Shut up, Maggie," Louanne hissed. "Aunt Michelle wouldn't let me visit if there was anything to worry about."

"Louanne's right," I said, trying to convince myself. "Aunt Michelle would die before she let anything happen to Lou. You know that."

"I hope you're right."

"Okay if we read the notes?" I asked.

Louanne nodded.

The first list was written in black ink:

1. *Michelle and Mother want to control everything I do.*
2. *O'Malley wants to arrest me—he's full of shit.*
3. *People hurt me—don't go near them.*
4. *People lie—never believe anything they say—they spy on me.*

Another list, written in purple, was about UFOs. He had past, present, and future columns for his sightings. The last list was labeled "Commitments." It was divided into two neat columns—hospital admission dates were written in green, and hospital discharge dates were written in blue. Uncle Tony had had four admissions already this year. I leaned in closer to see the actual dates and pulled back when something jumped against the other side of the door.

"That's Gabriel," Louanne whispered. "Be quiet."

The Dodds called him Gabriel, but most people in town called the black cocker spaniel "Uncle Tony's familiar," a demon sent to do his bidding—on an Easter Sunday, of all days. The parishioners had been outside the church saying goodbye to Father Flanagan after Mass and showing off their Easter finery when Louanne's uncle rode by on his bicycle. One of the Moore boys hurled a rock at Uncle Tony, knocking him off the bike. A little dog came out of nowhere, raced up the street, and licked the blood off of Uncle Tony's forehead, freaking everybody out. The churchgoers tried to shoo the cocker spaniel away, but his eyes turned red, his fur stood up, and he snarled like a wolf.

Doc ran over and helped Uncle Tony to his feet. He calmed the dog down and steadied Louanne's uncle while he climbed back on the bike. The little dog followed Uncle Tony home and moved right in.

The parishioners were afraid of the black dog and that's when they started calling him "Uncle Tony's familiar." Doc said they were all damn fools, and he was glad Tony finally had a friend—even if it did have four legs and a tail. Aunt Michelle didn't like dogs, but she agreed with Doc. Uncle Tony named him Gabriel, which means "warrior of God."

Louanne grabbed Maggie's hand and pulled her toward the attic stairs. "Come on, before Gabriel wakes up Uncle Tony."

"Are you sure Uncle Tony can't hear us up here?" I asked, taking one last look at the notes. "I don't want to wake him up."

"Don't worry," Louanne said. "Just shut the attic door. He won't hear a thing."

"If you say so," I said, tiptoeing up the stairs just in case.

The attic had low ceilings and was really hot; in fact, it felt a bit like a tomb, but it was nowhere near as hot as Mr. Kutter's furnace room. Nobody had taken off the storm windows, and the place smelled musty, like old books and dust. There was an exhaust fan, but it wasn't working. Spiderwebs hung down from the beams, and the wooden floorboards creaked when you walked. One whole corner was filled with old toys and stacks of board games that we used to play with. The four steamer trunks were in a semicircle in front of the mirror—right where we left them last summer.

Louanne's grandmother, Mrs. Dodd, loved her old clothes, and she kept most of them. When something went out of style, she put it in the attic for safekeeping. She'd say, "Eventually it will come back in style. Things always do." But they hadn't yet, and the trunks were filled with her fancy gowns, big hats, and high heels. A small white leather trunk lined with pink silk held her unmentionables—corsets, padded brassieres, and silk stockings. I couldn't imagine old Mrs. Dodd wearing any of them, but Doc said back in the day she'd been a looker.

Louanne took off her shirt and shorts and grabbed a black corset. She wriggled herself into it and smoothed the front with both hands. "They didn't have pointy bras back then," she explained. "Men liked flat breasts and no hips—just like Maggie."

"Are you out of your tree?" Maggie said. "Drop dead."

Louanne and I laughed.

"I'm just telling the truth," Lou said.

"I'm telling you perverts now," Maggie said, putting on one

new transistor radio to WPTR, which was playing "Wake Up Little Susie."

"That's the number one song," I said, lifting myself up on one elbow. "It's the Everly Brothers. Turn it up."

"This is the most stupid song I've ever heard," Louanne said, turning it up full blast. "Why would anyone get upset because they fall asleep at the movies? My father does it all the time. Sure my mother gets mad, but that's her."

"It's my favorite song."

Louanne ignored me. "Guess what? I want my parents to take me to Disneyland when I go home. Maybe they'll take you and Maggie too. I really want to see the Sleeping Beauty castle. It looks amazing on television. And it's close to Hollywood; we could see movie stars too. Wouldn't that be cool?"

"Wake Up Little Susie" ended, and a Camel cigarette commercial came over the air. "How mild, how mild can a cigarette be? Take the Camel thirty-day test, and you'll agree, that Camels suit you to a *T*."

"Hey," I said, turning over. "Remember how I was late?"

She nodded.

"Mr. Howe stopped me on my way over here."

"What do you mean?" she said, looking at me. "What did he want?"

"He said that Uncle Tony might go to jail. We've got to find the real arsonist before that happens."

"Why did he say that?"

"I don't know, but he sounded pretty sure of himself."

"I hate Mr. Howe," Louanne said, furrowing her brows. "I don't know what your mother sees in that man."

"Me either, but we need to find the real arsonist."

"We need—" Louanne stopped and looked out at the river. "Did you hear that noise?"

"Yeah," I said, turning my head.

"What the heck is it?"

"It's a boat. A motorboat," I yelled, jumping up. "It must've gone under the bridge. Come on, the beach…"

Vinnie's butcher shop was on top of the riverbank next to the old iron bridge. He butchered his meat on a wooden chopping block in front of a wide window that overlooked the Hudson River. When a boat went under the bridge, he saw it before anyone else. But not today.

"Where's Vinnie?" Louanne yelled as we ran toward the riverbank. "I don't hear his bell."

"Vinnie! Vinnie!" I screamed at the top of my lungs. "Your bell! Ring your bell!"

"Oh my God!" Lou screamed. "Where's Vinnie?"

Every summer tourists rented yachts from a marina in Schuylerville, about fifteen miles up the river from Stillwater. Sometimes they didn't understand how to operate them—or how the barge canal system worked. Vinnie noticed when the boats missed the buoy marking the canal and went to the right instead toward the dam. Then he'd swing into action, ringing his big cowbell like a crazy fool and yelling for all he was worth.

It was high drama several times a summer in Stillwater, and we loved it. I never saw a boat go over, but Doc remembered three of them crashing to pieces on the rocks below the dam. Secretly, I wanted to see that too.

Louanne and I raced to the edge of the steep bank and headed down the dirt path leading to her grandmother's beach. The stretch of water before the dam looked calm and peaceful, but under the still water, the Hudson was deep and treacherous.

The long white yacht was slowly moving down the middle of the river toward the dam. The low-level dam was about two hundred feet to the south of Mrs. Dodd's property, and unless you knew it was there, it was difficult to spot—especially from a boat. Doc said that low-level dams backed up the water as it flowed over the top before it dropped down and created a backwash that trapped and recirculated anything that could float—including boats and people. The swift current pushed everything against the face of the dam and then tossed it over.

"Stop," I yelled at the people on the boat. "Hey, stop!"

The closer the boat got to the dam, the faster it went.

"Louanne, we've got to stop them! Oh, stop, please stop!"

"Hey," Lou shrieked. "Turn around. STOP! STOP!"

"They can't hear us," I shouted, jumping up and down. "Oh, Lou, where's Vinnie? They're going over."

We screamed and screamed and finally Vinnie's cowbell rang out loud and long, but the people on the yacht didn't hear him; they were too busy laughing and drinking. Sunlight danced on the water, and white spray splashed up the sides of the boat as it moved closer and closer to the dam.

A tall lady in a white dress held her hat on her head with one hand and pointed back at the bridge with the other. The long red ribbons on her hat blew in the breeze, and she smiled and posed as a man in a black bathing suit took her picture. The boat's hull sliced through the water, and the hat with red ribbons flew off the lady's head and landed in the boat's wake. The people on the deck lifted their glasses and laughed.

"Stop!" I screamed as loud as I could. "You're going to die!"

The lady turned toward me with a questioning look.

I screamed again, "You're going to die! Turn the boat around."

She grabbed the man's shoulders and pointed to me.

"What the hell's wrong with you kids?" he shouted over the engine.

"There's a dam! You're going over the dam," Louanne yelled.

The man shaded his eyes with one hand and gazed down river. "Holy shit!" he yelled, running into the cabin.

The boat picked up speed as it passed our beach.

Louanne's face turned white, and her voice shook. "Please God, please God, please God."

Hail Mary full of grace…

A harsh grating sound came from the boat's motor. I held my breath and watched the pretty white boat shudder and slide sideways across the water. The engine coughed a few times—like Doc's car when it flooded—then it caught, and the boat slowly circled around and pointed upriver.

"Yes!" Louanne and I screamed and jumped up and down. "Yes!"

The hat lady and Speedo man were hugging each other tight. I took a deep breath, tried to slow my breathing down, and smiled at Louanne. Her face was pure white, but she smiled back.

"Piece of cake," I said, throwing my arms around her. "We didn't even need Vinnie."

"You saved our lives," the lady on the boat yelled. "Girls, what are your names?"

"Grace," I yelled, waving my arms.

"Louanne," Lou yelled, waving her arms.

The passengers raised their glasses. "Hip hip hooray! Thank you, Grace! Thank you, Louanne!"

"You're welcome! You're welcome!" we shouted as they moved upriver away from us.

"Piece of cake? You're crazy, Grace," Louanne said, linking her arm through mine. "I thought they were goners."

My grandfather said, "Sarah, there's been an accident. Dr. Whalen will explain." He gave Denny and me a strange smile and cleared his throat. "Come on, you two. Let's put those sandwiches away and go have ice-cream cones."

We hadn't even taken two bites of our sandwiches. I looked at my mother; she was never going to let us do that, but she had both hands over her mouth and was staring at Dr. Whalen with scared eyes. My heart started beating funny.

"Let's go, Grace," my grandfather said, lifting Denny out of his chair. "Come on, honey bunny."

I wanted to stay with my mother, but Denny grabbed my hand and pulled me toward the door. "Ice cream, Grace," he said. "Come on."

We weren't even down the porch steps when my mother screamed. I turned around to go to her, but my grandfather grabbed me by both shoulders and stopped me. I planted my feet and looked up at him. Tears were running down his cheeks, and I knew. I knew I'd never see my father again.

"Daddy?" I whispered, hoping with all of my heart Doc would say no. "Is it Daddy?"

"Yes, honey," he said, pulling me in close. "I'm afraid so." He rubbed my back and sighed a big sigh. "The angels came this morning and took your father to heaven."

That was a long time ago, but whenever I thought about it, part of me wanted to die too. I put my arms around myself and rocked back and forth, trying not to cry.

I glanced over at Maggie to see if she'd noticed how upset I was, but she'd moved to the far side of the swing and was staring straight ahead—like people do when they're not seeing.

"How did Louanne find out her father is leaving?"

"Her mother called and asked Aunt Michelle to tell her," I said.

"Maybe her father will change his mind," Maggie said. "Sometimes people do."

"Could be." I sure wished my mother would change her mind about Mr. Howe.

"You know, maybe it's not so bad," Maggie said in a low voice. "What if her parents hated each other and fought all the time? What if he was mean to Louanne?"

"No," I said, shaking my head. "Louanne would have told us."

"Maybe she didn't want anybody to know; maybe she was embarrassed." Maggie crossed her arms and looked across the street, where O'Malley the cop was mowing his lawn.

There's an arsonist on the loose, and what's O'Malley doing? Mowing his front lawn! They would never hire anyone like that on *Dragnet.*

He waved. "Hey, girls, want to trade places?"

We laughed.

It was a lazy day. Mr. Miller had taken the boys to the country to get sweet corn for dinner, and Mrs. Miller was running the vacuum in the living room. She never vacuumed when Mr. Miller was home because if she did, he went off of his rocker. He'd yell, "Ruth, turn that goddamn thing off! I mean it. I can't think straight."

Once I was there when she didn't turn it off fast enough, and he threw his magazine across the room and jerked the vacuum cleaner plug right out of the wall. Maggie acted like she didn't notice—just kept playing Monopoly like it happened every day—but he scared me.

Mrs. Miller was older than my mother. Her hair was white, she wore granny glasses and no makeup unless she was teaching or going to church. She looked like Mrs. Santa Claus, but she was very accident-prone—last year she broke her nose running into a door, and right before spring break, she broke her arm falling down the cellar stairs. The noise from the vacuum cleaner stopped, and Mrs. Miller poked her head out of the front door. "Grace, I haven't seen you in a couple of weeks. Where've you been, darling?"

I was about to say I hadn't been invited over when Maggie jumped in. "We've been at Louanne's house, Mom. You know that."

"Well, you girls had better start spreading your charm around here some more. I've missed you. In fact, when I'm finished cleaning, I'm going to bake chocolate chip cookies for the Nelsons. How about you help me?"

"Um, okay, Mom," Maggie said. "Call us when you're ready."

"That's a good idea," I said, my mouth salivating for some good cookie batter. Mrs. Miller always left a lot in the bowl for us. "That'll cheer the Nelsons up for sure."

"It will," Maggie said, watching her mother close the door. "My father said the Elks are collecting money for them too. He's the head of that committee."

"Oh, right. Doc told me that," I said, raising my eyebrows. "Who do you really think set Mr. Nelson's barn on fire?"

"Don't act stupid. I feel bad for Louanne, but we know it was her uncle." Maggie slapped a mosquito that had landed on her left arm and sucked the spot where he bit her. "He started the other ones too. Tony Dodd is always there before the fire truck. And don't pretend he doesn't go berserk and try to kill Mrs. Dodd and Aunt Michelle every chance he gets. Remember when he snuck into the attic to spy on us?"

"That was your fault," I said, blowing some air over my top lip. "You turned the music up."

"So what? He scared us half to death. Even Louanne was scared."

"Okay, Uncle Tony acts scary," I said, agreeing with her. "But

Doc says it's because he forgets to take his pills. What if he didn't start the fire? I think he's innocent."

"Yeah, right."

"We need to find the real arsonist and prove—"

"Grace, you've completely flipped your lid." Maggie stopped the swing with her feet and glared at me. "We could get into so much trouble—like we did with Mr. Kutter."

"How could investigating a crime get us in trouble?" I said, wanting to shake her. "Why are you so afraid? What's wrong with you?"

"Wrong with me? Wrong with me?"

"You didn't used to be afraid."

"Don't take this the wrong way, but in some ways you're lucky your dad is dead."

"Stop," I said, furious. "That's—"

"When my father found out I went into the basement with the janitor," she interrupted, "he beat me with his belt. He said I humiliated him." She leaned back and closed her eyes.

"His belt?" My mouth went dry.

"Yes, his belt."

Maggie was talking faster, but I didn't want to hear any more. I wanted her to shut up. Her words were going round and round in my head, making me sick.

"My father said he was going to show me what it was like to be humiliated. He made me pull down my pants and bend over the arm of the couch—right in front of my mother and Jimmy. Then he whipped me. He whipped me good." Maggie's face was flushed. She pulled her knees up against her chest and looked away from me.

My mother did things I didn't like, but she'd never let anybody hurt me—not even my father.

snowplow by putting your skates in a *V*, toes almost but not quite touching. Any questions?"

Louanne and I nodded, letting the boys know they were in the hands of three bike-skiing experts. Denny tightened his belt two notches and pursed his lips like he always did when he was nervous. I walked toward him to tell him he didn't have to go but stopped when he grinned and gave me a thumbs-up.

"Okay, now you guys listen to me," Jimmy said. "Don't go fast at the bottom of the hill. Last time was way too fast."

"Hey, wieners, no more orders," Maggie said, pointing her finger at them.

"Giddyup, guys," I yelled. "The ride is about to begin."

We rode around the schoolyard twice and then headed out on School Street. It was a quiet afternoon—sunny and hot, and the street was empty. Maggie and I rode side by side, the boys a few feet behind us swerving left and right like they were skiing.

"Ladies and gentlemen, presenting the Amazing Jimbo and DenDen the Great!" Louanne yelled, bringing up the rear. "Come on, boys, make us proud."

Denny lifted the rope over his head. "Woo-hoo!"

"Good start, DenDen," Lou said positively. "Now the slalom moves. Boys, show 'em what you've got!"

Jimmy whined. "I paid a lot of money for this. Go faster."

Maggie and I picked up the pace. At the top of School Street, I glanced down the hill.

Mrs. Hogan's yard was empty, her spring tulips long gone, replaced by a bed of bright orange marigolds. Kingfish, her fat, old basset hound, was stretched out on the front porch.

The Stephenson twins came around the corner holding chocolate ice cream cones. One twin noticed us and nudged her sister. This wasn't good—the twins were the town squealers. If they told their mother, and she called my mother, I'd be grounded for the rest of my life.

Maggie and I exchanged worried looks.

"Just what we don't need," Lou called out. "Snitches."

"Too late now," Maggie said, waving. "Hi, Twinnies. How's the ice cream?"

The twins—everyone called each one Twinnie; it saved time trying to tell them apart—didn't say anything. Their mother was a registered nurse. She never let them do anything fun because she was afraid they'd get hurt. Rumor had it she kept a big supply of penicillin in the house, and whenever they had as much as a sniffle, she'd whip out a needle and give them a shot. I guess the only fun they had was eating chocolate ice cream and tattling. Good thing they had each other because no one liked them.

Jimmy and Denny were yelling like banshees as we started down the hill. Maggie and I stood up to pedal faster, like I did when I raced with my father. He'd get way ahead of me and then slow down to let me catch up, and he'd act so surprised when I passed him. I took a deep breath; the wind felt warm on my face, and the run was almost over—so far, so good.

A car pulled up beside us, honking the horn, and Mr. Kutter leaned out of the driver's window. "Hey, kids!" he hollered.

My stomach knotted, I slammed on the brakes and my mouth went dry. Maggie's bike plowed into mine, and I flew over the handlebars, biting back a scream as my head hit the pavement. I skidded across the asphalt scraping the skin off my hands and knees before I came to a stop a few feet away.

The next thing I knew, a twinnie was yelling, "Oh my God! They're dead! They've killed themselves!"

"Twinnie," I said, trying to sit up, but everything went black and spun around. I felt sick to my stomach.

me to sit down, he poured me a glass of water and handed me a wet washcloth. I wiped my forehead with the cool cloth and waited for him to say something.

"It wasn't that long ago that you gave me your word you wouldn't tow Denny on the bike."

"I know. I'm sorry," I said, trying to figure out how I could convince him. "I really am."

"Let me make myself clear. You could've been killed if you'd swerved into the moving car. A hard fall like yours and a good knock to the head can kill a person. Do you know how lucky you all were?"

I nodded, but I didn't feel lucky. I'd known that Denny might fall and get hurt, but I didn't stop him from bike-skiing, and I never even thought about a car running over us.

I was pretty good at putting things out of my mind when I had to, like my father's accident, but I needed to get better at remembering. It was just so hard. Before my father died, things were different—everything was easy. I never got in trouble. My father always called me his good girl. Tears filled my eyes; nothing was the way it used to be. My mother was gaga over Mr. Howe, Lou's father left her, Maggie's father beat her, and everybody thought Uncle Tony was an arsonist.

"Grace, this is one time that crying won't help," Doc said unsympathetically. "You have to make better choices. From now on, take a deep breath, count to ten, and think before you act. I know you can do it—you're a good girl."

I buried my face in my hands and sobbed.

Dr. Whalen dropped by our house about four o'clock that afternoon to examine me. He always made us his last house call because after he finished with the medical stuff, he and my grandfather liked to relax over a couple of highballs.

I was in the living room lying on the couch with an ice pack on my head when he knocked on the door. My head felt better, but the cut on my elbow hurt whenever I moved my arm. My cuts and scrapes stung even though my mother made me take a bath and rub them with Unguentine before she went over to the Millers to check on Jimmy. I pushed my head into the rough couch pillow; I wanted my father.

My grandfather poked his head into the living room, and I turned over. "Grace, Dr. Whalen is waiting for you in the kitchen." He walked over to the couch and handed me his handkerchief. "Here now, dry those tears. You didn't anticipate what happened, but now you know. You've learned a valuable lesson—the hard way."

I dragged myself into the kitchen. Dr. Whalen was sitting at the table. He turned his chair sideways to look at me. I'd bandaged the cut on my elbow and was wearing a long-sleeved sweater so he wouldn't notice it. I didn't want him checking it out because he'd probably say the s-word—stitches.

Dr. Whalen fingered the purple bump on my forehead. "Look up; follow the light," he said, shining a small silver flashlight into my right eye. "Now look left; right; down. Do you have a headache?"

He asked me more standard concussion questions. "Can you remember what you had for breakfast?"

"Uh," I lied, thinking about the orange Popsicle I snuck from the refrigerator that morning. "Orange juice, I guess."

"If you feel nauseous or light-headed, have your mother call me, but Grace, I think you'll live. Did your bike make it?"

"My bike's fine," I said with a sigh. I glanced down at the bloodstains on my new white sneakers. "Uh, how's Jimmy?"

"He'll live too, but with a cast on his wrist for the next six weeks. Damned shame, because summer's just started."

"Did you see Maggie? Is she okay?"

"She was upstairs in her room, but her father said she was fine. Now you get outta the kitchen and let me talk to your grandfather." Dr. Whalen patted me on the shoulder. "And girl, take off that sweater, it's hot."

I was so worried about Maggie that I couldn't even feel truly glad about no stitches. I walked outside to get my bike. The kitchen window was open, and Doc was saying, "She's a good girl, but she changed some after her father died. She's more impulsive—doesn't always think things through. Almost like she's afraid to think because if she did…"

"Well, that kind of a death is tough—especially on kids. Makes 'em feel powerless and out of control."

Death was tough all right. I got on my bike and rode over to the Millers; my mother and Denny were there visiting Jimmy. Instead of riding down the road like I usually do, I rode down the sidewalk because my legs felt wobbly. I looked for Louanne when I passed the Dodd house, but the only sign of life was Gabriel peering out of Uncle Tony's bedroom window.

A dog would be nice—someone who loved me no matter what.

When I got to the Millers', Jimmy was spread out on the couch in his Roy Rogers pajamas. He had a big plaster cast that covered half of his arm and his wrist. Denny was so busy signing it that he didn't even look up when I walked in. Comic books and candy wrappers littered the coffee table; Jimmy was probably on a sugar high and not feeling any pain. In fact, the Amazing Jimbo looked like he was in his glory.

"Want me to sign your cast?"

"Sure, Grace," he said, holding it up. "Good thing you got here while I still have room. Mom says you guys have to give me my money back."

I drew a rainbow on his cast, ignored the money comment, and wandered into the kitchen, where my mother and Mrs. Miller were sipping tea.

"Your grandfather just called, Grace," my mother said. "I thought you were fine, but it was a load off my mind to hear Dr. Whalen thinks so too." I walked over and put my arms around my mother. She smelled fresh—like lemons. She hugged me and then sat back and frowned. "But you know, it won't be a very nice summer for Jimmy."

She had a bad habit of saying something nice and I'd feel good, but then she'd say something else and make me feel bad. My head started to hurt again.

"I know." I looked at Mrs. Miller. Her knees were bouncing up and down, and she seemed about to jump out of her chair. "I'm sorry he got hurt, we didn't think…"

"You're right, Grace. It's a shame," she said as Maggie walked into the kitchen. "Right, Maggie?"

Maggie had on a pair of blue slacks—the same ones she'd worn the last week of school, and she looked like she'd been crying. "Mom, I said I was sorry."

I looked at Maggie, and she looked the other way. It was pretty obvious Mr. Miller had whipped her again. I felt sick to my stomach.

"Your father called me from the mill. He's upset that Mr.

The cut on my elbow didn't hurt as long as I didn't hit it on anything; if I did, it hurt like heck and started to bleed again. In case that happened, I bandaged it extra and had on a dark long-sleeved shirt. The scrapes on my leg looked gross, but they were healing. Maggie was wearing Bermuda shorts, and, along with the cuts on her chin and scrapes on her knees, there was a long red welt on the back of her right leg. It made me sick to look at it.

Louanne hadn't been hurt in the crash, but she hadn't been herself since she found out her parents were separated. Every day she was different—sometimes she was sad, sometimes she was mean.

"It's too bad it's not a Halloween parade because then you wouldn't have to worry about costumes—you could pick up some crutches and go as accident victims," she said, crossing her arms and smirking. "And how come I have to wear all white? Am I supposed to be your nurse or something? White is not my color; I look all washed out."

"It's a good thing you're not our nurse," Maggie said, giving her a sad look. "Because you have no compassion."

Louanne's eyes watered, and she looked away.

"Louanne, you'll be beautiful," I said, smiling. "You'll look like a lovin' little angel in your white outfit."

"You wish," she said, but she smiled back.

Maggie laughed and ran inside to get the flags just as O'Malley the cop drove into the Millers' driveway. He parked over by the garage and got out of his car.

"What's he doing here?" Louanne asked, watching him walk over.

I shrugged.

"Bikes look good," he said, nodding. "How're you feeling after yesterday's crash, Grace?"

"I'm okay," I said, feeling guilt wash over me now that the law was here. I wouldn't make a good criminal. I can never remember my sins when I go to confession, but put a uniformed policeman in front of me, and I'll tell you anything. "But Jimmy broke his wrist; he's in a cast."

"He's tough," O'Malley said, smiling at me, "just like his old man. He'll be outta that cast before you know it."

A picture of Jimmy lying on the couch in his Roy Rogers jammies popped into my mind. He's tough all right.

"Maggie's father said you saw Nick Kutter just before your accident?"

I nodded.

"Well," Louanne said, jumping into the conversation, "we didn't really see him. He drove up behind us and honked his horn. He scared us half to death. Maggie and Grace crashed into each other, and the boys rolled down the hill."

Mr. Miller and Maggie came out of the house. Her arms were full of flags and crepe paper.

"Hey, O'Malley," Mr. Miller said, holding out his hand. "Thanks for coming over. What did Kutter have to say for himself?"

"Nothing much, Ted." O'Malley pulled a pack of Pall Malls and a lighter out of his pocket.

I poked Louanne, and Maggie nodded.

O'Malley lit up and took a long drag.

"Well, he must've said something," Mr. Miller said impatiently.

"Hold your horses, Ted, no reason to get your dander up," O'Malley said, checking him out. "He said he recognized two of the kids and honked the horn—just being friendly. He didn't see them fall."

"See, Dad, I told you he didn't mean—" Maggie interrupted.

"I'm not asking you, Missy," Mr. Miller said in a mean voice.

Maggie looked down and seemed to shrink into herself.

"Let me ask you something, Ted," O'Malley said. "Did you know Saint Mark's let Kutter go?"

"Ruth told me last night."

"Well, the guy's got it rough," O'Malley continued in his stern "I'm a policeman" voice. "Honking a horn's not illegal. I'm sorry the kids took a bad spill, but Kutter didn't break any laws. Leave it alone." O'Malley dropped his cigarette on the ground and crushed it with the toe of his shoe. He nodded once and walked back to his car.

CHAPTER 15

AT PRECISELY 4:00 P.M. on the Fourth of July, O'Malley the cop revved his engine, turned the siren on, and slowly cruised up Hudson Avenue. This was the official signal that the parade was underway.

People in Stillwater had lined the street to watch. They sat on their front porches or on the curbs, and they filled the sidewalks cheering and clapping when O'Malley drove by. Little kids bounced up and down on their tiptoes, waved their arms, and shouted. Men wearing aprons with deep pockets and carrying big bunches of balloons, flags, and cotton candy weaved their way in and around the crowd, hawking their wares.

The Stillwater High School band, resplendent in their maroon-and-white uniforms, followed O'Malley's car playing "God Bless America." They were pretty good this year—except for Greg Simmons, the tuba player.

"All blow and no show," Maggie said matter-of-factly. "He should be a drummer."

Next came an old town tradition—the E. I. Wood Steamer antique fire engine pulled by the town's tow truck because it had been out of commission since the 1930s. The new fire truck followed the old truck, and several volunteer firemen sat up on the top throwing wrapped candy to the kids.

People went wild when a stoic-looking Mortie the mortician drove by in Stillwater's long black hearse, which did double duty as the town ambulance. He waved his black top hat at the people, and they screamed, "Mortie! Mortie! Mortie!"

After that came the veterans—the brave heroes we honored in all our parades. They were wearing their military uniforms, and they marched to the music like they were still on active duty.

Mr. Walters led the Boy Scout troops. Two of the oldest, tallest Eagle Scouts carried a "Boyhaven" banner—the name of their summer camp at Saratoga Lake.

"I love courageous men in uniform," Louanne shouted as they passed. "Can I visit Boyhaven?"

Mr. Walters turned around and glared at her.

We giggled, and she yelled, "Three cheers for Boyhaven! Hip hip hooray!"

The plucky 4-Hers marched—well, wandered, actually—behind the Boy Scouts, waving little American flags.

Then came my favorite part: about thirty kids riding bikes, each one decorated to the hilt. The older kids had attached playing cards to their back tires with clothespins so their bikes would sound like motorcycles. Nobody was fooled, but I gave them an A for effort.

Jimmy and Denny rode in the front of the pack. The Amazing Jimbo had decorated his cast with bright yellow stars and blue stripes, and he proudly held it up like he was the Statue of Liberty. Denny's eyes sparkled, and he couldn't stop grinning.

His new blue Dodger cap set the red-white-and-blue streamers on his bike off nicely; he loved riding in parades.

Louanne, Maggie, and I rode down the center of Hudson Avenue side by side—just like the stripes in the American flag. I was wearing red shorts and a red-and-white-striped long-sleeved T-shirt; Maggie had on her blue slacks and a blue-and-white gingham blouse. We looked good, but Louanne looked sensational. She rode between Maggie and me dressed all in white—a white lacy shirt, white pedal pushers, and new white sandals.

"You were right, Grace," Louanne said, waving at the crowd. "We're definitely the most original bike riders in the parade. Nobody else comes close."

People clapped and whistled at us. My mother and Doc waved their flags and stood up and cheered when we rode by. Mr. and Mrs. Nelson did too, and Sylvia made us stop so she could take our picture with her new Brownie camera.

Most of the crowd stepped into the street the moment we passed. There was some good-natured pushing and shoving as the townspeople followed the parade to the veterans' monument in the small park on the edge of town. Gun salutes boomed, and the little kids covered their ears; some of them screamed bloody murder. Mr. Martin played "Taps" on his bugle, and Louanne brushed away a few tears—her father had been in the service when she was little. The mayor said a few uplifting words about how important the veterans were to our country and how grateful everyone was for their service, and the jubilant crowd went wild. The band struck up "God Bless America," and everyone sang their hearts out.

After the ceremony, most people trooped over to the American Legion Hall for beer, burgers, and ice cream. Vinnie the butcher supervised the barbeque, and he gave the three of us the biggest hamburgers on the grill.

We ate outside on an old picnic table behind the building. Vinnie's hamburgers were so good that we gobbled them down and went back for seconds. We ate so much we couldn't finish our hot fudge sundaes. It was too early to go home, so we wandered out of the hall to the baseball field, where some kids were starting a baseball game.

"I'll be umpire," Jimmy volunteered. "I can't play 'cause of my cast."

It was getting dark, but there was enough light for an inning or two. My team was up first. We had two outs, and Louanne had made it to third base when I hit a line drive hard enough to bring us both home. I rounded second base and noticed Uncle Tony and Gabriel over by the woods watching the game. When I reached home plate, I looked again, but they'd disappeared.

"Hey, I saw Tony Dodd," Jimmy said, running over to Maggie. "Take me home."

"Don't be a baby," Louanne said, sighing heavily. "There's no law against him watching us play ball. Why are you afraid?"

"Because he's a nut," Gary Cannon yelled from the pitcher's mound. "Stick up for your crazy uncle, Louanne! Whose house is he gonna burn down next?"

Gary Cannon was my next-door neighbor. He was a year older than me, and he hated girls. We didn't much like him either.

Louanne threw her mitt down and raced over to the pitcher's mound. "Take it back, you no-good wiener!"

To my utter amazement, she punched him hard in the stomach. He doubled over, his feet flew out from under him, and he hit the ground with a thud. He was taller and heavier than Louanne, but she'd taken him by surprise. Before he could fight back, she threw herself on top of him, punched him in the ribs, and yelled, "Take it back! You take that back."

"Lou!" Maggie screamed, running over to them. "Stop; you'll get hurt."

The twinnies were over by first base yelling, "Fight! Fight!"

Lou had Gary pinned, and he kept trying to push her off. They wrestled around in the grass—each one trying to hurt the other one.

"Take it back, jerk," Louanne said, spitting the words through her teeth.

It was only a matter of time before Gary got control and hurt her. I tried to drag her away, but she wouldn't let me. Finally, Maggie and I grabbed her arms and pulled her up. Gary's nose was bleeding, his face was scratched, and he was sweating like a pig.

"You stuck up little bitch! If you weren't a girl…" he said, jumping up and wiping the blood off of his face with the back of his hand. "You're as crazy as your uncle."

That's all it took—Louanne wrenched away from us and went after him again. Maggie jumped on his back; I piled on, and the three of us took him down to the ground. He was swinging wildly, and one of his punches got me smack in the eye.

The next thing I knew, Vinnie the butcher jerked me to my feet. "You kids stop. Enough! What's this about anyway?"

Louanne straightened her shoulders, pushed her hair out of her eyes, and pointed at Gary. "He called my uncle crazy and me crazy too."

"You girls are crazy. You're just like your stupid uncle, and Grace is like her father, crazy." Blood poured out of Gary's nose—his shirt was ripped.

"Oh yeah? You're the crazy one, wiener," Louanne said. "Letting a girl beat you up."

The twinnies giggled like wackadoos.

Vinnie wagged his finger at us. "Everyone go home. The party's over."

"Just wait, bitches. You'll be sorry," Gary said.

"Watch your language, Mister," Vinnie said, giving him a push. "You get on home before I go back in the bar and find your father."

"Hurry. Let's get out of here before my father comes," Maggie said with a worried look. "He'll be mad I was fighting."

I touched my left eye—it wouldn't open all the way. My new red shorts were grass stained, one of the pockets was torn, and my elbow was bleeding again. Louanne's white outfit was a mess—she'd never be able to wear it again. My mother was going to kill me, but nobody was going to get away with calling my father crazy and insulting my best friend's uncle—especially not Gary Cannon.

We walked our bikes back to my house, washed up, and took some sodas and chocolate chip cookies outside to the tree house. The moon was high in the summer sky. We watched the lightning bugs flash in and out of the lilac leaves and tried to pull ourselves together.

"My mother called this morning," Louanne said, taking a deep breath. "My dad's not coming back—he wants a divorce."

"That stinks," Maggie said, shaking her head, "But at least you'll see your dad sometimes. The Smiths are divorced, and it's not bad."

Mandy Smith was in my class at school, and she always looked sad to me.

"Mandy's dad never yells at her," Maggie continued, "and he always buys her presents. Your dad will do that too. It's not like he's dead or anything."

"Maggie," Louanne gasped, looking at me. "What are you saying?"

"Oh my God, Grace," Maggie said. "I'm sorry; I forgot all about your father."

"It's okay," I said, thinking sometimes it was okay, but other times I'd give anything if my dad were alive. Some nights when I couldn't sleep, I pretended to have conversations with him, and I tried to feel his bear hug, but it was getting harder and harder to remember his voice—his laugh.

"Maggie's right, Lou," I said. "If I could see my dad every other weekend, I wouldn't care about the presents."

"Grace," Louanne said. "I don't want to make you feel bad, but I don't know how…"

I waited for her to go on.

"Look. It's different for me," she finally said. "You know your dad loved you. He was in an accident. He couldn't help leaving you. My dad doesn't love me enough to stay."

No one said anything for a long time.

"Let's just hold hands and promise that we'll always be there for each other, no matter what," I whispered, holding up the little fingers on each of my hands. "Pinky swear."

"Pinky swear," Lou and Maggie whispered, twining their pinkies around mine.

said, looking sad. "I know it's been an awful day, but if you eat a little something, you'll feel better."

"We're just not hungry, Mrs. Bryant," Lou said. "Can I have my cake for breakfast?"

"Sure you can," my mother said, getting up from the table. "And if you girls do the dishes, I'll take Denny and Gabriel out for a walk."

I washed the glasses and rinsed them in cold water, and Louanne polished them until they sparkled. Maggie washed off the kitchen table and emptied the trash.

When we were finished, the three of us flopped down on the rug in my bedroom to play Monopoly.

"Louanne, do you think Uncle Tony could've had a breakdown because we found his fire truck?" I asked after we'd been playing for a while. "He didn't seem that upset in the carriage house—he even used his blanket for the kittens."

"Don't forget the fire last night," Maggie said. "My father said Uncle Tony and Gabriel were there—O'Malley told him."

Louanne shook her head. "It wasn't either one of those things. Aunt Michelle said she was making chicken and waffles for lunch and Uncle Tony lost it. He said waffles were breakfast food and she was deliberately fixing them to make him mad. It didn't have anything to do with the fire truck or the fire at the Baileys'. She never knows what sets him off."

I thought about the note on his bedroom door—"Michelle deliberately irritates me." Poor Aunt Michelle—she tries to make everyone happy. It must be hard for her.

Lou said that Aunt Michelle had told him she'd make him anything he wanted, but it was too late—he threw the waffle batter on the floor, then the waffle iron, and finally the syrup. He yelled so loud that Aunt Michelle got scared and called Vinnie the butcher.

Maggie scratched her head. "Was your aunt wigged out?"

"Wigged out?" Lou said, raising her eyebrows. "She felt awful."

"This is Uncle Tony's fifth hospitalization this year," I said. "Remember the list on his door?"

"I sure do," Maggie said, looking at her wristwatch. "Hey, what time is it? I forgot to wind my watch again."

"Almost eight," Louanne said, checking the clock on my nightstand. "What time do you have to be home?"

"Crap!" Maggie said, jumping up. "I have to be home by eight. It's my father's night off."

"Hurry," I said. "That's only five minutes."

"Damn," she said, running out of the room.

Two hours later, the house was quiet. My mother and brother were sleeping, and Doc was still at his weekly poker game in Saratoga—about ten miles away. Most of his games lasted until midnight, so we had plenty of time to look at my father's file.

"I'm going downstairs, Lou," I said, taking my shoes off so I didn't make any noise. "Want to wait here or come?"

"I'll come, but what for?"

"I found my father's funeral file in Doc's office. There was a lot of stuff in it, but I didn't have time to check it out then. I have to know how he died, so I hid it."

Louanne frowned and put the Monopoly game back in the closet. "I thought it was an accident."

"But what kind?" I said, moving toward the door. "Leave your shoes here, because the stairs squeak. I don't want my mother to wake up."

Doc had cleaned the office so well I could even see my

reflection on the desk, but he wasn't a furniture mover. The file was right where I had stashed it.

"Grace, don't go through that here," Louanne said in a worried voice. "Let's take it upstairs in case your mother wakes up."

"She won't wake up," I said, spreading everything out on Doc's desk. "She never does."

The first thing I picked up was a dried red rose with a white ribbon tied around the stem. It might have been beautiful once, but now the petals were flat and faded. I held it up to my nose and sniffed, but the scent was gone, and it was turning to dust—just like my father.

Setting the flower aside, I picked up a sympathy card. "Thinking of you" was inscribed in blue cursive letters on the front, and inside it was a note in handwriting so small I could barely read that said, "Dear Sarah, Things will never be the same without Den, but we'll always remember his smiling face. Sincerely, Margaret and Bill Walinsky."

The Walinskys were right; things weren't the same. I couldn't hold my father's hand, kiss his cheek, or hug him; the list of things that I couldn't do after he died went round and round in my mind like a song that never ends. I took a deep breath and picked up another card. "I'm so sorry to hear about Denny's death. I cannot imagine what you're going through, Ava and Sam Smith."

"Can I see them?" Louanne whispered.

"Sure," I said, handing them to her. "They're sad."

The next one I opened was from the Jensens—the minister and his wife. It was a pretty card; there was a white dove on the front flying over a green valley, but on the inside under the printed verse, Mrs. Jensen had written, "God needed him."

I threw the card in the trash can. Mrs. Jensen didn't know what she was talking about—we needed him more than God.

"How could she write that?" I whispered. "How?"

"Please, bring Daddy back, God. I need him." I'd beg to God after my father died. I'd kneel beside my bed, fold my hands, and look up at the ceiling, praying that when I woke up, he'd be in the kitchen waiting for me. I thought if I prayed long enough and hard enough, God would work a miracle, but he never did. I grabbed the card from the trash can, ripped it into a million pieces, and stuffed them in my pocket.

"Grace, what are you doing?" Louanne whispered, looking concerned. "What's wrong with you?"

"It's that Mrs. Jensen," I said in a low voice. "She wrote 'God needed him,' which is ridiculous. God has everything; he doesn't need my father." I pushed the rest of the cards over by the rose and picked up the newspaper clippings. I unfolded the yellowed clipping on the top and gasped.

"Local Man Shoots Himself on Paper Mill Loading Dock"

My father's smiling face looked out of the front page right at me. He was wearing his favorite green hunting jacket. His deer rifle was slung over his shoulder, and a dead buck was lying on the ground near his feet.

"No! No! No!" Something inside me was screaming. "No! No! No!"

"Grace, what's wrong? You're shaking all over. You're scaring me."

"Lou," I said, handing her the yellowed newspaper clipping. "I can't read it. You do it. Please."

She took it from me, her eyes widened, and she tried to give the clipping back.

"Please. I can't read it," I said, shaking my head. "Please."

"'Dennis Michael Bryant, husband of Sarah, father of two children, Grace Anne and Dennis Jr., died early this morning from a self-inflicted gunshot wound to the head.'" She covered her mouth with her hand. "I can't…read…any…more." She handed me back the paper.

"It's not true. It's not true," I said, feeling this couldn't be real. "Please don't let it be true." I sank down on the floor, numb. Why would he do that? No way. He loved us too much. He wouldn't kill himself. There's some mistake.

I made myself look at my father's picture again. I gently touched his face with my finger. I moved slowly down his face to his lips and traced his smile; I loved his smile. I kissed my finger and traced his lips again and again and again. "Daddy. Daddy. Daddy."

I wanted to scream—to run and never stop—to throw myself on the floor and beat my hands on the rug as hard as I could. "I can't stand this," I said, sobbing. "I loved him so much. Why…"

Louanne wrapped her arms around me and held me while I cried my heart out. Her tears mingled with mine.

"My mother said he died in an accident. My mother lied—she lied," I said when I could finally talk again. I pressed my right hand against my heart. "Why?"

"Maybe she thought you were too little—"

A key turned in the lock; I held my breath and looked at the doorway.

"Sarah, are you in my office?" Doc said, walking into the room. He scratched his head. "What are you two…"

I held up the clipping and looked into his eyes. "Why, Doc? Why didn't you tell me?" I cried, pleading for an answer.

Running a hand through his thick white hair, he shook his

head and sighed. "I knew this day would come, Grace, but God help me, I prayed every day it wouldn't."

My mother walked into the kitchen looking dazed. She'd pushed her hair behind her ears and was holding her pink bathrobe together with both hands like she was freezing to death. She pulled out the chair next to me, screeching its legs across the linoleum. I'd begged Doc not to wake her up, but he wouldn't listen. He wouldn't let Louanne stay with me either. He'd sent her upstairs in case Denny woke up and needed something. Mom's face was pure white—like a ghost. She reached over to hug me, but I pulled back so she couldn't. A voice inside me was screaming, "No, No, No," and then I realized that I was actually screaming. My mother tried again to pull me against her, but again I pushed her away.

"Don't hug me. You lied to me. I hate you," I said through my sobs.

"Grace." Mom's voice sounded shaky. "Take a few deep breaths. Stop. Breathe. Take it slow."

I took a deep breath, but my chest was heaving.

"That's better. Keep breathing, Grace."

I wiped my nose on my sleeve, took another deep breath, and waited for her explanation.

"You were only eight years old, Grace—the same age as Denny is now—when your father died."

"So what? You still should have told me."

"I couldn't tell you. It was hard enough telling you that your father died in an accident."

"When were you going to tell me? When?"

"I should have told you before now," she said, starting to cry. "It's just so hard."

"How would you like it if you found out accidentally like I did?" I said, flooded with anger.

My mother shook her head and sighed.

I faced my grandfather. It was even harder for me to believe that he'd kept the truth from me. "You didn't tell me either," I whispered, leaning toward him. "Why didn't you?"

"We were protecting you," he said, taking his glasses off and wiping his eyes. "You had every right to know the truth, but you were too young."

"What is the truth? Why did he, how could he…" I started to cry again. I couldn't talk; I felt like I was drowning. I covered my eyes, laid my head down on the cool Formica tabletop, and sobbed. When I couldn't cry anymore, I sat back up and looked at Doc.

He set his cup down and handed me his handkerchief. Wishing I could die on the spot, I wiped my face and blew my nose.

"Grace," Mom said softly. "Look at me, baby. Your father was sick. He had mental problems. He was manic-depressive. You were little, but you must remember when he used to be home from work for weeks at a time. He'd get sad and depressed and couldn't do anything. He wouldn't even leave the house."

"But you never said he couldn't work," I looked at her. "You told me he was on vacation."

She brushed my hair off my forehead and continued like I hadn't interrupted her. "Sometimes he'd cry, Grace, and you'd say, 'Don't cry, Daddy, please don't cry. I'll be good,' but it had nothing to do with you. You were always a good girl. You tried to help him even though you were a baby yourself."

I choked back tears.

Mom reached for one of Doc's cigarettes and drummed it

on the table. Her hand was shaking so much she couldn't light it, so she handed Doc the lighter, and he lit it for her. "You were very young," she went on. "When your father couldn't work, there were days when he wouldn't get out of bed. He wouldn't shower or get dressed. He wouldn't play with you and Denny. Dr. Whalen prescribed Thorazine, but your father never took the medication like he was supposed to. He'd have to be admitted to the hospital. Shock treatments worked, but he hated them."

Shock treatments? My own father had shock treatments? I took a deep breath and blew it out.

She wiped some tears away and went on. "Then he'd feel better, but before long he'd get depressed again. He'd drink because he was depressed. That made it worse. I couldn't help him, Grace."

"What does that mean? Why didn't you make him take the pills? You make Denny take pills when he's sick. Didn't you care?"

"Grace, your father didn't think straight when he was sick," Doc said, pushing his cup in a circle on the table.

I sniffed and looked over at him. I couldn't think straight either.

"Once he felt good, he didn't think he needed the pills," Doc continued. "He forgot about how bad he'd felt. He thought he was okay. He didn't want to depend on pills—that can make a man feel helpless. Alcohol was his way of self-medicating his pain."

"He always did that," Mom said, taking another drag on her cigarette. "He'd tell me he was taking his medicine, but instead of taking it, he drank. He'd stop at Riley's Tavern after work and drink for a couple of hours."

I closed my eyes.

"We'd have a big fight when he got home, because I knew

he'd been drinking. Oh, he'd promise he'd never drink again, but the next day he'd head right back to Riley's."

I remembered their fights. Denny and I'd be eating dinner in front of the television when my father came in. He'd be really, really happy—he'd tickle us and make us laugh. Sometimes he'd sing silly songs, and Mom would come into the living room and start screaming at him because he was late. I'd turn the television up and sit real close to Denny so we couldn't hear them fight. And I'd think to myself, If I were my father, I wouldn't come home early either.

"I even made your father go to Father Flanagan and take the pledge, Grace. You were too young to know what that meant—you were only in kindergarten. Your father promised on the holy Bible that he wouldn't drink alcohol for a year."

That sounded crazy, but I looked at Doc and he nodded.

"At first, he didn't drink a drop, and it was wonderful. Every day he took his medication, and he felt good. We started to do family things that we hadn't done in a long time. When school let out, we went camping, and at night after dinner, we went for long walks in the country. He bought you a fishing pole and taught you how to catch fish over at Two Trees."

Camping on Lake George was fun. I did remember Mom and Dad laughing a lot—they didn't fight much at all. After dinner Mom would put Denny and me to bed on army cots in the tent; she always left the flap open so we wouldn't be afraid. Denny fell asleep fast, but I'd lay awake and listen to my parents talk. The smell of the campfire would drift into the tent; I loved that smell. Mom and Dad would sit by the fire, and Dad would play his harmonica. I'd fall asleep listening to him play "Put On Your Old Gray Bonnet with the Blue Ribbons on It" or "Daisy,

Daisy, Give Me Your Answer Do," but my absolute favorite was when he played "Amazing Grace."

"Well, before the year was over, your father forgot all about the pledge—he went back to drinking—even more than before." My mother sighed. "It was a vicious circle, Grace. I kept hoping he'd snap out of it, but he was sick. He couldn't take it anymore. Even the smallest things were too much for him. He was in so much pain that one day," my mother's voice broke, "he ended his life. I know how hard this is, Grace, but your father loved you and Denny more than anything in the world."

Killing yourself was not the way to show your kids that you loved them.

CHAPTER 19

LOUANNE WAS ASLEEP IN my bed when I went upstairs. I turned the light off, climbed in beside her, and stared at the ceiling. The curtains were open, and the moonlight filled the room. I closed my eyes, and my father's face stared at me. I opened them, and he disappeared. Memories flooded through me like bright ribbons—one leading to the next. My father smelled like Old Spice; he loved the way moonlight shimmered on the river; he loved buckwheat pancakes, venison, and singing. Only now the memories felt different; it was like he had died all over again.

Why didn't he love me enough to stay?

I started to cry, remembering how he'd change the words to his favorite songs to make me laugh. I looked out the window and tried to hear him singing, "Amazing Grace, the precious girl who fills my heart with joy…"

I should've stayed home from school the day my father died. He might not have done it if I had been there. I kept thinking about how I could never get that day back—that morning, the morning I lost my father forever.

One time, my dad was babysitting us, and when my mother came home, he was laughing and chasing Denny around the apartment, pretending to be the tickle monster. I was reading at the kitchen table. Mom asked me if my father had been drinking beer. I told her not much—he'd only had three cans. She got mad, and he got sad. I shouldn't have told her; I should have kept my mouth shut.

The bedroom door opened, and my mother walked in. I closed my eyes and pretended to be sleeping. She pulled the covers up around me, kissed my forehead, and tiptoed out. What if she died? And Doc—he was in his sixties. Who would take care of Denny and me? I snuggled deeper in the bed and tried not to think.

Louanne turned over with a little sigh. I wondered if Uncle Tony would ever kill himself. He didn't drink, but he didn't always take his medication. He seemed sad too; he didn't smile much. He loved Gabriel and riding his bike. Those were his happy things, and maybe they were enough to live for. I crossed my fingers.

The moon had moved higher in the sky. I rolled over on my stomach, buried my head in the pillow so Louanne wouldn't hear me, and cried myself to sleep.

Next morning, Louanne was still sleeping when the bedroom door opened and my mother came in. She walked over to my side of the bed and waited for me to open my eyes.

"Hi, Mom."

"Morning, Grace," she whispered, rubbing my shoulder. Her eyes were red and swollen; mine felt like they were too. "I looked in on you a couple of times, and you were asleep. I don't have to go to school today. I can stay home and spend the day with you and Louanne."

I did not want her hanging around watching me. I needed to think about lots of things in my own way and time. "Mom, go to work. I'm fine," I said, knowing I'd never be fine again—never fine.

"Grace, I can cancel my in-service. How about I make you and Louanne pancakes?"

"No, go to school. Honest, I don't want pancakes," I said, getting out of bed. "It's too hot for pancakes."

Louanne stirred and opened her eyes.

"We'll get cereal," I said, trying to act like it was a normal day. "We have to go over and feed the kittens."

"Morning, Mrs. Bryant," Louanne said, sitting up in bed.

My mother nodded. "Morning, honey. Doc and Denny just went to the gas station to get a new muffler for the car. They'll be back in an hour or so. If you're sure you girls don't need me, I might as well go to school."

"Great," I said, bending down for my slippers, which weren't under the bed where they were supposed to be. "Mom, did you take my slippers? Why do you always…"

She pointed to my slippers under the chair, where I'd left them yesterday.

"Sorry, Mom," I said, shaking my head.

She threw her arms around me and hugged me for a long time. "It's all right, Grace. I understand."

We grabbed a couple of doughnuts and walked over to Louanne's with Gabriel. Maggie met us on Louanne's back porch a few minutes later.

"How long is your aunt going to be away?" Maggie asked Louanne.

"I'm not sure," Lou said. "She'll probably call me today."

"What'd you do last night after I left?"

Louanne and I looked at each other. "Well, Lou won the Monopoly game," I said, tugging on my earlobe. "And…"

"And what?"

Louanne stuck her legs out in front of her, crossed her ankles, and looked off in the distance.

"I found out how my father died," I said, standing up. "He killed himself."

She shifted her weight from one foot to the other and said in a low voice, "I know."

Louanne and I exchanged looks.

"What do you mean, you know?" I said, squaring my shoulders.

"Look, don't get mad," Maggie said, tucking a lock of hair behind her ear. "My mother told me last year when Mr. Sanders killed himself. She didn't mean to. We were having breakfast when my father read about Mr. Sanders in the paper. He asked my mother how many years has it been since your father shot himself, and I freaked. She told me but made me promise not to say anything until you brought it up."

"So everybody knew," I said, beginning to cry. "Except me. Nice—and he was my father."

"I didn't," Louanne said, lifting her chin. "Honest."

"I couldn't tell you, Grace," Maggie said, grabbing my hand. "I didn't want to believe it myself. Please don't be mad."

I pulled away and whistled to Gabriel. I put him back in the dog run and filled his bowl with water from the hose so that Maggie wouldn't see how hurt I was.

The kittens pounced on us when we opened the carriage-house door. They were growing so fast. I scooped up the gray one; he wasn't skinny anymore—his tummy felt like a little round ball. Aunt Michelle said I could have him when he was big enough to leave his mother; I couldn't wait. I named him Ambrose because it means "immortal." If Ambrose was immortal, he'd never die.

We brought the kitties outside so they could play and chase butterflies. The mother cat stretched out close to her babies and closed her eyes. It was a perfect summer day. The grass was thick and green, and the climbing roses on the side of the carriage house had reached the rooftop. Bees buzzed around the flowers, but they didn't bother us or the cats.

"I should've figured out my dad killed himself a long time ago," I said, watching Ambrose bat a leaf around. "I knew it was strange that my mother and Doc wouldn't tell me what happened. And another thing…you know how everyone always eyeballs us and asks my mother how my brother and I are doing? 'How're the children doing, Sarah? They're so young. God bless them.' That always felt weird to me."

"Since my dad left, people ask Aunt Michelle how I'm doing right in front of me too. 'How's she holding up—poor little thing?'"

"Poor little thing is different than being a 'God bless 'em.' God bless 'em doesn't sound good," I said, swatting at a fly.

"I think God bless 'em is okay," Louanne said, twisting her hair around her fingers. "People probably feel sorry for you."

"I don't want people feeling sorry for me. I don't want people knowing secrets about me. I don't want to be a God bless 'em. I want to be normal."

"Yeah, I get it," Louanne said, sighing. "I'm not a poor little thing."

"Well, try having a father who beats you," Maggie said, crossing her arms. "I don't want that, either."

Louanne looked at me in surprise.

"Wow," I said, wishing I had a magic wand. "Everything sucks."

"Did you ever wish you were a Bobbsey twin?" Louanne asked. "The four of them have perfect lives. Their father and mother love each other and the kids. I think about that family at night when I can't sleep. I want to be Nan."

"It sounds nice," I said, reaching into my pocket. "I brought a 3 Musketeers bar—all for one and one for all, forever and ever."

None of us had a perfect life, but we did have each other.

A week later, things returned to normal—well, not for me, but the Dodds came home from the state hospital with Uncle Tony. Maggie and I sat on the floor watching Louanne pack. I couldn't wait until she was gone. It wasn't that I didn't love her, but things were different now. Since the night I found out about my father, everybody watched me, even Lou, to see if I was okay. And I wasn't—even when I tried my best to act normal, I couldn't. And knowing that Louanne, one of my best friends, was worried about me only made it harder.

Sometimes, for no reason at all, the tears would start rolling down my cheeks, and I'd have to run into the bathroom and lock the door so nobody would see me cry. And it wasn't crying like I'd cried before—it was "I can't stop crying no matter how hard I try" crying.

I had terrible nightmares about my father shooting himself. I'd beg him not to do it, but he'd smile at me and pull the trigger. One night, I dreamt that he shot Denny and me because we didn't drink all our milk. Night after night, I'd wake up screaming. Louanne would wake up too and try to comfort me. I'd be frantic and afraid to go back to sleep in case I had another terrifying nightmare. She was probably afraid to go back to sleep; if I was her, I would've been.

I wasn't hungry, and when I did eat, nothing tasted good. Doc tried hard to get me to eat. Three days in a row, he treated the three of us to root beer floats at the coffee shop, but I couldn't eat more than a couple of bites. Maggie had to finish them off.

My mother didn't say anything much, but she was extra nice. She didn't yell at me to pick up my room or make me do my usual chores. She made all of my favorite foods for dinner, mashed potatoes with gravy, chicken pot pie, raspberry pie, and strawberry shortcake. I pushed the food around my plate and pretended I was eating, but it didn't fool her. "Just take a couple of bites," she'd say, like I was a baby.

Doc kept telling me that he loved me and, even though he knew that I wouldn't believe him, in time I'd feel better.

Everyone was so nice that part of me felt bad that I got really angry at Doc and my mother when I found out. I knew Denny would feel like I did when he found out; it was like having your dad die again, but worse. There was no way I could tell Denny—not now, anyway, when he was so little.

When Louanne finished packing, we walked over to her grandmother's to help her settle back in and ran into Uncle Tony in the upstairs hall.

sick if smoke gets in your lungs. You told me you tried smoking before."

"I've tried..." Maggie said, holding her chest.

"No you haven't! You're a virgin smoker. A virgin smoker."

"Wait," I said, pointing toward the bend in the trail. "Someone's coming down the path."

The words were barely out of my mouth when the twinnies rounded the bend and ran toward us. We dropped our cigarettes on the ground and squished them into the dirt with our shoes.

"Do you think they saw us?" Maggie said, waving some smoke away with her hands. "Do you think they can smell it?"

"Not if you cover your mouth and stop coughing," I said. "They're too far away."

"Wonder what's got them all wigged out," Lou said, watching them.

"Boys! Skinny-dipping! Naked!" Twinnie Number One yelled as she raced past us. "We're telling. They're in big trouble."

"Disgusting," Twinnie Number Two yelled, following her sister back to the main road.

"Who?" Maggie called, but the twins were too far away to hear her.

"What difference does it make?" Louanne said, grabbing the lunch bag and heading for the creek. "Let's see for ourselves."

"Come on," Maggie said, pulling on my arm. "This is gonna be fun."

We traced the path the twins had taken, and when we got closer to the stream, we heard kids laughing and splashing in the water. Lou got there first.

"Oh my God!" she said, covering her eyes. "I've been waiting forever to see a naked man, and who do I see?"

"Who?" I asked. "Who is it?"

"Who?" Maggie echoed like an owl.

"Your weird brothers," she said, glaring at us. "Their little blue wieners look like turkey necks and gizzards!"

My jaw dropped.

Moving into the open so Denny and Jimmy could see her, Louanne cupped her hands around her mouth and yelled, "Hey, wieners. How's the water?"

Denny and Jimmy looked up in surprise. They screamed, grabbed their private parts, and ducked down in the stream.

"You dummies," Jimmy jumped back up and screamed. "You made me get my cast wet."

The water trickled over the rocks in the stream, making a cheerful bubbling sound, but it didn't drown out Jimmy's sobs as he made his way to the bank. The boys grabbed their clothes and headed for the bushes.

"My father's going to murder him," Maggie said, looking like she was about to cry too. "I wish we found the boys before the twins did."

My mother and Doc wouldn't be very upset when they found out about Denny skinny-dipping, but Maggie's father was another story.

"This place is cursed," I said, pulling off the rubber band and shaking out my hair. "Or maybe it's just us."

"It's this summer," Louanne said, nodding her head. "My parents are divorcing; everybody thinks my uncle's an arsonist…"

"Mr. Kutter got us in trouble. Jimmy broke his arm…"

"My father killed himself," I said, feeling sick to my stomach. "Let's get out of here."

We walked back to the bikes and slowly pedaled out to the road. Louanne and Maggie were riding behind me singing "Bye Bye Love" when I noticed an old green car coming down the road.

"Isn't that Mr. Kutter's car?" I said. "See?"

"You're right," Maggie said, catching up with me.

"Pull into that driveway," I said, pointing to Hogan's slaughterhouse up ahead. "Hurry."

We turned into Hogan's driveway just as Mr. Kutter drove by honking his horn like he did the day we were bike skiing.

"Let's wait here in case he comes back," I said, getting off my bike. I knew Mr. Hogan—he was nice. When I was little, I took tap dancing lessons with his daughter, and he drove in our carpool.

The front doors to the slaughterhouse were open, and we wandered in. Mr. Hogan was in the middle of the room facing away from us. He stood in front of a black-and-white cow holding a gun—a pistol like the one the Lone Ranger used.

The cow looked upset—almost panicked. She tossed her head back and forth and made funny noises deep in her throat. Her back leg had a metal band fastened to it just above her hoof. The band was attached to a chain that hung down from the ceiling. When the cow moved, the chain rattled and slid across the gray cement floor. The sound spooked the cow; she swished her tail, kicked her legs out behind her, and tried to spin around.

Mr. Hogan grabbed her head. The cow braced her legs and butted him hard in the chest. He swore, dropped the gun, and watched it skid across the floor into a pile of runny manure.

"Damn cow," Mr. Hogan swore, pushing her away. "Goddamned cow."

He picked up the gun and wiped the manure off on his apron. Taking a short step, he approached the cow from the side, murmuring, "Here, Bossy. Here, Bossy." After a few moments, the cow relaxed and let Mr. Hogan put his hand on her shoulder. He stood there stroking her gently until she calmed down.

My father probably told himself to calm down—just one more thing to do and his problems would be over.

Time slowed—almost stopped. It was as if Mr. Hogan and the cow weren't real—like they were on a screen in a movie theater.

"Easy, Bossy, easy," Mr. Hogan said, cocking his gun. He moved his feet farther apart and planted them firmly on the cement. "Stand still, girl. Stand still."

My father stood on the loading dock holding his favorite rifle.

I trembled.

"Oh no," Lou whispered. "Oh no."

Oh yes. Oh yes.

Mr. Hogan fired the gun. The cow's front legs buckled, and without a sound, she toppled over. Blood trickled out of her forehead onto the floor.

The cows in the corral next to the slaughterhouse sounded frantic; they bellowed and mooed, but Mr. Hogan didn't appear to notice. He flipped a switch on the wall. The chain slowly hoisted the cow up and swung her body around in a half circle while her legs twisted and jerked.

My father collapsed on his back on the loading dock in a pool of his own blood. His left leg twitched three times, and he was still.

Mr. Hogan grabbed a knife from his workbench and sliced through the skin on the cow's throat. Blood gushed out, spattering his apron and boots.

I choked on the fresh mineral smell of the cow's blood.

"Oh my God, Grace," Louanne said, hitting me on the back. "Are you okay?"

Mr. Hogan jerked around, holding the bloody knife. "What in the jackrabbit are you girls doing here? Christ a'mighty! You

CHAPTER 21

MY FRIENDS WERE WAITING impatiently for me on the other side of the bridge. Maggie stood next to her bike pointing down Hudson Avenue. Louanne had turned around and was waving her hands at me, trying to make me hurry.

"What's up?" I asked, pulling up beside Louanne.

"Can't you smell the smoke?" Maggie said, shaking her head. "There's a fire at the end of your street."

"Grace," Louanne said, her voice full of fear. "Could it be my grandmother's house?"

My fingers tightened on both handlebars, and I looked down the street—there was smoke everywhere, and it was impossible to see what was burning. Uncle Tony had only been back from the hospital a few days. Would he set his own house on fire? Doc would have told me not to jump to conclusions…

Louanne took off down the street like she had been shot out of a gun. Her long blond ponytail streamed out behind her as she crouched low over her bike.

I looked up the street. Doc was in front of our house talking with Vinnie the butcher and some of our other neighbors.

"I have to go," I said, needing to talk to Doc. Uncle Tony stepped back to let me pass, and he smiled when I walked by. I was so worried about what Doc was going to say that I didn't even think about Uncle Tony's smile until much later.

CHAPTER 23

AS SOON AS I got home, I told Doc I needed to talk.

"Come inside," Doc said, leading me into the living room. He pointed to the couch while he eased himself into his leather recliner. He leaned back, cupped his chin in one hand, and looked at me. "What's the matter, Grace?"

My mouth was dry, and my tongue felt like it was stuck to the roof of my mouth. "We saw Mr. Kutter coming down the road this afternoon when we were out riding our bikes. We didn't want him honking his horn at us, so we went into Mr. Hogan's slaughterhouse."

"Go on," Doc said, nodding encouragingly.

"The doors were open, and we just walked in," I said, choking up.

"It's okay, Grace," Doc said, crossing his legs. "Take your time."

I got up and knelt down on the floor next to him. "Mr. Hogan had a cow chained up so it couldn't get away. The cow was frightened; it made all kinds of awful sounds like it was begging him to stop. Mr. Parker didn't listen—he had a gun in his hand. He shot the cow in the head—right between her eyes. There was blood everywhere and the cow just fell over dead," I said, crying so hard I couldn't talk.

Doc put his hand on my shoulder. I made myself stop crying and pulled back so I could see his face while I told him the rest—the part that made no sense.

"But that's not the worst," I said, talking louder and faster. "When Mr. Hogan was killing the cow, I kept seeing my father kill himself. I was screaming, and my father looked at me like he didn't know me, but all of a sudden he recognized me and smiled."

I bit my bottom lip so hard I tasted blood. "Daddy cocked the gun, put it against his head, and pulled the trigger. I tried to make him stop, Doc, I tried to save him, but he…" I sank back down on the floor and hugged myself.

"Grace, come on, let's get you off the floor," Doc said, standing up. He sat down on the couch and patted the cushion beside him. "Come on up here beside me."

"Okay," I said, sinking down on the couch next to him.

"Whoa, Nellie," he said, taking his handkerchief out of his pocket. "Your lip's bleeding, Grace; put a little pressure on it, and make it stop."

I sank back on the couch and gently patted my lip. My blood made bright red splotches on the white cloth—just like the ones on the bloody slaughterhouse floor.

"Listen to me, Grace," Doc said, but then he paused and didn't say anything. Tears glistened in his eyes, and he tried to blink them away.

"Didn't he love me enough to put the gun away?" I whispered. "Why?"

"Of course he loved you. If love was enough, he wouldn't

have done it," Doc said, holding my face in his hands. "Your father was so sick that he couldn't think straight."

"I'm sick too, like my father and Uncle Tony," I said, watching Doc's face through my tears. "I thought if I let the cow loose, it was like I was saving my father."

"You're not sick, not sick at all. Finding out how your father died was a terrible shock, and you're not over it," Doc said, shaking his head. "It's on your mind all day long, and I hear you yelling at night when you have nightmares."

I hadn't realized Doc knew any of that; I'd thought I was doing a good job of hiding it.

"And I bet if you start to have fun and you forget for a minute or two, it pops back up, and you blame yourself for having fun. Right?"

"Yes," I said, blowing out a long breath.

"You're going through a tough time, Grace. Suicide's a horrible thing for a kid your age to come to terms with. But awful as it is, everything you're experiencing is normal—all of your thoughts and feelings are normal."

I sighed.

"I promise they'll go away eventually," he said. "You probably don't believe me, but they will."

I wanted to believe him. I wanted things to be normal again.

Doc put his arm around me and squeezed me hard. "Grace, you're not sick. It's grief, not mental illness," he said, shaking his head and smiling a sad little smile. "Don't worry about that anymore."

"Are you sure?" I asked, tears of relief pouring down my cheeks.

"I'm sure, honey," he said, folding me into a big hug. "You'll never forget your father, and you'll always miss him, but I promise potato chip sandwiches and bring your mom's oatmeal cookies? Maybe they'll make her feel better."

"Okay," I said. "See you soon."

Maggie's father must've gotten mad again. If my father had been like Mr. Miller, would I still miss him? Or would I be glad he was gone? I shrugged; it was too hard to imagine.

There wasn't any bread in the bread box and only a few chips in the bottom of the bag, so I ran down to the grocery store. Doc was standing at the counter talking with Vinnie.

"We were just solving all of the world's problems, Grace," Doc said, winking at me. "Did you need me?"

I explained that I was getting stuff for lunch because I was going swimming with my friends.

"Sounds like a great idea," he said. "Wish I had a bathing suit; I'd go too."

"Now that's something I'd pay to see," Vinnie said, laughing. "Your grandfather sunbathing at Belly Beach!"

Doc laughed too. "Well I'm not going to take your money, Vinnie. That's for sure."

I headed over to the bread aisle and picked up a loaf of Freihofer's bread. Making sure Doc and Vinnie weren't watching, I squeezed it gently to make sure it was fresh—my mother hated it when I did that. I was looking for the Wise potato chips—my favorite because they were so crispy—when the bell rang, and Mr. Kutter walked into the store.

I squeezed the bread so hard there was no way anyone could make sandwiches out of it. I stood perfectly still so he wouldn't notice me.

Mr. Kutter picked up a can of Maxwell House coffee and walked over to the counter, where Vinnie and Doc were still talking.

"Carton of Pall Malls," he said, slamming the coffee can down next to Doc. He pulled out his wallet, counted out some money, and put it on the counter.

"Sorry," Doc said, stepping aside. "Didn't realize you were there."

Vinnie pulled the cigarettes off of the shelf and put them in a bag with the coffee. He rang up Mr. Kutter's purchases and gave him his change.

"Ain't you the man who got me fired?" Mr. Kutter said, looking at Doc more closely. He stuck his wallet back into his pocket and thrust his chest out. "Yeah, you're that girl's grandfather. You got me fired."

I stayed still.

"Hold on, Mr. Kutter. I didn't get you fired," Doc said firmly. "You did that to yourself. You've no one to blame but yourself."

"Bull. Shit. You cost me my job," Mr. Kutter said, spitting his words out. "I ain't forgot." He grabbed his bag and walked out to his car.

"He's holding a grudge, Doc," Vinnie said, watching him peel away from the curb. Vinnie and everyone else in town knew that Doc had insisted the school do something after Mr. Kutter took Maggie and me down to the school basement—everyone in town did. There weren't many secrets in Stillwater.

"He knows he was wrong," Doc said, shaking his head. "He's embarrassed. Blowing off steam, that's all. Besides, he's working part-time for the city now, helping them clean up after the hotel fire. That'll keep him busy for quite a while."

I walked up to the counter and put my things down.

Doc put his arm around me. "He didn't scare you, did he?"

"A little," I said, wishing for the hundredth time I'd never gone into the school basement with Mr. Kutter.

splashed water in our faces and pushed us away. "My rock," she said, ducking Maggie's head underwater. "Mine."

"Louanne! You idiot." Maggie spit out a mouthful of water. "You're not funny; you could have drowned me." She made another attempt to climb on, but Louanne laughed and pushed her away again.

"Stop pushing me; the rock is slippery. I could get hurt."

"Maggie," Louanne said, striking her "I'm a mermaid" pose. "Say sorry for calling me an idiot if you want to get on."

"No way," Maggie shot back.

"Come on, Lou," I said, climbing up beside her. "Let Maggie on."

"Oh, go ahead and ruin my fun," Lou said, but she smiled and moved over so Maggie could get on.

"Hey, look how different it looks on Hudson Avenue," I said, pointing to the space up the river where the old hotel had been. "Reminds me of a missing tooth."

"Jeez," Maggie said.

"Do you think O'Malley will arrest my uncle?"

"Probably," Maggie said, slipping off the rock to float in the cool water.

"But he has to prove Uncle Tony did it," I said. "So many people smoke Pall Malls. How do we know which one's the arsonist?"

"We look for bad people, like Gary Cannon," Louanne said, slapping her forehead. "I know he smokes because I saw Gary down by the river. He and his friends were all smoking—I just don't know what kind of cigarettes."

"And remember," I said, "Gary and two of his friends got in trouble for breaking into the drive-in theater last year. They stole beer and cigarettes."

"I didn't know that," Louanne said, staring at me. "What happened?"

"They went to court, but they didn't go to jail. They had a curfew—had to be home by nine at night, and they had to meet with O'Malley once a week," Maggie said. "They could be the ones setting the fires."

"It's true," I said, shivering. "Doc always tells me that you look at the past to predict the future."

"Yeah," Maggie agreed. "They've already committed one crime."

"I wonder if O'Malley suspects them," Louanne asked. "How can we find out?"

"Wait—one more thing," I said, getting excited. "I was going to tell you this when I came over this morning, but I forgot because of O'Malley."

"What?" Maggie asked.

"I've been reading about arson for our investigation, and sometimes firemen are arsonists."

"No way," Louanne said. "That doesn't make sense."

"I know, but it's true."

"Go on," Maggie said. "What else did it say?"

"Well, they're usually regular people, volunteers, like Mr. Howe. They like the idea of fighting fires—that's why they learn about it. They want to save people."

"So?" Louanne said. "What's wrong with that?"

"Nothing, Lou," I said impatiently, "but if there aren't fires for them to put out, sometimes they set them so they can be heroes."

"Are you kidding me?" Maggie said. "Seriously, I don't believe it."

"It's true," I said, trying to convince her. "The fireman in the book I'm reading set a house on fire just because he wanted to save the people inside."

"Really?" Louanne said, shaking her head in disbelief. "What happened?"

"The fire burned too fast. Everybody in the house died."

CHAPTER 25

O'MALLEY'S VISIT UPSET EVERYONE, Uncle Tony most of all. He thought everyone was conspiring against him, and he went into a downward spiral. He refused to come out of his room, even to take Gabriel for a walk—Louanne had to do it. It seemed like the life had been sucked out of him, and two days later Aunt Michele had to call Vinnie and the ambulance. Uncle Tony was restrained and carried off to the state hospital again—only three weeks after his last hospitalization.

Vinnie the butcher, Aunt Michelle, and Mrs. Dodd made their familiar trek to Utica, and Louanne came over to stay with us. She threw her stuff on my bed, and I made her and Maggie lunch.

"Why did you make us soup?" Maggie complained, fanning herself with her napkin. "It's so hot today."

"If it's so hot, why did you wear a sweater?" Lou asked. "I like vegetable soup. It's good."

"It's a light sweater, and it goes with my shirt," Maggie said. "Can I just have watermelon?"

We were finishing our lunch when Doc walked in carrying his lucky sport coat and a racing form. He took an ashtray from the dish drainer, sat down at the table, and lit up a Camel.

"Louanne," he said, leaning back in his chair. "It's a shame about your uncle going back to the hospital." Doc set his cigarette in the ashtray and went on. "Did Michelle and your grandmother go out to Utica too?"

Louanne nodded. "Yes. Vinnie drove—he's keeping Gabriel until they get back." She wiped her mouth off with her napkin.

"Well, I'm glad you're staying with us," Doc said, smiling.

"Doc," Louanne said, leaning her elbows on the table. "Can I ask you a question?"

"Sure, honey," he answered in a serious voice. "What is it?"

"Do you think O'Malley's the reason my uncle got sick again?" Louanne said, raising her chin and looking straight at Doc. "O'Malley told him that the next time he came over, he was going to arrest him."

"Uncle Tony was really upset," I said, remembering the moaning sound that he'd made after O'Malley left the house. It sounded a lot like the cow in Mr. Hogan's barn when it knew it was going to be slaughtered.

"It could be," Doc said, stubbing out his cigarette. "O'Malley's visit must've weighed heavily on your uncle, and the poor fish couldn't take it." He reached across the table and covered Louanne's small hand with his big one. "O'Malley is feeling a lot of pressure from the mayor to make an arrest."

"From the newspaper too," Maggie said. "There was that story the day after the hotel fire that said if the arsonist isn't caught, more buildings will burn down—and somebody could get hurt."

"Tony is O'Malley's only suspect, but that doesn't mean he did it. O'Malley needs evidence to arrest him."

Doc glanced at his watch and stood up. "I've got to run if I want to make the Daily Double, but I'll be back about six." He picked up his things and looked at us. "Would going to the drive-in tonight bring smiles to your faces? *Creature from the Black Lagoon* is playing."

"Yes! Want to?" I asked, looking at Maggie and Louanne.

"That's supposed to be a really scary movie, Doc," Maggie said, pushing her sleeves up and fanning her face with both hands. "Are you sure you want to go?"

"If you girls are up for it, I can handle it," Doc said, staring at Maggie's arm. "What happened, Maggie? That's quite a bruise."

Maggie quickly pulled her sleeve down and folded her arms across her chest. "I bumped it on the door."

Doc raised his eyebrows and looked at her.

"It's okay," Maggie said with a nervous laugh. "Doesn't even hurt."

"Looks like it hurt when it happened," Doc said, shaking his head. "I've got to get going, or I'll never make the first race."

We followed Doc outside and climbed up the ladder into the tree house. I'd brought a cookie for Earl the squirrel, but he was nowhere to be seen, so I ate it. Denny and Jimmy were playing catch in the front yard, and except for their voices, everything was still.

Doc tooted the horn when he pulled his Dodge away from the curb. The heat bounced off Hudson Avenue in waves; some of the tar had even melted into puddles. A stray dog wandered aimlessly down the street. He stopped in front of our fence and whined.

"Don't go near him, Denny," I said, warning him. "He might be sick."

Denny yelled back. "He's not sick. He wants a drink."

opening Uncle Tony's bedroom door. "I don't want him to know we snooped."

"Me either," I said, following her into the room. The blinds were closed, the curtains were drawn, and the room smelled like stale smoke. Uncle Tony's bed was made, and there was a water glass on his nightstand next to some books and magazines. There was a Bible open on his bed, and I picked it up. The verse Romans 12:19 was underlined: "Beloved, never avenge yourselves, but leave it to the wrath of God, for it is written, 'Vengeance is mine. I will repay, says the Lord.'"

I handed the Bible to Louanne, and she read the verse out loud. "Vengeance. Maybe that means he's going to let the Lord take care of O'Malley," she said.

One of the books on the nightstand was *Fahrenheit 451*, a novel by Ray Bradbury. The book jacket said it was about a future American society where books are outlawed and "firemen" burn any that are found. I turned the book over and read the blurb on the back: "The system was simple. Everyone understood it. Books were for burning, along with the houses in which they were hidden. Guy Montag was a fireman…"

"Lou," I said. "You've got to see this."

"Holy shit."

"I know," I said, shaking my head. "This scares me."

Maggie grabbed the book from Louanne. "What does this mean?"

"It's just a book," Louanne said in a low voice. "It doesn't mean anything."

I turned out the light, and we walked downstairs in a daze. The book had sucked the life out of our investigation; we were unsure what to do next.

"Do we still check the dates at the library?" Maggie asked as Louanne locked the front door.

"That was our plan," Louanne answered, pulling on the door handle to make sure it was locked. "We can't quit now."

The library was across the street, catty-corner from the Dodds, a one-room clapboard cabin, rundown and plain. It was an eyesore among the stately homes and businesses on Hudson Avenue. Once painted bright yellow, the library had faded to a shade of dirty white, and the wide-plank porch sagged in the middle. There wasn't much paint left on the porch steps, and they creaked as we walked up to the front door. A clay pot filled with red geraniums sat beside the door, giving the place a splash of color, and the mat in front of the door said "We come" instead of "Welcome."

The librarian, Doris Fitch, was an unpaid volunteer, but she took her position seriously and kept regular hours. Every morning at nine, she unlocked the front door and turned on the porch light—the signal that the library was open for business. Doc said you could set your watch by her.

"Oh, girls," Miss Doris said when we walked in. "I was just leaving for lunch; I hate to keep Mrs. Teaford waiting." Mrs. Teaford was an Abyssinian cat, and Miss Doris loved her more than anything in the world—even books. She pushed her oversized glasses up on her head, smoothed down some strands of thin gray hair, and started to get up.

"Can we keep the library open while you're away?" Louanne asked, knowing the answer would be yes.

"Of course, dear," Miss Doris said, heading for the door. Before she opened it, she turned around and gestured to the metal file box on her desk. "But when you arrange the cards in alphabetical order—remember, it's the last name, not the first."

said, sliding closer to me. "Who sets the fires? Jimmy said it's Uncle Tony."

"Nobody knows," I whispered, wishing Jimmy would just shut up.

"Doc's old, almost a hundred," Denny went on. "If somebody set our house on fire, he's too old to save us."

"Doc's not that old," I said, sighing. "He'd save us, but nobody is going to set our house on fire."

"I wish Daddy didn't die."

"Me too," I said, turning my head to look out the window. "Dad watches over us though, kind of like our own dad guardian angel."

"That's funny," Denny said. "Dad guardian angel."

"Sometimes I pretend he's here."

Denny buried his head in my shoulder and said in a muffled voice, "You do? I don't remember him. Tell me about him; Mom never does."

"He was the best father in the whole wide world," I said, putting my arm around him.

My father smelled like Old Spice; I loved that smell. After he died, I took his bottle of Old Spice from the medicine cabinet and hid it in my top dresser drawer. At night I'd sprinkle a few drops on my pillow, and it smelled like he was right there with me.

"What else, Grace?" Denny's voice broke into my thoughts. "What did he do?"

"Don't you remember anything?" I said, feeling sorry for Denny. "He tickled us with his whiskers before he shaved; he'd rub his scratchy chin on your fat belly. You'd giggle, and then he'd tickle you even more."

"I was a funny baby," Denny said, bouncing a little in the bed. "Mom told me that. What else?"

"Daddy read us stories at night. You wore blue pajamas with feetsies, and he would throw you up in the air so high you'd almost touch the ceiling."

"I did?"

"Yep, and Dad would be singing 'Bye baby bunting, Daddy's gone a hunting to get a little rabbit skin to wrap his baby Denny in.'" I sighed—it all seemed so long ago.

Denny pulled my face so close our noses touched. "What else did he sing, Grace?"

"'Rock-a-bye baby in the tree top. When the wind blows, the cradle will rock. When the bough breaks, the cradle will fall, and down will come Denny, cradle and all.' Then he'd kiss you a hundred million times and put you back in your crib."

"You're right; he loved me so much," Denny said, closing his eyes.

But then came the day when love wasn't enough.

Later that night my father came to me in a dream. He was sitting in his special chair in the living room when I walked in wearing a crown of red roses and my favorite white lace nightgown.

"My beautiful girl," my father said, smiling. "Grace, my beautiful girl."

"What about me?" Denny chirped. "Am I your best boy?"

"Yep," my dad said. "My best boy."

"Play with us, Daddy," we said, tugging on his arms. "Please."

"I'll get you," Daddy cried, jumping out of his chair. He held his arms straight out in front of him like Frankenstein and wiggled his long fingers back and forth. "You can't get away from the tickle monster. I'll catch you, little missy and mister."

We screamed and ran around the coffee table and right out the front door into the yard. The sun was high in the sky, and the birds were singing in the trees. Earl the squirrel ran up the lilac tree, chattering all the way to the top branch.

"Daddy, watch this," Denny said, performing a perfect backward somersault. My father laughed and blew him kisses.

I twirled around and around like a ballerina, and my father cheered and clapped his hands.

"Encore," he shouted. "More, more."

Denny bowed and I curtsied; then we did our tricks all over again.

But this time when I curtsied, the sky turned pitch black. My father's eyes filled up with tears, and he turned and walked toward the house.

"Don't cry, Daddy," we yelled. "Daddy, please don't cry. We love you."

My father walked up the porch steps, stopped when he reached the front door, and covered his face with his hands. He moaned like an animal caught in a trap, like Uncle Tony did after O'Malley threatened to arrest him; then he straightened up, opened the door, and disappeared inside.

"Daddy," I screamed, desperately trying to open the door. "Come back. Please don't leave us."

"Open," Denny yelled, pounding his little fists on the door. "Please."

"Daddy," I said, collapsing in a heap on the porch. "What'll I do if you leave me? Don't leave me."

There was a loud crack, and the door opened wide. A fierce wind sucked Denny and me into the house, but it wasn't our house—it was the boiler room at Saint Mark's School. A large furnace hissed and shot yellow darts of fire at us. We tried to run away, but we couldn't. Our feet were stuck to the floor.

A scary devil floated above the furnace near the ceiling. He had a giant red balloon head with two horns on the top. Sulfur-smelling smoke swirled out of the horns. Somehow I knew that the devil was Mr. Kutter. He opened his mouth and flicked his long-forked tongue at me and laughed; a long black cape drifted behind him like an ominous thundercloud.

"Look in there, girlie," he ordered, pointing to the furnace. "Look deep inside. That's where your father is."

I screamed and closed my eyes. "Open your eyes, Grace," Mr. Kutter said. "Open your eyes."

I opened my eyes. Denny had disappeared, and Uncle Tony was standing in front of me.

"Help me, Grace. Please help me," he said, pointing at the furnace. "I don't want to..."

"How?" I said shakily. "But how?"

Uncle Tony's eyes were dark. He stared at me and didn't say anything else.

The next thing I knew, my mother was shaking me and telling me I was okay.

My heart was pounding, and I couldn't catch my breath. Denny was kneeling at the bottom of the bed—his eyes wide, watching me.

"It's all right, Grace," my mother said softly. "You had a nightmare, a bad dream. It's all right, baby."

"Mom," I said, sitting up. "You don't understand. Daddy was...Uncle Tony..."

"Shhh, Grace, baby," Mom said, hugging me tight. "Let it

"It's Louanne and Maggie," Denny shouted from the hall. "They want you, Grace."

"Bring them in here," I said, clearing off the rest of the table.

"Did you hear that O'Malley tried to arrest my uncle?" Louanne said, storming into the kitchen. "He didn't know how the fire started, and he—"

"Doc just told us," I said, interrupting her. "That's awful."

"How's your uncle doing?" Doc asked, getting up from the table.

"He was pretty upset, but Aunt Michelle and Vinnie calmed him down."

"O'Malley must be so embarrassed," Maggie said.

"Things aren't always what they seem," Doc said, shaking his head. "O'Malley shouldn't have assumed Tony set the fire before he knew the facts. I'm sure he won't make that mistake again."

"He better not," I said.

CHAPTER 27

"MRS. FERRELL'S A FINE woman," I said, jumping down her porch steps two at a time. We'd picked up the books she was donating to the library, all romances, and she'd made us oatmeal cookies and root beer floats.

"Mighty fine woman," echoed Louanne. "That was so good."

"Since we're over here," Maggie said. "Let's stop at Two Trees."

Two Trees was a small beach on the barge canal where the older kids hung out. They wouldn't be there now though—they got there in the late afternoons.

The most exciting thing about Two Trees was the rope swing that went out over the canal. The city took the rope down the summer after Billy Thompson fell off it and drowned. They nailed a "No Swimming" sign to the tree to prevent more accidents, but someone had taken the sign down and put the rope back up.

My father used to take Denny and me to Two Trees to fish for stripers, but he never let us swim because the canal was so deep. He'd cast our lines into the weeds growing out of the shallows, and we usually caught one or two fish before we had to go home. He caught more fish than we did, but when he didn't think I was watching him, he'd take the fish off of his line and put it on Denny's or mine. Then he'd say, "Look you've got a bite—looks like a big one."

Louanne and I pulled off our sneaks and bobby socks and waded into the water. Maggie sat on a flat rock and watched.

"I'll play lifeguard," she said, folding her arms. "I'll save you if you start to drown."

"Just don't tell Aunt Michelle. She'll kill me if she finds out I went into the canal."

"No sweat," Maggie said. "But you're not swimming—only cooling your feet."

Louanne and I waded for a few minutes and then sat down beside Maggie.

"Scoot over," Lou said. "You're taking up all the room on the rock with your big butt."

"Am not," Maggie said, moving over.

I stretched my arms up over my head and yawned.

"Tired?" Louanne asked. "You look kind of sleepy."

"I didn't sleep much last night," I said, yawning again. "I had a nightmare."

"I hate nightmares," Maggie said, looking at me. "What was yours about?"

"It was strange—scary," I said, searching for the right words. Even thinking about it made me shiver. I wrapped my arms around myself. "My father was burning up in a furnace. He started out playing with Denny and me inside the house and ended up in the furnace at Saint Mark's."

"Saint Mark's," Louanne said. "That is weird."

"Uncle Tony was there too," I said, taking a deep breath.

"Uncle Tony?" Louanne said, raising her eyebrows.

"Right. He asked me to help him."

"Did you…"

"No, my mother woke me up," I said. "The thing that bothers me is my father." I chewed my fingernail. "Do you believe that if you commit a mortal sin you go straight to hell?"

"My religion doesn't have a hell; what is a mortal sin?" Louanne said, puzzled.

"Eating meat on Friday, missing Mass on purpose on Sunday," Maggie said, rattling off a couple of biggies. "Catholics have lots of things that are mortal sins. If you commit one and die without confessing it, you go straight to hell."

"Suicide is another one," I said, lowering my voice. "Sister said when you break God's laws, he punishes you. He doesn't forgive, and when you go to hell, you're there forever."

"What are you saying?" Louanne asked. "Are you talking about your father? That's nuts."

"I used to think the worst thing was losing my dad in an accident," I said, my voice cracked. "Then I thought his suicide was the worst thing, but what if he's suffering forever in hell…"

"Your dad was sick," Maggie said, in a reassuring tone. "He didn't know what he was doing."

I know he was sick, but…

"Maggie's right. Sick people don't go to hell," Louanne said.

"Remember, Maggie," I asked, "when Sister John the Baptist said I was going to burn in hell just like him?"

"She should burn forever for saying that to a kid," Louanne said.

"My feet are cold," I said, getting up. "I'll wait for you by the bikes."

"Okay," Maggie said. "We'll be there soon."

I purposely scraped my bare feet all the way up the gravel path to the top of the bank. The stones were sharp, and by the time I got to the top, the bottoms of my feet were bloody. The pain from the thousand little cuts on my feet stopped me from thinking about my father burning in hell and Sister John the Baptist. I found a grassy spot under the tree, sat down, and wiped the blood off my feet with my socks. When they were clean and dry, I put on my sneakers and settled back against the hard tree trunk. Maggie's and Louanne's voices drifted from the beach, but I couldn't tell what they were saying.

The rope moved a bit in the breeze, and I grabbed it and pulled on it. It seemed strong—about an inch thick and rough. I gave the rope a good swing and watched as it moved out over the water, thinking how good it would be to swing out and never come back.

Shading my eyes with both hands, I watched a motorboat towing a water skier about a half a mile away. The skier was having a tough time standing up even though he stayed inside the wake. Sometimes I felt like that—even when I was on dry land. I watched until he disappeared around the river bend; no other boats were in sight.

Maggie and Louanne walked up the path carrying their shoes.

"You okay?" Louanne asked.

I nodded and shook the rope at them. "Let's try this thing just once before we go. It can't be that hard."

"We'll get in trouble," Maggie said. "What if someone finds out?"

"It looks like a storm's coming," Louanne said, pointing to the clouds that were moving toward us. "We should start home. I don't want to get my hair wet."

"I think it's going to blow over," I said, tightening my fingers on the rope. "You don't have to try the rope, but I'm going to." I raced off of the bank, and seconds later, I was right back on the grass where I started. It was a great feeling, flying out over the canal; I wanted to do it again and again.

"It's fun," I said, handing Maggie the rope. "Come on, just try it."

"I'll probably kill myself," she said, gripping the rope for dear life. "What if it breaks?" She walked the rope over to the edge of the bank and looked down at the water. "That's a long way to fall."

"Come on, the rope won't break, but if it does, you'll fall in the water, and then you swim to shore," Louanne said patiently. "Easy peasy—as long as a barge isn't coming."

"Run fast and don't let go," I added, more than willing to give her advice now that I was the expert. "Hold on tight."

"Are you chickening out?" Louanne asked, flapping her arms and clucking like a chicken.

Maggie crossed her arms over her chest. "I am not a chicken. Maybe you don't remember, but I do have a major fear of heights."

"Okay, then don't do it," Louanne said, taking the rope. "I will." She raced off the bank and tucked her legs up behind her knees. Her pink pedal pushers slipped down below her hips, revealing white cotton panties for the entire world to see. "Oh no, my pants!"

Maggie and I laughed so hard that I almost wet my pants.

"NOT FUNNY," Louanne shouted, landing beside us.

"We see London. We see France," Maggie and I chanted.

"Good thing you were wearing underpants," Maggie added.

"Shut up! Thank God I'm not the nervous type," Louanne said, pulling her pedal pushers up. "You made so much noise; you almost gave me a heart attack."

"I'm going one more time," I said, flinging myself off the bank

Spice drifted away, and I was engulfed in the smells of gasoline and motor oil from the barge.

"Faster, Grace, swim."

"I love you, Daddy," I said, taking a deep breath and swimming for shore as fast as I could.

Lou threw her arms around me as soon as I reached the beach—even though I was soaking wet. "Grace, you almost died. The boat was so close to you."

I looked back at the water—no sign of my father. I sniffed—no hint of Old Spice, but I knew without a shadow of a doubt that my father wasn't in hell—he'd always be with me.

Maggie grabbed us both and hugged us tight. "Grace, are you okay?"

The waves from the boat's wake crashed against the shore, washed over my feet, and retreated back into the river.

I was more than okay.

CHAPTER 28

MY CLOTHES WERE ABOUT dry when I got home, but my sneakers were sopping wet, so I changed everything and brushed my hair before Doc and Denny saw me. I guess I looked normal because Doc gave us money to buy hamburgers at the coffee shop for lunch.

"If your grandfather knew you fell off the rope swing at Two Trees and almost drowned, he wouldn't have treated us to lunch," Louanne said, drenching her french fries with ketchup.

"I'd be grounded for life," I said, sighing dramatically. "But he doesn't know, and he's not going to."

"You shouldn't have gone on the rope," Maggie said, wiping mustard off her mouth. "I told you it was dangerous, but you had to do it."

"That's the kind of person I am," I said, smiling at her. "I live my life on the edge."

"Or you're a lunatic with a death wish."

"Seriously, Grace," Louanne said softly. "I don't know what we'd do without you."

"I would've drowned if it wasn't for my father," I said, watching their expressions.

"What do you mean?" Louanne asked, raising her eyebrows. "Really, what?"

"I mean, obviously, my father's dead, but when I fell into the water, I couldn't move—like I was frozen." I paused to see what they were going to say. They sat there staring at me with their mouths open, so I went on. "Then suddenly my father was in the water with me. I smelled his Old Spice. I felt his arms around me."

"You must've been hallucinating," Maggie said with a condescending smile. "That happens sometimes in near-death experiences. I read about it in *Reader's Digest*."

"Then what happened?" Louanne said, her voice smooth and soothing like she was talking to a baby.

"Don't look at me like I'm a moron," I said, blushing. "I admit it's weird, but my father swam me toward the shore and told me what to do. He was really there; I know it."

They looked at me like I had two heads.

"And remember how I had that nightmare? Where I was afraid my dad was in hell? He's not."

"Where is he? The canal?" Maggie asked, looking around the coffee shop. "You are seriously creeping me out."

"It's not creepy at all," I said, trying to explain. "I feel so much better because I know he loves me and he's with me all the time. Maybe he's with me more now than he ever could have been alive. Do you know what I mean?"

"I know what you mean," Louanne said, leaning forward.

"My father's not dead, but he's living someplace else. Sometimes I feel him with me, telling me he loves me."

We finished eating and rode over to the library to give Miss Doris the books, but she wasn't back from lunch. I glanced at my Timex—the one Doc gave me for my twelfth birthday—the one I had on in the canal. Still ticking, and Miss Doris was an hour late.

"She should be here any minute," I said. "Let's just wait on the steps."

"I hope nothing happened to her," Louanne said. "She's never late."

"There she is," I said, pointing up the street. "She's coming."

Miss Doris walked down the street and up the library steps. "Girls, thank you for picking up the books," she said, unlocking the door. "Sorry I'm late."

She sat down behind her desk and absentmindedly lit a cigarette. "I haven't been myself lately, and driving all the way out to the country for the books was out of the question." Miss Doris glanced sideways at Louanne. "Today when I went home for lunch, my front gate was wide open."

"Are you sure you closed it?" Maggie said. "Maybe you accidentally left it open."

"Everyone knows that I never leave my gate open," Miss Doris said indignantly. "It's the third time in the last two weeks that someone's unlatched my gate. The third time."

"Wow," I said. "That's weird."

"When I went home for lunch, Louanne, your uncle was way down the street on his bike riding out of town with that dog of his," she said, sitting up straight. "He looked like he was in a big hurry."

"Well, sometimes, Miss Doris, it gets really hot in Uncle Tony's bedroom," Louanne said, looking puzzled. "Then he goes out on his bike to cool off. But he wouldn't open your gate."

"Well somebody did—and Mrs. Teaford is gone." Miss Doris put her left hand over her heart. "The cat always sits on her pillow on the side porch waiting to have lunch with me." She sniffed. "I looked in all of her favorite spots in the yard, behind the birdbath near the back wall, combed the entire neighborhood, but she's disappeared. She's never left the yard before. Something's happened to her." Miss Doris's voice broke. "I know it."

Louanne walked around the desk and hugged the librarian. "Mrs. Teaford probably chased a bird or mouse out of your yard, Miss Doris, and got a little lost. She'll come back; I know she will."

Miss Doris shook her head and cried.

"Oh, Miss Doris, don't cry," I said, feeling sorry for her. "We'll ride around and look for your cat."

"And we can make posters," Louanne said, her eyes lighting up. "We'll put your phone number on them so when someone finds Mrs. Teaford, they'll know who to call. What about a reward?"

"Thank you," Miss Doris said, sniffing. "That's a wonderful idea—I'll offer a five-dollar reward." She took off her glasses, dabbed at her eyes with a wrinkled hankie, and pulled a pack of Pall Malls out of her purse.

"Miss Doris," I said, worried about the report I had seen on the television set a couple of nights ago. "Did you know smoking causes lung cancer?"

Before she could say anything, Denny burst through the door and smiled—a big smile that lit up his whole face. "Miss Doris, have you got the new *Sports Illustrated* magazine? Doc paid me a quarter to come get it."

CHAPTER 29

"DO YOU THINK ANYBODY found Mrs. Teaford yet?" I asked Louanne and Maggie. We'd ridden all over the town looking for the cat, and we were back at my house getting something to eat. I rummaged through the pantry for the potato chips while Maggie made bologna sandwiches and Louanne looked in the refrigerator for drinks.

"Maybe. Lots of people must've seen our posters," Maggie said, smearing ketchup on three slices of bread. She licked her fingers and put the top back on the bottle. "People like rewards; God knows I could use five dollars."

"We should've put Mrs. Teaford's poster next to the wanted posters, not on the bulletin board," Louanne said. "I blame myself for not doing that."

"Blame away, Lou," I said, sampling some chips. "But the cat's not wanted for murder; she's just old and lost."

"So, so funny; I forgot to laugh."

We brought the food and our notebooks out to the tree

again, smiled at herself, and snapped the lid shut. "Why did you have brothers, anyway?"

"Our parents are Catholics, and they can't use birth control," Maggie said without missing a beat. "Sometimes the rhythm system doesn't work."

"Maggs," I said, laughing. "Come on. If they're not here when my mother gets back, she'll have a cardiac arrest."

My mother worried when Denny and I were late. She worried when we got hurt. She worried when we weren't hungry. She turned into the worry queen when my father died—she didn't want to lose us too. Me? Not a worrier, but…

We rode our bikes over to the corner store and got there just as Bert the bum was walking out of the door.

"Hi, Bert," I said, getting off of my bike. "Did you seen Denny and Jimmy?"

"Nope," Bert said, taking a swig of something from a bottle in his bag. He sat down on the steps and wiped his mouth off on his sleeve. "They ain't in the store."

"Thanks," Maggie said. "Let's check my house."

The boys' bikes weren't on the sidewalk in front of the Millers' porch, so we knew they weren't there. Instead of going in and scaring Mr. and Mrs. Miller and getting "How could you'd" to death, we turned around and pedaled back toward my house. The night had turned muggy, and it looked like a thunderstorm was brewing. You could feel and smell the electricity in the air. The wind picked up, and the leaves in the trees rustled and turned themselves inside out.

The sky darkened, and the lights in the houses went on as we rode by, but some of the neighbors were out on their front porches rocking and relaxing after their supper. They waved, and we waved back.

My father used to take Denny and me on walks up there when Whitman's was open. He'd wink and hand me a loaf of Freihofer's bread.

He'd pick Denny up and put him in my old gray stroller and kiss my mother on the cheek. "We're off to feed the duckies, Sarah," he'd say with a laugh. "The lucky duckies."

My mother would put her hands on her hips and eyeball him. She'd say, "Really, Dennis? Is that all you're going to do?"

"Sarah, can't I even take the kids on a walk without you accusing me of something?"

"A walk is fine; just make sure that's all it is. And don't take your eyes off them even for a second."

My father's face would turn red, and he'd push the stroller up the street as fast as he could, humming under his breath. I'd half run and walk behind him, struggling to keep up before he'd remember me and slow down. I liked it when my father was happy and silly, but my mother always ruined it.

Sometimes Doc brought us to feed the ducks, and he taught me his duck-feeding technique. He showed me how to break off small pieces of the bread and gently toss it far away so that the ducks, especially the babies, wouldn't be scared. After a while you didn't have to throw it out so far, and the birds would come in closer and closer. Once a big mallard with a bright green head waddled up and ate right out of my hand. Doc patted my shoulder and said, "See, Grace? Good things come to he who waits—or in this case, *she* who waits."

On the other hand, my father would break the bread into big pieces and throw them fast—like he was in a hurry. And Denny was another story. He never threw the bread to the ducks. He'd stuff it in his mouth and almost choke to death before we could get it away from him.

My father never waited very long before he'd say in his "I'm so sorry" voice, "Grace, I'm going to go check on Old Man Whitman—see what he's up to. You're a big girl; you'll be all right here. Just don't let Denny get out of the stroller and into the river. You're responsible. When you're done feeding the duckies, bring Denny up to the bar. I'll be waiting."

I never said anything back, but my stomach did flip-flops. I'd bite my lips until I tasted blood instead of crying. I'd watch my father walk all the way back up the long driveway, climb the wooden steps, and disappear into the bar without even once looking back. The first time it happened, I was five years old. How could I have kept Denny in the stroller if he'd tried to climb out and run into the river? If he'd drowned, it would have been my fault.

The bar looked like it was a million miles away. Usually there were some people fishing; others were sitting around the picnic tables drinking beer, but I didn't know any of them, and if I needed help…

Nothing ever happened. Denny stayed in the stroller, and when our bread ran out, I'd push him up the dirt driveway to the bar, avoiding the deep ruts as best I could.

There was a picture window in the bar that overlooked the water, and when I got close to the building, I would check for my dad's face. When he saw me, he'd smile and wave and point for me to sit down on the wooden porch steps. If Denny cried, I'd take him out of the stroller and chase him around the porch, which went all the way around the building. Eventually my dad would come out holding a Saf-T-Pop for Denny in one hand and a 3 Musketeers bar in the other hand for me.

He'd be happy again, and he'd cup my face in his hands and sing. "Lavender blue, Gracie Gracie, lavender green. If I was king, Gracie Gracie, you'd be my queen." Then he'd lower his voice and go on. "Grace, don't tell your mother I went into Old Man Whitman's. She'll be mad I got you a candy bar. Our secret, right?"

I would nod, fingering the unwrapped candy bar in my pocket. I would share my 3 Musketeers bars with my best friends Louanne and Maggie. I'd feel sad though, and I wouldn't know why. Thinking back, I knew why now, and it made me even sadder.

We weren't supposed to go to the old marina because Doc and my mother said you never knew who might be there, and if something happened, no one would know. Of course, that made the place more attractive to us, especially in the summertime. Bert the bum was usually there. He slept behind the boathouse and was nice. In the mornings, he collected night crawlers and sold them to the fishermen so he could buy beer and food.

Denny and Jimmy used to sneak up to the marina too. They'd bring Bert the bum cookies, and he'd give them night crawlers and help them bait their hooks—if they had gotten out of the house with their fishing poles.

We peddled up Hudson Avenue to the marina. It was getting darker—the streetlights turned on. When we turned into the marina's long driveway, everything was a dark, hazy blur.

"Check the docks first," Maggie said, speeding up. "I bet that's where they are. Watch out for the holes."

Louanne followed Maggie, and I followed Louanne. The wind picked up; we were riding into it. The ruts in the driveway were deep, close together, and almost impossible to maneuver around. Old Man Whitman used to fill them with crushed stones every spring, but he'd been dead so long that the holes had become craters.

"Their bikes are here," Louanne shouted over her shoulder. "Right by the dock. Jimmy, Denny, where are you guys?"

"Jimmy!" Maggie yelled into the wind. "Hurry up; it's going to rain. Mom and Dad are going to be really mad."

We dropped our bikes and walked down to the edge of the river. The wind had churned the water into whitecaps that crashed impressively on the shore and slid back into the dark Hudson.

"Shhh," Louanne said, slowly turning her head from side to side. "Did you hear that?"

"It's nothing," I said, cocking my head and listening. "Just the wind."

"I don't know; maybe Old Man Whitman is coming to take back his property or"—Lou's voice changed to a deep, raspy tone—"to get revenge and savagely murder the three of us."

"Louanne! That's not even remotely funny," Maggie said, sounding anxious. "You're not helping."

"Just kidding," Louanne said. "But I did hear somebody yelling."

Across the river, lightning flashed, and a minute later we heard the distant rumble of thunder. The trees bent back and forth in the wind. It started to sprinkle.

"We need to get away from the river," I said, looking at the sky. "We could be struck by lightning. There are so many trees."

Another bolt of lightning lit up the area, and Maggie yelled and pointed at her feet. "Look! Somebody wrote 'STOP GET OU' on the dock."

"That's how Uncle Tony writes," Louanne said.

"Shhh," I said. "Now I hear something."

"It could be the boys," Louanne said.

"Yeah," Maggie agreed. "It could be."

I cupped my hands around my mouth and yelled over the wind. "We're over here."

Nobody answered.

"Maybe it was the wind," I said. "Or Bert the bum."

"He couldn't be back here already," Maggie said, shaking her head. "He doesn't walk that fast."

A white curtain of rain was moving toward us over the water. Flashes of lightning lit up the marina, followed by deafening cracks of thunder. The skies opened up and let loose the rain. No sign of Denny and Jimmy.

I shouldn't have let them play marbles on the sidewalk. I shouldn't have taken my eyes off them. Hail Mary full of grace…

"Run to the bar," Louanne shouted, grabbing my arm. "Seriously, we have to get out of here. Don't touch the bikes; they're metal."

"But they have rubber tires," Maggie yelled.

"Forget the bikes," Louanne shouted. "Hurry."

Maggie and I followed her up the driveway.

"There," Louanne shouted, pointing to the heavy door on the bar, which was swinging back and forth in the wind. "The boys must've gone in and left the door open."

"Hurry up," I said. "It's getting worse."

The wind blew the rain straight into our faces, and it was so dark we couldn't see three feet ahead. Branches from a tall oak tree broke off and crashed to the ground as we rushed past. A lightning bolt struck the tin roof on the boathouse, and sparks flew everywhere.

"It's so scary," Lou cried. "Maybe Old Man Whitman does haunt this place."

"Don't think about it," I said, wiping the rain out of my eyes. "Worry about us making it to the bar in this storm."

"Someone is behind us," Louanne screamed. "I'm not kidding—run, run."

"Denny?" I called out over the noise of the storm. "Is that you?

Nobody answered.

We dashed up the steps, out of the rain. Lightning lit up the night, and bursts of thunder rumbled so loud that the wooden porch trembled under our feet. The boathouse roof blew off and clattered down the driveway toward the beach. The hairs on the back of my neck stood up, and prickles shot up and down my spine. I had my hand on the doorknob when Maggie shouted.

"Danger! Danger!"

The sky lit up as lightning struck the tallest oak about fifty feet away from the porch. The tree exploded, split in two, and crashed to the ground. The pungent smell of ozone filled the air, and sparks danced in the sky where the tree was a minute ago.

"Oh my God," Louanne said, grabbing me. "That was like an atom bomb. We just ran under that tree—we could've been killed." She ran her fingers through her wet hair. "Maggie, how did you know that was gonna happen?"

"I didn't know," Maggie said, hugging herself. "What do you mean?"

"You yelled 'Danger! Danger!' right before the tree exploded."

"Because," Maggie said, pointing to the bar door. "'Danger! Danger!' is written on the door!"

"It's your uncle's writing, Louanne," I said, peering at it. "Like the writing on the dock—and his bedroom door."

"But why?" Louanne said. "Why would he write 'danger'?"

"I can't make sense of crazy," Maggie said impatiently. "Maybe your uncle hangs out here, and he wants to scare everyone else away."

"Even if it says 'danger,'" I said, "we have to go in. Denny and Jimmy are in there."

"Would your uncle hurt them, Louanne?" Maggie said, grabbing her shoulder. "Maybe we should go get help."

"Leave me alone," Louanne answered, pulling away. "He wouldn't hurt anyone."

This was worse than my worst nightmare. I wished I could go back to the start of this whole mess and make Denny stay with me.

"Your uncle wrote 'danger' on the door for a reason, Lou," Maggie said, raising her voice.

"My uncle wouldn't hurt them," Louanne repeated.

The heavy door swung back and forth on its old hinges—creaking every time.

"Shhh," I said as a beam of light lit up the dark bar. "Duck."

"What if Uncle Tony caught the boys?" Maggie whispered, catching the door with her hand. "What if he—"

"Maggie," I whispered back. "Don't."

Thunder rumbled overhead. The rain kept pouring down.

"We don't have a choice. We have to find them," I said, slipping past Maggie into the bar.

Hail Mary full of grace. Make Denny and Jimmy be in here safe, and I'll never sin again. I'll even give up potato chips.

It was dark inside the bar. I took a few tentative steps to the right. Louanne and Maggie were behind me. If I remembered correctly, the shuffleboard table was flush against the wall. When my dad brought Denny and me to the marina and it was too cold outside to let us feed the ducks, he'd bring us into the bar and let me slide the pucks back and forth on the shuffleboard table. I swept my hand back and forth in front of me until I touched the table. Running my hand along the side of it, I moved forward one small step at a time.

The rain pounded down on the bar's tin roof like bullets. Lightning lit up the room, followed by a barrage of thunder that sounded like a fireworks finale on the Fourth of July. The door slammed shut behind us. I took another small step, and a hand closed around my right ankle.

I shrieked and jumped back.

"SHHH," Jimmy said in a stage whisper. "Shhh. Quick, under the table."

"Jimmy, you gave me a heart attack," I said, slithering under the table. "Thank God you're okay. Where's Denny?"

"SHHH!" Louanne joined us. "Someone's coming."

"Jimmy," Maggie whispered, moving in beside us, "are you—"

A door opened, and I turned my head in the direction of the sound—the kitchen door. A flashlight beam was slowly moving back and forth across the room, heading right our way. All the person had to do was shine it lower, and he'd see us. We were trapped.

"Goddamn little fools," a deep voice shouted in a voice I couldn't place. "I know you're in here. You ain't gonna get out alive."

Jimmy gasped. Maggie stuck her hand over his mouth and shook her head.

The man walked down the aisle past the shuffleboard table, his footsteps crunching on the dirty floor just inches away from where we were huddled together. It was so dark I couldn't see his face. He locked the main door and dragged chairs and tables over in front of it, stacking them up on top of each other so we couldn't escape.

We pressed ourselves against the wall as his footsteps pounded by us on his way back to the kitchen. My heart was thumping and bumping faster than it ever had before.

Jimmy whimpered, "Louanne, don't let your uncle hurt us."

Louanne didn't say anything.

"Where's Denny?" I whispered in Jimmy's ear. "Where is he?"

"Uncle Tony grabbed him," Jimmy said with a sob. "I ran and hid, but he got Denny."

Time stood still. I was paralyzed—unable to speak or move. We had to get out of the bar and go for help, but I didn't know how. The door closest to us had furniture piled in front of it. But then I remembered that the kitchen and the storeroom were behind the bar.

"We have to get to the storeroom," I said in a low voice. "There's another door in there."

"That's a bad idea," Jimmy said. "I'm not going."

"Stay with me," Maggie hissed. "You'll be okay."

"No," Jimmy cried. "I'm scared, I don't want to."

"You have to," Maggie said.

"No I don't. I'm not going."

"Shut up," Maggie said. "Come on."

In the end, only three of us went. Jimmy was adamant; no matter how much we pleaded, he wouldn't come.

"We'll get help and come back for you," Maggie said. "Just stay back against the wall, and don't make a sound."

I slithered out from under the table on my stomach and went straight back to the inside wall; then I crawled left along the baseboard until I felt the storeroom door and opened it.

"Where are we?" Louanne whispered, standing up. "I've got slivers in my knees."

"In the storeroom," I said, trying my best to see. "Close

the door behind you; I'm going to find the back door so we can get out."

The walls were lined with shelves, and I slid my fingers along them, making my way to the back. Something soft crunched under my shoe, an animal howled in pain, and I screamed bloody murder. The thing scrambled up the shelves, knocking everything over trying to get away.

"Grace," Maggie said. "Are you okay?"

"I stepped on something—maybe a rat," I said, trying to calm myself down. "It scared the heck out of me."

"Rats don't make that kind of noise, but cats do," Louanne said.

I felt my way along the back wall to the outside door. The door on the left that went into the kitchen was closed and locked from the other side. "Oh no. Don't tell me…"

"What?" Maggie said. "Is it a rat?"

"There's a bookcase blocking the back door," I said, rubbing the back of my neck. "We've got a bigger problem than a rat."

CHAPTER 30

THE STORM HAD PASSED; everything was quiet except for a faint splashing sound out in the bar.

"What's that noise?" Maggie whispered. "It sounds funny."

Someone was stomping around the bar throwing liquid on the walls and floor. I sniffed—the undeniable smell of gasoline seeped into the room.

"Oh my God, Louanne," Maggie hissed. "That splashing sound is gas—your uncle is going to burn us alive."

"We need to move the bookcase," Louanne said. "We've got to get out."

"It won't budge," I said, pulling one side of it with all my might.

Maggie pulled the other side. "It's so heavy; I think it's filled with bottles."

"Get the boxes off it. Hurry," I said.

There was a loud whooshing sound in the bar—the building was on fire.

"We're going to burn up," Louanne said. "We're going to die!"

"Don't, Lou," Maggie said, breathing hard. "Keep working."

"There's so many of these stupid things, and they're heavy," Louanne cried, grabbing another box.

"Hurry!" Maggie said. "We've got to get out."

"Fire!" Louanne screamed. "Hear that? Fire!"

Smoke seeped in under the doors, immediately heating up the room.

"The fire's moving so fast," Maggie said, throwing the boxes off the shelves as fast as she could.

"Take off your shirts, and jam them under the doors," I said, peeling my shirt off. "That will stop the smoke from getting in."

"My blouse?"

"Louanne," I said, stuffing my shirt in the crack. "Do it. It's easier to breathe by the floor." I grabbed my chest. "But we've got to move the bookcase."

We lifted the last few boxes off of the shelves and tried to move the bookcase.

"Maggie, grab this side with me, and pull," I said.

"There's nothing to grip," Maggie said. "My hands keep sliding."

"I know, but we've gotta try."

We pulled as hard as we could, and after a while the heavy bookcase moved a little.

"It's giving," I said. "Come on; it's coming."

Maggie coughed and slumped down on the floor. Louanne took her place, and after tugging as hard as we could, there was room for me to wedge myself between the bookcase and the door. I held my breath to make myself smaller and squeezed in. I tried to open the door, but it opened into the room—the only way out was to break the window, but I had nothing to hit it with. The fire crackled louder, my eyes stung from the smoke, and it hurt to breathe.

I smelled Old Spice, felt my father's presence, and punched my fist through the glass as hard as I could over and over. The rat screeched again, leaped past my head, and hurtled out the window. Everything went black; I couldn't catch my breath, and I fell back against the bookcase.

When I came to, I was outside on the grass with Denny, Maggie, and Louanne. Blood seeped out of the cuts on my right arm; I cradled it with my left hand, trying to stop the pain. Maggie was crying hysterically, and Louanne was attempting to comfort her.

It sounded like every emergency vehicle in the county was coming. O'Malley, the fire truck, and the ambulance roared into the marina, one after the other. Mr. Nunnalley and his assistant jumped out of the ambulance and hurried over to where we were sitting. Firemen raced around the building assessing the situation. Captain Steele dashed inside Whitman's carrying a long-handled axe—where had that been when we needed it? Mr. Howe and another fireman threw a ladder against the burning building and climbed up on the roof.

"Mr. O'Malley," Maggie screamed, pointing at the burning building. "Please, Jimmy's inside. Under the shuffleboard table."

"Mrs. Teaford, too," Denny shouted. "She's hurt bad."

"I knew it was a cat," Louanne said. "Where is she?"

"If that was Mrs. Teaford," I said, "she's okay. I saw her jump out the window."

"Shuffleboard table?" O'Malley shouted back. "There's no way to get through those flames."

"Shuffleboard table," Maggie mouthed, but no sound came out.

I closed my eyes, leaned against Denny, and prayed.

Mr. Nunnalley and his assistant immobilized my arm and tucked thick blankets around us. They checked our blood pressure, listened to our chests, and gave us water. Mr. Nunnalley squirted something in our eyes to stop the burning, but they still hurt, and I couldn't stop blinking.

A roar went up from all of the firemen as O'Malley walked out of the front door with Jimmy in his arms.

"Tony got the kid and handed him over to me. He's the luckiest little son of a bitch I've ever seen," he said, dropping him on Maggie's lap. "The kid was right there under the shuffleboard table curled up against the wall—low enough to protect him from the smoke. What the hell were you kids doing in there?"

The chief ran out of the building. "Out! Roof's gonna give. Stand back."

Mr. Howe and the other fireman scrambled down the ladder.

"Where's Dodd?" O'Malley raced toward the front door. "Quick, he's inside."

Uncle Tony appeared in the doorway with someone flung over his shoulder. His knees buckled, and he fell to the ground. The building collapsed with a loud roar, covering both men with piles of burning debris.

"Shovels! Train the hoses there," Captain Steele yelled, pointing at the place where Uncle Tony went down. "Hurry!"

Firemen rushed over with shovels and pried the burning beams off the two men as fast as they could. When the beams were pushed to the side, O'Malley knelt down beside the men for a minute or two, and then he pushed himself to his feet and quickly motioned for Mr. Nunnalley.

Mr. Nunnalley and his assistant raced over with the stretcher and picked up one of the men, who was screaming and thrashing around. They loaded him on the stretcher while Mr. Howe ran around to the back of the ambulance and grabbed a white blanket. The firemen stepped aside and watched Mr. Howe cover the other man. They dropped their heads and stepped back when he pulled the blanket all the way up.

"Somebody get Mortie over here ASAP," O'Malley shouted. "Tony Dodd just went to his last fire."

CHAPTER 31

DR. WHALEN INVITED US to his house that night; it was easier for him than making house calls at three different places, and we all wanted to be together.

Mrs. Whalen brought coffee, cold drinks, and a tray of cookies into the parlor. She passed them around and left the rest on one side of her long mahogany sideboard so we could help ourselves to more. My mother, Doc, and Denny were there, along with O'Malley the cop, the Millers, Aunt Michelle, Louanne, and Vinnie the butcher.

"My mother will never get over this," Aunt Michelle said quietly to Vinnie. "Tony was her baby." Her shoulders slumped, and she covered her face with her hands. He took his handkerchief out of his pocket, handed it to her, and draped an arm over her shoulder.

O'Malley the cop sat at a small desk at the end of the room talking on the phone in a low monotone. He shook his head several times and frowned.

I looked around the room. Preposterous as it sounded, none of us were badly hurt. It was a miracle. We were stunned, of course, but physically fine. I was hurt the worst. Dr. Whalen had just finished stitching my cuts, setting my arm, and casting it. He gave me something that tasted like cough syrup for the pain, and I felt sleepy and a little woozy. I had to wear the cast for eight weeks because it was a bad break, but the doctor said it would heal just fine.

We all suffered from smoke inhalation, but Dr. Whalen had given us oxygen and told us we'd be hoarse and coughing for a few days, but as long as we weren't spitting up blood or having trouble breathing, there wasn't a problem.

O'Malley ended his phone call and walked over to the middle of the room. "Bring a few more chairs in here so everyone can sit," he said, gesturing to Vinnie.

"I'll sit on the floor," I said, dropping down slowly on the rug. "I don't need a chair."

"Good idea, kids on the floor."

"I'm staying here," Louanne said, sitting on the arm of the couch beside Aunt Michelle. It was hard seeing everyone so sad—especially Lou. She was the one who always said funny things and made everyone laugh, but there wasn't anything to laugh about tonight.

Dr. Whalen walked into the room. "Michelle, I couldn't be sorrier about your brother. I just got off the phone with Mortie. He offered to come over, but I told him you'd make the funeral arrangements in the morning. Not much he can do tonight."

"Thank you," she said, looking up at him. "You're very kind."

O'Malley said, "Christ, we're all sorry, Michelle. Make yourself comfortable, Doctor. We've been waiting for you."

The doctor sat down beside my mother and rested his chin on his hand.

"Everyone settled?" O'Malley paused and rubbed his forehead. "Here's what I've pieced together: Kutter set the fire."

"Who?" I asked, looking around the room at the stunned looks on all of the faces. "Mr. Kutter the janitor?"

"Kutter's the arsonist—the person who set all the fires this summer."

Mr. Kutter wasn't even on our list.

Doc got up and crossed the room to the window. He turned around and looked back at O'Malley. "Well, I'll be damned. Kutter," he said, shaking his head. "I should have known."

"That bastard," Vinnie said through clenched teeth.

"Wait—Uncle Tony grabbed Denny," I said, wrinkling my forehead. I looked over at Jimmy. "You saw him. Right, Jimmy?"

Jimmy's head bobbed up and down.

"Tony took Denny all right, but not to hurt him. To protect him." O'Malley frowned and looked at Jimmy. "He wanted to get you boys out of Whitman's."

"What are you saying, O'Malley?" Doc asked, glancing at Dr. Whalen. "Any ashtrays here? I need a cigarette."

"Right here," Vinnie said, passing over an ashtray from the end table.

Doc pulled his Camels out of his pocket, lit up, and inhaled deeply.

"Here's what happened," O'Malley continued. "Tony rode his bike to Whitman's earlier that afternoon. When the storm blew in, he started for home but stopped when he noticed Kutter's car hidden behind the bar. He watched Kutter carrying gasoline, Cut-Rite wax paper, and Mrs. Teaford into the place."

"Mrs. Teaford?" Louanne said. "Why?"

"Tony didn't know why either, but he figured Kutter was gonna set the place on fire. Tony had patience; he waited and watched. While he waited, he scrawled warnings on the dock and doors to scare people away. 'Danger,' 'Keep away'—that sort of stuff. Everybody with me?"

Louanne nodded and rested her head on Aunt Michelle's shoulder.

"So far," my mother said, leaning forward.

"Kutter snatched Mrs. Teaford from Miss Doris's yard earlier in the day. He knew everyone in town would be looking for that cat—especially the kids. He waited until the boys were by themselves and told them that Mrs. Teaford was at the marina and that she was hurt. Of course, the boys jumped up and went after her," O'Malley continued. "Kutter beat them to the marina and hid his car again."

"We thought the cat was down by the docks," Jimmy interrupted O'Malley. "But she wasn't."

"Kutter snuck out on the porch with the cat and twisted her leg so she'd cry out. The boys ran into the bar to find her, but before the janitor could set the place on fire, Tony grabbed Denny, and the boys screamed."

"I thought Uncle Tony was the bad guy," Jimmy said, shaking his head.

"Nope," O'Malley went on. "Then the girls went in looking for the boys. Kutter trapped them too and set the bar on fire."

"Why?" Mrs. Miller gasped.

"To get revenge on Doc for getting him fired from Saint Mark's."

Doc pulled back a little and looked O'Malley in the eye. "I never thought he'd go so far as to hurt the kids."

"He's a piece of work," O'Malley said. "But getting back to what happened: Tony sent Denny to Vinnie's for help."

"Denny?" I said in disbelief. "He sent Denny?"

"Denny?" echoed Louanne, shaking her head.

Denny nodded. "Gabriel went with me; I wasn't afraid."

O'Malley smiled at Denny, who buried his face in my mother's lap. "That kid's a pistol. Tony wasn't sure which part of the building the kids were in. The place went up fast. He was running around trying to figure out how to save them when Grace broke the window and screamed. He got her out and went back in for the other two."

I remembered strong arms grabbing me and a man's voice telling me I was okay, but nothing else.

O'Malley went on. "Tony found Jimmy hiding under the shuffleboard table."

"Uncle Tony's a hero," Louanne said, sighing. Her eyes were red and watery from the smoke, and she rubbed them with her fingers.

"Then damned if Tony didn't go back for Kutter," O'Malley blew air out of his mouth and looked around the room. "Gave his life trying to save the goddamned arsonist who tried to kill the kids."

"How did you find this out, O'Malley?" Doc asked.

"Kutter confessed, and Tony had told Denny a lot of the story so he'd go get help. I pieced the stories together. I know exactly what happened."

No one said anything; over on the desk, Doc Whalen's clock ticked off the seconds, reminding me that things change every day—every minute.

"It's not fair. I wish Uncle Tony had lived and…" I said, breaking the silence.

"You ain't alone, Grace," O'Malley said sadly. "None of us like the way this went down. I should've realized it was Kutter. I never connected the dots."

Aunt Michelle cleared her throat.

O'Malley looked down and rubbed his jaws with his fingers.

"Was there a reason he burned those places?" Doc asked, sitting down.

"Each place that burned had a connection to Saint Mark's—where Kutter used to work."

I remembered the day he came into Vinnie's store and yelled at Doc. I was worried he might do something to Doc; I never thought he might try to kill Denny.

"So he set fires at places tied to the school. Remember the Nelsons' barn? Nelson sold janitorial supplies to Saint Mark's. The Bailey farmhouse burned: Eleanor Bailey made muffins for the school on First Fridays. Sulley bartended at the old hotel that burned: he coached the school's baseball team. And Mrs. Phillips gave the school pizza."

"But Kutter worked at those places—helped clean up after those fires," Mr. Miller said. "They hired him."

"And nobody suspected him," O'Malley said.

"What about Whitman's?" Doc said, taking a puff on his cigarette. "I don't see that connection."

"No connection. Kutter hung out there," O'Malley said. "I guess you could say he was a squatter. He stored his arson supplies in the kitchen."

"Are you absolutely sure?" Mr. Miller asked.

"Ab-so-lute-ly! Kutter signed a confession before he went into surgery," O'Malley said, raising his eyebrows and scratching his head. "Damn fool doesn't want to burn in hell if he dies."

CHAPTER 32

I DIDN'T WANT TO go to the wake, but my mother and Doc made me. Uncle Tony would still be alive if I'd watched Denny and Jimmy better. Doc had told me over and over that they would never have left the sidewalk if Mr. Kutter hadn't tricked them, but I still felt guilty.

"You don't have to go inside the house, Grace," Doc had told me when we were walking over to the Dodds'. "You can sit on the porch, but Tony gave his life to save you kids, and the least you can do is to be there today and show him proper respect."

I flinched and dropped back to walk with my mother. She looked nice; her hair was pulled back in a bun, and she wasn't wearing much makeup. We'd gone shopping the day before in Troy for funeral clothes, and she had on the black dress that she'd bought at Frears Department Store. She saw me looking at her and smiled.

"You'll be glad you went," my mother said, trying to encourage me. "I know it's hard, Grace, but someday you'll thank us for making you go." She smoothed the back of my new navy-blue dress. "I'm glad you chose this color. I don't like black on girls your age."

"I know." I stiffened my back, wishing my mother would stop talking about the dress. I'd picked the one she liked so we could get out of the store and go home, but I hated it. I hated my new patent leather shoes too; they were stiff, and they hurt my feet. There wasn't much I liked about anything today—I just wanted it to be over. I watched the back of Doc's head, hoping he'd change his mind, but he looked straight ahead and kept walking. He didn't know that Uncle Tony's death had brought back my father's suicide, and no matter how hard I tried, I couldn't get either one of them out of my mind.

The nights were the worst. I was afraid to go to sleep because I had the same nightmare over and over. The burning building was caving in on Uncle Tony, and my father was holding a gun to his own head. I'd scream "No, Daddy, no!," and he'd look at me and pull the trigger. I'd yell "Run! Run!" to Uncle Tony, and he'd look at me, and the building would collapse. Everything in the dream turned red from my father's blood and the flames. Mr. Kutter floated overhead on a cloud of black smoke, laughing and laughing. I'd wake up in a cold sweat screaming, and my mother and Denny would run into my room to see what was going on.

My mind couldn't even be trusted when I was awake. A couple of times, I was sure I saw Uncle Tony riding his bike down the street. Thoughts about the fire burst into my head with no warning. It was so real—as if it were happening again. I couldn't save my father, and I couldn't save Uncle Tony. It was always my fault.

Doc stopped when we got to the Dodds' to let my mother and me go up the steps first. Maggie and Louanne were sitting at the end of the porch on the railing.

"Louanne, Maggie," he said, nodding his head. "Don't you girls look nice."

"Hi, Mr. Flynn," Louanne said. "Thanks for coming."

My mother and Doc went inside. I walked over to Louanne and Maggie and carefully climbed up on the railing next to them.

"My father's here," Louanne said, smiling a little. "He came last night. I'm going home with him tomorrow after the funeral." She turned and looked at me. "He said that he and my mother are trying to work things out."

"Oh, that's great," I said, smiling back. "What happened?"

"I guess when Uncle Tony died, he realized he could lose us forever too. He doesn't want that."

I threw my good arm around her shoulders. We sat there quietly, watching people walk up to the house and file inside. Almost everyone in town came. Most of them dropped their eyes and nodded when they came up the steps; others looked straight ahead.

Mrs. Earl and her nephew walked over when they noticed us. She had on a somber black dress and matching pillbox hat; her nephew had on a shiny blue suit and white shirt. He brushed his hair back and looked down at his feet.

"I'm so sorry, Louanne," Mrs. Earl said, throwing her arms around Louanne.

Maggie stuck her finger under her nose and made a face.

"Thank you, Mrs. Earl," Lou said, pulling back a little.

"It's a sad day, dears," Mrs. Earl continued as she steered her nephew toward the door. "We'll see you inside."

"She didn't smell that bad," Louanne said. "I think even Mrs. Earl cleans up for a wake."

Maggie murmured in agreement.

Inside the house, Mrs. O'Malley was playing "Amazing

Grace" on Aunt Michelle's old upright piano. I closed my eyes for a moment and remembered my father singing that song to me. The music calmed me down, and I closed my eyes and tried to relax. It was one of the hottest days of the summer—or at least that's what it felt like. I rested my cast on my knee and flexed my fingers a few times, trying to make them stop tingling.

"Here come the Cannons," Maggie whispered. "Brace yourselves."

I took a deep breath and sat up straight.

"Afternoon, girls," Mr. Cannon said, walking up the steps. He held the door open for his wife and son, Gary. They saw us and stopped.

Mrs. Cannon pulled her black sweater tight across her chest and said, "We came to pay our respects—to say some prayers for our—I mean, Tony Dodd's—soul."

Gary nodded and mouthed "Sorry" before he followed his mother into the house.

Louanne rolled her eyes and sniffed.

"Let it go, Lou." I rubbed my cast and sighed. "Maybe they finally understand."

"I'm not sure," Louanne said, swinging her feet back and forth. Her shiny blond hair was pushed back under a black headband, and she was wearing a white linen dress and white-strapped sandals. "Remember Gary calling my uncle crazy and blaming him for setting the fires—right in front of everybody? Remember?"

"Yeah, but you didn't let him get away with it," I said.

"You knocked the heck out of him," Maggie said. "In front of everybody."

"So?"

"So, he said he was sorry," I said in a low voice. "We're all sorry."

Mrs. O'Malley went right into "The Old Rugged Cross."

"Grace, I know you don't want to, but please come in," Louanne said, sliding off the railing. "Aunt Michelle will feel bad if I stay here any longer. And my father wants me to mingle, but I don't know how to mingle today. I can't do it alone. I need you and Maggie."

"Remember how we said we'd always be there for each other?" Maggie said, holding out her hand. She was wearing a headband too, but a white one that looked good with her black-and-white polka-dot skirt. "Pinky swear?"

"Pinky swear," I said, knowing I couldn't let them down. Grabbing Maggie's hand, I maneuvered myself awkwardly off of the railing. Doc was right—you can always use a hand, sometimes to help you up and sometimes to hold. Today I needed both.

"Yoo-hoo," someone called from the sidewalk. "Yoo-hoo!"

The three of us turned and watched Miss Doris hurry up the walk toward us.

"I'm sorry I'm late. I just came back from the veterinarian's office," she said, breathing heavily. "Mrs. Teaford came home last night. The poor thing smelled like smoke and was covered with soot, and her front leg was broken, but the vet fixed her up. She'll be fine."

"Mrs. Teaford was trapped in the bar with us," I said. "We thought she was a rat."

"I knew it was a cat," Lou said, smiling at Miss Doris. "I just didn't know it was Mrs. T."

"Well, you three get the reward money," Miss Doris said, pulling five dollars out of her pocketbook. "Here. You take it and spend it on something fun."

"Thank you, but Jimmy and Denny deserve it more than we do," I said, taking the money. "Do you mind if we give it to them?"

Maggie and Louanne nodded in agreement.

"Not at all, dear," she said, opening the door into the house. "Not at all."

CHAPTER 33

UNCLE TONY WAS LAID out in a coffin on the far side of the parlor. Aunt Michelle, Mrs. Dodd, Louanne's father, and Vinnie the butcher stood next to him, speaking in hushed tones to the people who had lined up to pay their respects. The curtains on the windows were closed, except for one window in the front, which was wide open. The gold-framed mirror hanging over the fireplace had been covered with Aunt Michelle's long black shawl. My mother knelt on the bench in front of the coffin with her head buried in her hands; her shoulders were shaking. I bit my lip and started to walk away.

"Wait, we have to sign," Louanne said, pointing to the guest book on the small table beside me. "Now, before anybody else does."

"What do we say?" Maggie whispered, turning around to face me. "I never did this before."

"Me either," I whispered back.

Louanne looked at the book. "Mr. Cannon wrote, 'Our

sincere deep condolences to all of you,' and the O'Malleys wrote, 'We are so sorry for your loss.'"

I picked up the pen and wrote, "I'm so sorry for everything, Grace Denise Bryant."

After Maggie and Louanne signed, we checked the cards on the flower arrangements to see who sent the biggest one. My mother and Doc had sent a medium-size spray of white gladiolas, so it definitely wasn't us.

"The mayor wins the contest," Louanne said, tilting her head in his direction. She pointed to a gigantic wreath of white roses with "Our Hero" on a blue banner across the front. "That man definitely has a guilty conscience."

Maggie and I smiled.

Mrs. O'Malley switched to "I'll Fly Away," which seemed a very lively song to be playing at a wake, but no one except me seemed to notice.

Aunt Michelle gestured to Louanne to come over and sit with the family.

"I have to go over there for a while," Louanne said under her breath. "Don't worry. I'll come back soon."

Maggie and I watched her go before we wandered into the dining room. There was food everywhere. Salad bowls, platters of sandwiches, casseroles, two hams, and a turkey covered the dining room table, and there were so many desserts that the sideboard looked like a bakery. The strawberry shortcake was melting, and its sticky red glaze dripped off the white platter and onto Mrs. Dodd's white crocheted runner.

"How come there's so much food?" I asked, feeling sick to my stomach. "I didn't know you ate at a wake."

"You always eat when somebody dies," Maggie said. "Didn't they do that when your father died?"

"I wasn't there," I said abruptly. "Remember?"

"Oh, sorry," Maggie said. "Don't be mad; I forgot."

I shook my head, and we walked into the kitchen to get something to drink. Father Flanagan was standing in front of the window sipping whiskey and looking at his notebook. He nodded but didn't say anything. I looked past him, out the open window, where Doc and Mr. Miller were crouched down on the back porch, putting beer and soda in coolers.

"I'll never lay a hand on them again," Mr. Miller said, choking up. "I don't know why I've treated them so bad."

Maggie and I backed up so they couldn't see us but not enough so that we couldn't hear. Maggie's eyes were wide open, and she took a deep breath. I put my good hand on her arm and squeezed.

"That's right, Ted," Doc said, pouring a bucket of ice in the cooler. "You've got a nice wife and two kids. It's not right to abuse them."

"I'm so ashamed, Doc," Mr. Miller said, adding another layer of bottles. "That's what my old man did to me, and I hated him for it."

"Sometimes you repeat the past without realizing it," Doc said, standing up. "Be careful. Sometimes you become who you hate. But if you realize it, you have the opportunity to change."

Mr. Miller stood up too, and Doc patted him on the back. Mr. Miller took a deep breath and sighed. "Doc, I swear to you on Tony's grave that I'll never lay a hand on my family again."

"I believe you, Ted. Good for you."

I filled two glasses with water and handed one to Maggie. Her eyes were full of tears, but she gave me a big smile.

"Almost time for the service," the priest said. "You girls better get in there."

"Okay, Father," I said, gulping my drink. "We will."

There weren't any seats left when Maggie and I got back to the parlor. We maneuvered to the other side of the room and leaned against the wall. A lot of the men, and women too, were puffing on cigarettes. The room smelled like smoke and sweat and perfume and flowers. Doc and Mr. Howe brought in two kitchen chairs, put them at the end of my mother's row, and sat down. Mrs. O'Malley pounded out the last notes to "How Great Thou Art" just as Father Flanagan walked up to the lectern. He paused and looked out at the crowd.

I tensed and moved closer to Maggie. The room went still.

"In the name of the Father, the Son, and the Holy Ghost," the priest began in a deep, reverent tone. "We're here tonight to pray for the soul of Tony Dodd." He looked at Mrs. Dodd and Aunt Michelle and Louanne's father and lifted his hands. "Life was not easy for this misunderstood man. None of us walked in his shoes. None of us know the agony he endured during his short life. *Not one of us!*"

Tears welled up in my eyes and dripped down my cheeks, and I wiped them away with the back of my hand.

Father Flanagan cleared his throat. People looked down at their laps, avoiding his gaze.

"Sadly, many of us here made fun of Tony Dodd. Many of us here judged him. Many of us here feared him because he was different." The priest's voice rose, and he struck the lectern with the palm of his hand. "Few called him friend!"

I reached over and squeezed Maggie's hand. She squeezed back.

Father Flanagan looked back at the Dodds and nodded. "Yes, this man suffered greatly, but his spirit never faltered. When the children he cared about were in danger, he put his own life on the line and saved them. What an example this man was. He gave his life attempting to save a man many would say wasn't worth it. Many would say the arsonist was wicked and would have let him die." The priest's voice rose, and he shook his head. "But not Tony Dodd. He believed every life was sacred. *He did not judge!*"

Father Flanagan paused—a long, unsettling pause.

"His favorite verse was Romans 12:19. 'Beloved, never avenge yourselves, but leave it to the wrath of God, for it is written, "Vengeance is mine. I will repay," says the Lord.'"

Sounds of sniffling, quiet weeping, and the creaking of chairs filled the room as people shifted around uncomfortably in their seats.

"And now, please bow your heads and pray. Pray for this good man, Tony Dodd, who I believe is sitting at the right hand of the Father—right now—watching us, grateful that we are here for him and his family. Here to pay him respect. Here to call him friend. For it is never too late to call him that. Let us pray."

I bowed my head and sobbed.

Mrs. O'Malley softly played "Nearer My God to Thee." Everyone got up from their seats, waited respectfully until Father had left the room, and slowly made their way to the dining room. A few folks headed out the front door, but most of them stayed. They filled their plates and talked to each other in quiet voices about the fire—about how brave and unselfish Uncle Tony was.

Maggie, Louanne, and I took our food outside on the back porch and sat down on the steps.

"Did you notice that Father Flanagan didn't say 'thee apawsels' even once?" Louanne set her plate down and smiled.

The deep voices of the priest and the men in the kitchen drifted out the open window—along with a cloud of cigarette smoke.

"Anyone need a drink?" Doc asked.

"I'll have one," Louanne's father said. "Thank you."

"Hell, yes," Dr. Whalen answered. "After that sermon, I bet everyone wants one."

"It sure hit home for me," Mr. Howe said. "Make mine a double."

"Father Flanagan was right," I said, surprised and impressed that Mr. Howe had admitted he was wrong. Maybe there was even hope for him. "Nobody knew your uncle, Lou; nobody walked in his shoes."

"They didn't," she said, wiping her mouth off with her napkin. "They were positive that he set the fires."

"Now that Uncle Tony's gone," I said. "Maybe they'll do that with—"

"Shhh," Louanne said, holding her finger up in front of her mouth. She pointed at the open window. "Listen."

"Fellas, this old house has been sad for a long time," Dr. Whalen said. "Ever since Tony got sick, Michelle and Mrs. Dodd have carried quite a load. It was bad enough dealing with his schizophrenia, but how the hell did they cope with the whole town thinking he was the arsonist?"

"Dr. Whalen knows how," Louanne whispered. "Pills. My grandmother's on tranquilizers, and he's the one who prescribed them."

"What?" I wrinkled my brow.

"True," she said. "They did help her."

"Nobody knows what goes on behind closed doors," Doc said. "People think they do, and they like to talk. Tony proved them wrong in a big way."

"You're goddamn right," O'Malley said. "The Dodds can hold their heads up high. No one's ever going to forget what Tony did."

"Easy for O'Malley to say that now," I said, remembering what he'd said about Uncle Tony.

Mrs. O'Malley started banging out "My Wild Irish Rose," and the men started singing along. When I was little, my father used to sing that song to my mother.

"Where's my girl?" Mr. Miller said softly as he stepped out on the porch. "Ready to go, Maggie?"

Maggie's lips trembled, and she stiffened.

Mr. Miller reached down and held out his hand, and Maggie flinched. Stepping away, he said, "I deserve that, Maggie, but I was just trying to help you up."

Maggie cautiously reached her hand toward her father; he put both of his big hands around her small one and gently pulled her to her feet.

"Let's go home, Maggs," Mr. Miller said, hugging her tight.

"Daddy," she said, hugging him back.

"Let's go up and read Aunt Michelle's *Cosmo*," Louanne said after they left. "I'm so tired. My father wants to leave right after the funeral tomorrow morning. I'm definitely going to bed early tonight."

I hated that Louanne was leaving; everything was going to be different without her. I was going to miss her so much; it hurt my heart. I'll think about it when she's gone, I said to myself. Tomorrow night, not now.

We went upstairs and got comfortable on Lou's double bed. Her suitcases were all packed and in a row next to the door. I laid my head on her shoulder while she flipped through the pages in *Cosmopolitan*. She held the magazine up in front of my face so I could see one of the featured articles: "Are Our Children Too Soft to Face the Future?"

"I don't think we're too soft to face anything, Grace," she said, resting the magazine on her chest. "Do you?"

When I was little, I thought bad things happened to other

people—not to me. I was wrong; bad things can happen to anybody. Maggie, Louanne, and I'd each had bad things happen, but we'd faced them together—the three musketeers, one for all and all for one.

I started to tell Louanne my brilliant observation, but she'd fallen asleep, and I didn't want to disturb her. Quietly, I got up and went downstairs; the house was dark and empty. The people still here were out on the back porch talking and laughing.

The grandfather clock in the hall chimed nine times as I walked by. The living room lights were off, but the white candles in the cut glass candleholders glowed on the tables, and a spotlight was trained on Uncle Tony's coffin. Gabriel was lying on the rug not far away. He raised his head when I came in. Louanne was taking him with her tomorrow; she said she'd always wanted a dog.

Doc said it was customary for the family and close friends to sit up with the body the night before the funeral. He and my mother planned on sitting up with Uncle Tony and the Dodds and other close friends, but I was going home.

I walked over to the coffin, knelt down, and forced myself to look at Uncle Tony. You'd never know a burning building had collapsed on him; he looked like he was asleep. His eyes were shut, and his hands were folded peacefully on his chest. Louanne had helped Aunt Michelle pick out the new pinstripe suit and red tie that he was wearing. She'd scattered forget-me-nots around his head on the white satin pillow and tucked her teddy bear, Sir Laurence Olivier, under his arm so he'd never be alone.

I pulled the thank-you note I'd written Uncle Tony out of my sock. I'd stuck it there because my dress didn't have pockets. I hadn't been sure I'd even give him the note, but I wanted him to know how sad I was that he was gone, how bad I felt for not really knowing him, how much I liked it when he smiled at me the day I let the cow loose, how much I had wanted to hug him when he was being taken away on the stretcher, and how, even though I'd been afraid of him, I'd always loved him because he reminded me of my father.

Kissing the note three times (once for him, once for my father, and once for me), I stood up on the kneeler and slipped it into the front pocket of his suit. I reached inside the coffin and gently rested my good hand on top of his.

"Something inside me, Uncle Tony, tells me you already know the things I wrote in this letter because you're in heaven—even Father Flanagan said so. You probably know I need a favor—a big one." I stopped talking and squeezed his cold hard hands.

"But in case you don't, would you please tell my dad that I forgive him for leaving me? I don't hate him anymore. I know he loved me, but he hurt so much—like you—that he just had to make it stop. Please, Uncle Tony, tell him I love him. I'll never forget him."

I leaned in and whispered in his ear. "I'll never forget you either. I love you."

ACKNOWLEDGMENTS

I COULD NOT HAVE brought *Stillwater* to fruition without the generosity, help, and support of my family and friends.

My husband, Victor, my four children and their spouses, Jackie Hernandez, Steve Hazard, and Anne Jagger, Tory and Maureen Hazard, and Jennifer and Mark Giacalone were my cheerleaders. My brother, Bob Dellinger, and my sister, Jane Waring, backed me right from the start.

My writing group buddies, Larry Andrews, Eddy Bay, Judy Bayer, Gil Beall, Julie Mayerson Brown, Dolores Davis, Jeff Guenther, Laura Hines-Jurgens, Lisa Manterfield, Tom Mooney, Paula Reuben, James Flaherty, and Jean Shriver, critiqued my early drafts and urged me on.

Mark Sarvas, professor at the UCLA Novel Writing Intensive Workshop, helped polish my very first paragraph, and Book Coach Jennie Nash, Julie Artz, Jade Eby, and Laura Franzini, of the Author Accelerator group, improved my revisions. Dan

Blank, Founder of We Grow Media, helped me identify ways to connect with readers.

Teri Case, Brian Peyton Joyner, Jack Schaeffer, and Maya Rushing Walker read my last draft and encouraged me to publish.

My book club members, Jerri Beall, Barbara Case, Kathleen Cunningham, Tami Eaton, Jan Faris, Dorothy Jacobi, Grace Mascola, were behind me, and one member, Becky Tortorice, was my first editor.

I'm grateful to my granddaughter, Molly Lowe White, who helped organize and format the manuscript, something I could never do.

My heartfelt gratitude to Naren Aryal, Kristin Perry, and the rest of the staff at Mascot who took my manuscript and made it a book!

I could never have done this without help. As Helen Keller wisely said, "Alone we can do so little; together we can do so much."

NOTE TO READER

ALTHOUGH IT HAPPENED FORTY YEARS AGO, my father's death by suicide is still painful—a wound that never truly heals. Working on my "coming of age" novel helped me put things in perspective, see his death in a more positive way, and let others who have lost a loved one this way know that they are not alone.

My novel, *Stillwater*, is set in upstate New York in the '50s. Back then, mental illness was considered a disgrace; people with those kinds of problems were ridiculed and feared. People were ashamed to talk about their emotional problems, and if they did seek help, there wasn't much out there.

As for my target audience, the protagonists are twelve, so it's really not YA. It's definitely not middle grade. I see it like *To Kill a Mockingbird*—dealing with mental illness, not race. I see the audience as adult women who grew up in the '50s—women who have someone in their family who is mentally ill, or has committed suicide, or struggles with alcoholism. Most people have a loved one, or know someone, who has emotional issues or has committed suicide. Everyone seems to have a connection and is "unfortunately, in the club."

Since *Stillwater* is a "coming of age" novel, I think it's easier for readers to connect with the topic. They're older, but they can easily identify with Grace and see, as well as feel, what she's going through. The book gives the readers hope, Grace gets over her anger at her father for choosing to leave her and realizes that he was in so much pain he was only thinking of a way out. It wasn't his fault. Big step forward.

Today we have better help, suicide prevention programs, better medications, and therapies. There is a lot of help and support—even in our workplaces and schools. People don't have to be alone.

If you or someone you know is considering suicide or struggling with mental health, please contact the National Suicide Prevention Lifeline at 1-800-273-TALK (8255) or the National Alliance on Mental Illness at 1-800-950-6264.

If you or someone you know is a victim of domestic violence, please contact the Domestic Violence Hotline at 1-800-799-7233.

ABOUT THE AUTHOR

MARY JO HAZARD, M.A., M.F.T., is a licensed psychotherapist, the author of three children's books, and a contributor to *Palos Verdes Peninsula News*. She loves living on the Palos Verdes Peninsula—a place with crashing waves, rolling hills, and colorful peacocks in the trees. Mary Jo and her husband love traveling and spending time with their ten grandchildren. Her mission is to remove the stigma of mental illness and help others live their lives to the fullest.